D0758157

WORKING THE LAND

Journeys Into the Heart of Canada

DAVID CRUISE & ALISON GRIFFITHS

VIKING

VIKING
Published by the Penguin Group
Penguin Books Canada Ltd, 10 Alcorn Avenue, Toronto, Ontario, Canada M4V 3B2
Penguin Books Ltd, 27 Wrights Lane, London W8 5TZ, England
Penguin Putnam Inc., 375 Hudson Street, New York, New York 10014, U.S.A.
Penguin Books Australia Ltd, Ringwood, Victoria, Australia
Penguin Books (NZ) Ltd, cnr Rosedale and Airborne Roads, Albany Auckland 1310,
New Zealand

Penguin Books Ltd Registered Offices: Harmondsworth, Middlesex, England

First published 1999
10 9 8 7 6 5 4 3 2 1

Text design and typesetting by Laura Brady

Printed and bound in Canada on acid free paper ∞

CANADIAN CATALOGUING IN PUBLICATION DATA

Cruise, David, 1950–
    Working the land: journeys into the heart of Canada

ISBN 0-670-87741-7

1. Canada – Description and travel. 2. Cruise, David, 1950–   – Journeys – Canada.
3. Griffiths, Alison, 1953–   – Journeys – Canada. 4. Canada – Biography – Anecdotes. I. Griffiths, Alison 1953–   . II. Title.

FC75.C78 1999   917.104'648   C99-931241-3
F1017.C78 1999

Visit Penguin Canada's website at **www.penguin.ca**

To Faye, Michael, Adriane and Alexandra

CONTENTS

ACKNOWLEDGEMENTS

We usually leave our editor to the end. This time we've decided to promote him. After sticking with us for nearly fifteen years, after hearing our excuses for being late (which never change from book to book) and after cutting thousands of words that we snuck back in, we feel that David Kilgour deserves to be first in something.

Along the back roads of rural communities across Canada, we have met so many wonderful people who, with a word or two, gave us enlightenment about those who work the land. We never learned their names or even, in many cases, what they do, but they have added an important layer to our tales of this country. They are people we met in gas stations, corner stores, in fields and barns, on buses, in processing plants and at roadside produce stands. To all of you, thank you, and keep welcoming strangers like us into your midst.

There are fifty or sixty people for each section of this book who should be singled out for thanks, but we will have to limit ourselves to only a few.

PEI holds a special place in our hearts and we would love, one day, to call its gentle landscape home. A big part of the reason we feel this way is the people. Michael, Alexandra and Adriane Gaudet and Faye Pound are good friends and without them we would never have discovered the potato to be the exciting veg it is. Special thanks to the busy farmers who gave us their time; Elmer MacDonald, the Hardys—John, Sydney, John Jr. and Matthew, Barry Cudmore, Raymond and Gerrit Loo. Also we are grateful to and admiring of Sharon Labchuk and Phil Corsi. And we appreciate the help of potato inspector Glen Campbell as well as the proprietors of the Silver Fox Inn in Summerside.

We are particularly grateful to Randy Turner, John MacDonald and all the individuals associated with Winspear Resources Ltd. who gave us their time and valuable information. We are especially grateful to Jennifer Irwin, Greg Burroughs, Nick and Lucy Pokhilenko, Sergei, Mikhail, big Matt and little Matt, geologists who introduced us to the story of the diamond. There are also many in Yellowknife who were terrific sources of insight—including Brian and Penny Weir, Mary and Wayne Bryant and Walt Humphries.

We've been involved with Quarter Horses for nearly three years and couldn't begin to list all the people who have helped us gain knowledge and entertained us with stories. This short list will have to suffice: Chris and Tina Gaul, Helen Wolf, Mark Grice, Dave and Judy Hickey, Lindsay Grice, Joanne Black, Nancy Clements and innumerable others who freely gave their time and information. Very special thanks go to the cowgals— Babs, Lynn, Cathy, Barbara, Joanne and Kelly. And finally, the Portuguese Cowboy.

In Yukon we could not have stumbled upon a more interesting group of people than the trappers who allowed us to tag along and learn about the traditions and techniques of trapping—Poncho and Tammy Rudniski, Linch and Bob Curry, Alex Van Bibber and Danny and Dorothy McDiarmid. Nor can we forget Ivan, Bruce and Henry from the 8th Avenue Trappers' Association. Our thanks also to Mark Smith for his insights about and entrée into the trapping world.

On the west coast the Lallys and Bainses introduced us to the intricacies of berry growing and dairy farming and opened the door to their own intriguing culture and religion. Darshan, Sarbjit, Gurts, Harbans, Mr. Bains, Rajinder, Sukhi, Raminder and Rajvinder were welcoming hosts and good teachers. We also appreciate the time Jack Wessel, Tom Sterns and Bill Weismiller took in explaining their part in the berry industry and the Sikh community. David's old friend Rick King was also very helpful in the initial stages.

Our neighbours, Bill and Steve Bogert, fixed many things that kept breaking down on our farm, while Irma and Vicky Bogert commiserated. Susan Simmons lent a helping hand with various ailing critters.

To our children Claudia and Quinn, sorry for all the crabby days, early mornings, late nights, endless commands of "don't bother us now" and rambling discussions about farming and the land. We'll return to being parents for a while—until we write another book.

We thank Cynthia Good and Penguin for asking us to write this book. We are also very grateful to have had Wendy Thomas once again backstopping us on the copy-editing front. The last thank-you goes to editor Meg Masters, who came up with the idea for *Working the Land*.

FOREWORD

Working the Land has been an extraordinary voyage of discovery for us. We started out smugly believing we knew a lot about this country. With one of us from the east coast, the other from the west, and having lived collectively in eight provinces over our lives, we were fairly confident we had a good understanding of Canada and Canadians. On top of that we had written six books about our national heroes and villains, our past and present. Surely we were experts on the subject of this land and its people. Wrong, dead wrong. Within months of embarking upon the research, we were forced to humbly admit we knew little about this vast country or those who live here. We weren't alone.

Canadians really don't know very much about each other, but we discovered, happily, that, given the opportunity, they are quite fascinated by their countrymen and women. Up north, trappers marvelled at stories of the Sikhs in the Fraser Valley and the war hardworking potato farmers wage against nature. Potato farmers were intrigued by the characters who populate the Quarter-Horse industry. And almost everybody we talked to couldn't believe that diamonds were being mined in Canada. "How come I didn't know that!" was a common comment as we went around the country telling stories of our various travels.

Conventional wisdom has it that we are shaped by the forces, largely foreign, of popular culture: film, fashion, television, magazines, music, sport. That may be true on the surface. But deep down, deep down where our hearts beat, who we are is rooted in the land. Though Canada is one of the most urbanized countries on earth, it is the land that has moulded us. And though most of us live in cities, our passion for the land is strong. Our dreams of it fill us up and find outlets in our little gardens, our weekend trips to farmers' markets, our cottage and camping holidays and our walks in city parks.

NO BOOK ABOUT WORKING the land in Canada could be comprehensive, but we were unrealistic enough to think we could cover much of the terrain. One thing we knew was that we wanted to explore both clichés and the unexpected. We began with about two dozen potential chapters; time and circumstance whittled them down to five. We sadly abandoned a chapter on Newfoundland, realizing that it should be a whole book in itself. The constraints of space forced us to put aside our chapter about the maple sugar industry in Quebec. Similarly, we couldn't include the fascinating story of native groups who harvest Saskatchewan wildflowers to be used in a host of products ranging from cosmetics to medicine.

After more than eighteen months we have enough ideas and information for at least two more books and a cast of lovely characters sufficient for a dozen television series. We have also discovered in ourselves a fascination with corners of this land we never realized existed. Like many of our age, education and experience, we were weaned on the value of working with our minds and the importance of university degrees. Through writing this book—and toiling alongside the men and women who populate its pages—we have learned about the hardship and pleasure of work done by hand. We have also discovered that some of the brightest, most innovative people in this country can be found on the seat of a tractor, in the cool dark of a barn or striding across the landscape searching for a particular rock.

We hope *Working the Land* makes our readers feel the same way.

WORKING THE LAND

CHAPTER ONE

EAST

IN SUMMER THE LAND IS gentle and alluring, accented by a green the gods must have conferred over for centuries before creating. On its own the verdant colour of Prince Edward Island is lustrous enough, but what lends special depth and uniqueness is the contrasting red of the Island soil. They play with each other, these two hues, doing in nature what would be tiring to the eye anywhere else. Red follows you down clay roads that disappear over a swell and along the tidy furrows of soil that invade every nook and cranny of the land. Dust speckles clothing, and after a few days exposed to the colour you swear there is a red scent in the air.

One becomes so enveloped by the dusky rouge, there's a small sense of surprise to visit the famous sand dunes that create a fifty-kilometre-long smile on the province's north shore. They aren't red or even pinky white but ivory. The wonder of it is where and why the red gave way.

Colour defines the Island. The shades of the rainbow appear in sharper relief, perhaps because the land is not aggressive here. Its ups and downs are tempered, its stands of trees approachable, their size intimate. And though the climate can be as ferocious as any northern maritime island, the weather is not matched by the land. Areas of geological sharpness are few; a cliff here and there, a hill that seems steeper than it ought to be, a cove of boulders that would be more at home in the Rocky Mountains than in this place. Without the severe emotion of a violent landscape the eye can concentrate, be drawn to colour.

The farm fields in late fall and early spring are long ribbons of red-brown furrows. On and on they march, like crumbly worms, until they smack into the sky and are gobbled up. Find the right spot at the bottom of a gentle valley, lie back in a soft patch of grass and you can follow their journey from earth to heaven. The mind easily saunters up the incline to grab a piece of blue.

People add patina to the Island. During a two-week visit a few years ago we gorged on lobsters at every opportunity—a fat claw goes very nicely with morning coffee. One night, intending to have spaghetti, we were gripped by a crustacean urge so powerful we rushed to the car and belted thirty minutes down the road, hoping to catch the New London pound before it closed for the day. We scooted into the parking lot just as the doors were being bolted. "No prablam," said the agreeable man, "I ain't taken my apron off yet." Into the cavernous fish "barn" we went, sloshing through water from the freshly hosed concrete floor. Two pound-and-a-halfers had our names on them and they were out of the tank and bagged in no time.

Then came the prablam. Money. We had two fifties, he had no change. Off he went into the restaurant that shares the same site, but the waitress had just sent the deposit off to the bank. She checked her purse, he checked his wallet. At the back of the restaurant a group of middle-aged cyclists were expanding their Lycra shorts wading through great piles of fish and chips. They checked their fanny packs. "Travelling light," grinned one, patting his belly and brandishing only a credit card. The lobsters were getting impatient. Finally, all avenues explored, the man in the rubber apron shrugged. "Bring it tomorrow." We offered instead to leave a fifty and return for the change. "Nah, tomorrow's soon enough."

Whether it's a vision conjured up by Lucy Maud Montgomery's novels, one manufactured by PEI tourism or simply the *idea* of the Island, people come to PEI laden with images that rarely disappoint, even when the northwesterlies blow so hard you wonder if morning will find you and the Island on Dorothy's doorstep.

We sat down for lunch in a coffee shop in the tiny resort village and found out, without much obvious prying, that the owner was from Kingston, Ontario, a Ph.D. who works like a dog during the short summer tourist season for the privilege of living on PEI all year long. Another couple we met, heading into their late forties, he an academic, she a nurse, contract themselves out all over North America in order to spend the six warmer months here.

Just north of Charlottetown we stopped at a roadside corn stand manned by an elderly farmer who looked and spoke as if his ancestors came over with the Westcountrymen back in the 1800s.

3

He dropped vowels, consonants and words like a character from a James Herriot novel. "Just called vet'nry." After an impromptu tour of his dairy operation with an extended stop in the barn while our ten-year-old had her fingers well sucked by a calf, we asked the grizzled Islander how many generations of his family had been on the farm. "None," was his amused reply. Turned out he was a teacher from Winnipeg who got fed up with city life and ill-behaved students less than a decade earlier.

Alison, an air force brat, enjoys a certain cachet when visiting because she was actually born on the Island. As a baby, she lived there briefly in a house on an abandoned fox farm complete with tomb-like fox houses that terrified her mother when night fell. Many postings later, her family returned but once again was forced to live off the base because married quarters were in short supply. The family camped out for a few months in the fishing village of Victoria on the south shore. It was a magical place for an eight-year-old—milk delivered by horse and cart and a hulking wooden pier jutting out into the Northumberland Strait where the whole town seemed to congregate.

Alison and her brother and sister spent many happy hours hanging over the pier and dropping rocks into the water, trying to split the giant jellyfish in half. Modest utilitarian houses rimmed the main street, in fact just about the only street in town. The fields ran down to the shoreline and stretched out in every direction. To a child the village was a storybook oasis wedged between the endless ocean on one side and the endless land on the other.

The school was a two-room wooden structure, grades 1 to 6 in one room, 7 to 12 in the other—a row of desks for each grade. The two hard-working teachers kept order with a form of academic musical chairs. When you finished the material for one grade, the teacher simply moved you farther down the row.

When you reached the bottom of one row, you moved to the top of the next. Each morning the students checked the seating chart on the blackboard to see which part of which grade they were in. Alison managed to complete two grades, or two rows, in three months. At that pace, had she stayed, she would have graduated at thirteen and finished a Ph.D. by seventeen.

The short cut to school was across the fields of a farm on the edge of town. A strange young man worked there. "Crooked in the head," the farmer solemnly explained to Alison after he caught his employee trying to give an anatomy lesson to her and her sister one morning. "He's a good fella, just keep away from his hands," he advised the girls, who spent the rest of the walk to school pondering the connection between crooked heads and hands.

One day in late May, just before recess, the schoolchildren were busily engaged in workbook computations when a loud clanging started in the school yard.

"They're here!" several boys shouted in unison, leaping from their desks and rushing to the door. "I'll be planting potatoes in your backside if you don't sit down," the teacher bellowed in a voice that could easily have served as the lighthouse foghorn. Quickly she rattled off the lessons they were to do on their own in the evenings. Knowing each child's farm and circumstance, she adjusted their workload accordingly. Some with small acreages would be back in a week, others not for a month. Even those who didn't live on farms helped out, so no one commented as Alison, who had no idea what they were doing or where they were going, flung herself out the door and onto the waiting hay wagon with the other children.

Oh glory! Oh freedom! The air never tasted so sweet. The wagon, pulled by Robin and Candy, two dark chestnut Clydesdales with flaxen manes and tails, dropped the children off at various points. Alison simply stayed aboard until the last stop. Within the hour, she was belly down on a different wagon, handing out potatoes to fill up planters' apron-like burlap bags as they walked slowly along the furrows dropping slices of seed potatoes into the ground, careful that each piece contained an eye.

Alison's childhood sojourn in PEI imprinted itself deeply on her but, in spite of extensive travel, it wasn't until thirty-five years later, with David and two kids in tow, that she was able to revisit the dream.

Victoria was little changed, though the milk lady was gone, the houses had somehow shrunk and the pier was now shorter, to an adult's eye. Everything once working had been re-created for tourism. A restaurant and souvenir shops occupied the end of the pier and the lighthouse had become a charming "attraction." The village inn was still an inn but many of the houses along the main street had been converted to cafés and boutiques that, thankfully, stocked minimal amounts of Anne. Near the lighthouse a small, ancient house had become a used bookstore with tilting floors and rough-hewn board walls polished by generations of hands. When Alison lived in Victoria, a man easily as old as the house owned it and kept a pig in the front room. The farm on the edge of town was still there but the fields that once held cattle and horses were planted in potatoes. There was no sign of the man crooked in the head.

We had a wonderful time, two of the best weeks of our lives together. We rented a cottage in Thunder Cove on the north shore of the island and melted into the place as if we'd been there forever. The sea changed daily from a friendly blue to a stand-offish green to a roiling, angry grey, and once, in the morning, nearly a hundred metres of brown-grey froth lay on the beach like a dirty moustache. We were in the water every day. We made friends, the rare kind you know are forever within five minutes of meeting—Faye Pound, Michael Gaudet and their two children.

Through them and our own explorations, we were being slowly steeped in the culture of the potato. During the summer, the ebbs and flows of the spud are reported on the front page of the paper as if it were the Queen come to visit. There are daily evaluations from the government agriculturalist about the shape, colour and condition of flowers, reports on the incidence of disease—the dreaded blight, recommendations about what and when farmers should be spraying and, of course, the current price per pound. Island farmers, like most elsewhere in Canada, use a pidgin form of measurement—pounds for this, kilometres for that and acres for something else.

We visited the potato museum in O'Leary, an earnest place seemingly designed to cement for all time the potato's boring image. Out front, impaled on a pole, is a large brown object looking more like a giant carbuncle than a spud.

"Hey, you guys should write about the potato," Faye urged us late one evening, when we were all deep into cognac and Cuban cigars. "There's all kinds of interesting stuff." We distinctly recall our dismissive response. But the potato was growing into us just as surely as the Island itself. For the simple truth remains that PEI is potatoes and potatoes are PEI.

The Inuit have a multitude of words to describe snow, the thing that most defines the pattern of their lives. Similarly, Islanders have a variety of ways to pronounce potatoes. The four consonants and four vowels are combined with remarkable results. In the earthiest version, the p becomes b and the two t's are d's. Bodadoes. There's a gutteral quality to this version, the word rising up out of the lower part of the throat with each syllable receiving equal emphasis, and the voice remaining flat

7

throughout. It's fairly rare to hear this most elemental pronunciation of the word. More common is the form favoured by veteran spud man Elmer MacDonald. At the end of his hearty phone message, he encourages callers to "eat beef and potatoes," except it comes out as "podadoes."

Then there are potadoes and podatoes and even, occasionally, potatas, potadas or bodatas. Who would have imagined such a humble veg would give rise to such variation? Normally the word is spoken with a thud, like a spud dropped on a wooden table— a sound, despite the variations, as plain and no-nonsense as the potato appears to be. Sometimes though, when uttered with the rounded corners of an Acadian accent, a hint of lyricism envelops the vegetable.

ABOUT THE ONLY THING that Island potato farmers agree on is that it's no longer possible at current prices to start a farm from scratch. Land sells for between $2,500 and $3,000 an acre and it's now simply too expensive for the average person to buy enough land to make potato growing economic. But at $3,000 an acre, if you haven't already acquired your stake, then it will likely never be.

A generation ago, two hundred acres was a big holding capable of supporting a family in style; now it's barely enough. And that is what haunts so many farmers on the Island. Potatoes are greedy, pulling nutrients out of the land faster than farmers can replace them. That, plus the incidence of blight, means the land needs to rest for two to three years after a potato crop, and some believe a four- or five-year rotation is healthier for the land. So three hundred acres means, at best, only a hundred acres in spuds every fall. The rest of the land is planted in hay or grain, but the prices are so low it isn't even worth trying to market that crop so the harvest gets used for livestock on the farm. That's why most potato farmers have something four-footed on the land—to eat up whatever gets planted in the fields after harvest.

Potato farmers don't dare think of splitting their land among their children. Today, the average farm size is six hundred acres, and dividing that between even two children can turn a viable farm into a marginal one, with both limping along until they're forced to give up and the land is devoured by a bigger farmer or one of the corporations that are buying increasingly large chunks of PEI.

"I'm hoping to die accidental," hollered one farmer with a mouth full of scallop burger at Shelley's Diner in Alberton on the western section of the Island, "with just enough of my insurance left over to take care of the two younger ones." A full holler was apparently his normal speaking voice.

His companion guffawed, almost choking on his burger in the process. "Ahhh Harvey, we should be so lucky to see you gone before your time!"

"I'm serious, I've got it all figured out. If I kick over before I'm seventy, then there'll be some insurance. Sammy'll have the farm and be land-rich and cash-poor—just like his old pa. And the others'll have money in the bank but no land. I'd say that's a fair trade-off. But if I live till I'm eighty, the insurance will be piss-all."

"Well," observed his companion, wiping a dollop of tartar sauce from his lips, "we'll have to shoot you. That's all there is to it. Otherwise you're likely to live till you're a hundred. You're stubborn enough."

"Stubborn? Look who's stubborn. Who told you not to plant those blue potatoes last year? Me! And who said he was going to make a fortune on the fancy pants market? You! Who was right? Me!"

His companion acknowledged the truth of it with sheepish good nature. With "gourmet" blue and purple potatoes retailing at three times the price of the standard table varieties, he thought he could balance out the lower priced potatoes destined for the French fry market with twenty acres of two specialty varieties— almost black-skinned on the outside with exotic blue flesh shot through with purple on the inside. Then came the problem of marketing a specialty product. He thought he'd sold over half the crop to a wholesaler who supplied the giant Sobey's chain. But the man never showed up to truck the crop away. Hurriedly, he made a deal with an agent on the Island at twenty-five cents a pound, only to get beaten down to eighteen cents a few days before the load was to be shipped. Five thousand pounds went at that price, and he hung on until January with a heaping pile of spuds resting in his barn gambling on a late-season surge in prices. It never happened and he ended up averaging less than he got for his French fry crop.

Farmers complain bitterly about the prices paid to them by Cavendish Farms, owned by the omnivorous Irvings. It's barely break-even, they grouse, but the relationship with Cavendish or McCain, the newcomer to the frozen chip industry on PEI, carries a precious bonus—a contract, a guarantee.

With no quota system or marketing board setting prices and controlling production, such as exists with milk and eggs in most parts of the country, farmers have no idea when the seed goes in the ground how much they will be able to sell and at what price when the tuber is disinterred nearly five months later. A contract in hand means certain money in the pocket. Appealing to many —anathema to some.

The image of the potato farmer is universally staid, as unchanging as the earth, conservative to the core, practical to a fault. We

10

think it may have something to do with the potato itself, which is hardly the stuff of romance. William Tell didn't shoot a potato off his son's head. The wicked witch didn't offer Sleeping Beauty a poisoned spud. Nor was Adam tempted by a tuber. The potato has something of an image problem, and calling it the apple of the earth isn't fooling anyone.

But as with the potato itself there is more going on under the farmer's skin than meets the eye. Tease the surface of a surprising number of farmers and you will find the soul of a gambler. There are plenty of stories of high stakes games played among growers, with fields and farms being won and lost on the turn of a card.

Less dramatic, but also risky, is refusing to sign early contracts for French fry or table potatoes. Some farmers hold their crops off the market, paying storage fees throughout the early winter months, betting prices will rise. All the while they know there's a chance their pile of potatoes will end up a pile of mush—caused by mould or blight—by the time they turn around to sell them.

FIVE MINUTES IN THE company of Elmer MacDonald is like an adrenalin injection. Lassitude departs and you suddenly feel the urge to organize yourself—clean out a closet, tidy the glove compartment of your car, purge an address book—anything to make life click along more smoothly, unfettered by the detritus that so often slows us to a crawl.

Elmer could have been many things: a battlefield general, the administrator of a large institution like a hospital, a university president, a traffic cop, a night club comedian—anything requiring self-confidence and sufficient strength of personality to convince those around you that the right thing has been done or said.

For a time Elmer struggled against his fate. His mother, born and raised on the Island, was an only child. She married his father in 1941, and her family farm eventually came along with the union. It was a typical eighty-acre mixed farm of the time: cereal crops, cows, swine, potatoes. "We still had a laying flock," Elmer recalls. "And it wasn't the potatoes that brought in the money, it was the weaner pigs."

Elmer, born in 1943, was well saturated in the culture of the land but his first two career attempts would have set him on the urban path. He took his booming voice, as impressive as the late Lorne Greene's, and applied for a job as a radio announcer. The station said no thanks. His father had started a small insurance company to make ends meet during poor crop years, so Elmer decided the world of business deserved a look. He went to Household Finance for a position as a loans officer. He didn't pass muster there either. Finally he edged closer to the land and applied for a job artificially inseminating cattle. Elmer was eminently qualified for the work as he'd grown up with cattle, and piping bull semen into vaginas was something he could do with his eyes shut. But the cattle breeder sent him on his way.

"I thought, the Lord, or somebody, is giving me a message. I might as well go home and farm." Another message was waiting for him there. One day in 1968, not long after his return to the farm, Elmer went into the barn to find his father hanging from the rafters. To this day no one knows the hows or whys. Looking back, Elmer is grateful that he and his brother, Earle, had the responsibility of taking care of both the family farm and the insurance business. It kept him from thinking too much, wondering why a man who had led a successful life could not, one day, face another morning. "It's not one single thing that makes a person what they are," he says, having long ago put the tragedy into a cupboard in his mind marked "no answers." "Some things are not for us to understand."

Over thirty years Elmer and Earle, who is the business manager, have carefully and deliberately expanded their holdings from 80 acres to 1700, absorbing nearly a dozen small farms or parts of farms in the process. The brothers' farm is an average sized one, just as it was in the days of their father. The MacDonald spread perfectly reflects what has happened to PEI in the last quarter of a century. From supporting primarily mixed farms, the land is now given over to potatoes with some beef cattle or pigs to clean up the leftover spuds, provide manure for the fields and generally make the farm more efficient. "The way I look at it, my brother and our two boys make up a production unit. Back when we took over the farm there were more than two thousand production units on the Island. Now there's only six hundred."

The brothers have expanded the insurance agency begun by their father and write policies for many farmers in the area. They've also teamed up with a group of other farmers to create a packing and processing company, Mid-Isle Farms, to wash, package, market and ship their crops instead of sending it out, as most farmers do, to one of the big plants on the island. Elmer's proud of what the two families have accomplished, but his recitation of their progress is underlain by the barest hint of remorse. Though he knows the growth of the MacDonald farm was necessary and inevitable for survival, he recognizes that their success has helped hurry along the end of PEI's old way of life. "Those farms we bought, each were separate parcels. Each were run by separate families, eking out a living the day my father died."

Elmer is that rare beast—a natural-born salesman. Life insurance policies fly out of his hands because he fervently believes in the concept and feels his price is fair. People trust him because there's no doubt about his beliefs and the passion underlying them. And the single thing that Elmer is most passionate about is . . . well, potatoes.

"Do you know that the potato is the only vegetable that can be whipped?" he demands. "It's incredibly versatile! You can put it in ice cream, fry it, freeze it, boil it, mash it. You can do it up all elegant or it can be a lowly man's meat and potato."

Elmer invites Alison to ride along one morning in October as he harvests the last of his fields for the season. Early morning frost had kept them waiting for the soil to warm. Among its many peculiarities and sensitivities, the potato has a powerful aversion to frost. Unlike some tuberous veggies such as leeks, parsnips and carrots, which actually enjoy a jolt of sub-zero temperatures, firing up their sugar content in response to the onslaught of cold, the potato shrinks from it, a princess bruised by a pea.

When the crew pulls over to the side of the field for lunch, Elmer quickly turns the conversation to his favourite topic. He maintains that the spud has the temperament, if not the looks, of a movie star. "It's a peculiar animal," he says while digging into a hard-boiled egg. Fussy about its growing conditions and as susceptible to ailments as an over-corseted Victorian woman was to fainting, the potato cannot be taken for granted. He presses his thumbnail into a spud's skin. It gives a little pop of resistance as the nail digs into the flesh. "Hear that? That snap means it's okay. The pulp of the tuber will injure very, very easily if it's too cold."

"You know," he sums up with a note of sympathy, "it's a living organism and when you consider it, it doesn't really have any great life. Lots of things can get at it."

Elmer has 150 acres planted in Russet Burbank—the brick, farmers call it. Long, blocky and heavy yielding, its squarish shape has made it every man's potato, a versatile form of the vegetable

14

that bakes, mashes and fries equally well. The French fry companies love the Russet Burbank because its regular, elongated shape yields the maximum number of long, skinny chips with minimum waste. But the potato gives nothing away easily. Though simple to market, it needs one of the longest growing seasons, 130 to 140 days, forcing farmers to plant early in the spring when the ground is still wet and keeping them harvesting late in the fall when frost is common. The harvesting season is so late farmers often can't get a cover crop of hay or rye on the field to stabilize the soil and return vital nutrients. Elmer picks up an average-sized fairly round potato the harvester missed. "These are Sierra. I decided to plant them for fun. It's a little bit of excitement, doing something different just to see what will come up." He turns the potato over in his hand. "Jeepers, it's kind of nice to be doing something with a little excitement to it!"

As he excavates the last bit of egg from its shell, Elmer looks out over the neat furrows. "This is a business, no mistake about that. But I tell you, it's something to walk out in a field and say those are my cattle and that's my potato field." Elmer loves the land as much as the next guy, but before you get too spiritual about Mother Nature he'll bring you back to earth. "You can talk about ways of life and all that. But this is a business we're running here."

"Pitter, patter, let's get at her!" bellows the warehouse foreman to the small crew of men and women lounging in a hedgerow, finishing their lunch. The foreman, a small, hustling man, is actually a carpenter by trade but takes his temporary job of organizing Elmer's warehouse during planting and harvest very seriously.

"He gives us orders!" Elmer laughs as the foreman shepherds the crew back on to the machinery like a border collie with sheep. "And we take them. No questions asked." He swings up into the cab of the harvester, beckoning Alison to follow. "There's not a whole heck of a lot of room in here. I'm not slim. No, I'm not." He's big all over, a bear-like burliness that radiates strength, confidence and vigour. So it's almost impossible to believe that he's survived two battles with cancer. "I'm glad to be here. Every day's a great day!"

You would think a man who'd faced down that terror would be content to coast on the labour of a lifetime, perhaps even sell off a bit to one of the voracious mega-farms on the Island. It's an idea that raises steam from Elmer's collar. "We're not going to be forced away from what is ours! Not for any reason!"

Elmer's voice hasn't softened with his nearly six decades, nor has his enthusiasm for new directions. In his spare time, a bit of an oxymoron in the farming business, he calls horse shows and tractor pulls, both requiring a stentorian voice and a ready supply of comedic jabber to fill in the down times. He's also a skilful back-room negotiator and communicator, so he was the obvious choice to chair the highly charged 1996 provincial Round Table on Resource Land Use and Stewardship, set up by the government to investigate land use practices in the province. Elmer, with seventeen hundred acres, wasn't big enough to alienate the smaller farmers, but he was successful enough to talk to the corporate farmers; he wasn't too environmental for the more conservative farmers, yet he was open enough to satisfy most environmentalists—in short, he was Elmer.

"Now why would you deliberately set up something that's going to piss everyone off and satisfy no one," observes one potato inspector sagely, "except perhaps a bunch of bleeding-heart ecotypes who could then point to it as some kind of Holy Bible which is then going to piss people off even more? I'd be lying to you if I said when they set the thing up there were more than three people on the whole island who thought it could work." He pauses for a moment as if trying to summon up the three in his mind. "Elmer would be one of them, that's for sure."

The Round Table was a blueprint for disaster, surely created by a sly machiavellian back-room boy hoping that its various factions would punch themselves out on each other before the issues got back to the politicians for action. Farmers of all sorts, thrown together with environmentalists and a sprinkling of ordinary citizens and academics, were asked to come to sensible, workable conclusions about the serious land use problems facing PEI. Each of them had their own flag to wave, their own spot of turf to defend to the death.

Against all expectations it worked—after a fashion. Despite having to fast-track their report after a change in government, a page near the end of the document tells the entire story—sixteen signatures. Every member signed, indicating they agreed with the far-ranging, often radical recommendations, including legislation to make it the owners' responsibility to protect land from erosion and a law barring farmers from planting potatoes in a given field more than once every three years.

"I know it sounds real silly, but it was a labour of love," Elmer says. "The government gave me some tremendous people. We danced for a few meetings. Then all of a sudden we coalesced into a unit doing a job. I was pleased to come up with a document everyone signed, but there were reservations within the industry." The industry being, of course, the potato industry.

"They wouldn't come forward, they were largely silent," says Elmer in disgust. "Since 1990 we've had an increase of forty per cent in the land devoted to potatoes but we didn't get an increase in management skills. Something has to be done. We can't do anything about the price of chemicals or potatoes and we sure as

17

hell can't control the price of machinery, but we can change how we work the land, how we use it. Let's face it, the best piece of land on your farm is your garden. You baby it, put manure and seaweed on it. We don't do the same with potato land. It would be stupid for me not to look after the land. Ultimately, it's one of the few things we can control."

The industry is rapidly becoming a juggernaut, consuming the land, tearing down trees and hedgerows and ploughing right to river's edge to squeeze in an extra few acres. Elmer recognizes that he and his success are part of that juggernaut. He thinks about cod when he worries about the future of potatoes. "I flew to Europe a while back and I asked the attendant to tell me when we'd flown two hundred miles out to sea. I wanted to gaze down and see where there were no more codfish, to get a sense of how big that area was. It's quite a thing to fish out an ocean. There's a lesson there for everything."

One day David accompanies Elmer into Summerside, a former air force base, now a pleasant seaside town, to pick up tractor and car parts. Every second person knows him and expects a word, an exchange of pleasantries or a discussion of crops. Elmer indulges them all. In three hours he chats with twenty people he knows well and greets another two dozen acquaintances. He looks like a man totally at home in his environment.

"Sometimes I wish I lived in a big city like Toronto," Elmer sighs. "You're anonymous. Sometimes I come into town, I don't want to talk to anyone, I'm thinking about something, or worried about something or just don't feel like talking. But if I snub just one person, it'll be all over the island that Elmer MacDonald is a stuck-up son of a bitch who forgets his friends."

Visitors to PEI can entertain themselves by seeing what reaction they can provoke among farmers with the mention of the name

Irving. Complaining about the family, rumoured to be the wealthiest in the country and among the top ten in North America, is a way of life on PEI. People loathe them and all their various companies and holdings so much that the McCains, with their mammoth food processing empire, look like good guys in comparison. Well established outside PEI, the McCains also fall into the devil-with-a-bulging-wallet category, but they're newcomers to the Island French fry industry, and potato farmers take a perverse joy in contemplating a pit bull–like fight to the death between the two corporate entities.

Over the past few decades, the Irvings have gone a long way toward making PEI the world's largest company town. Not only do they own the biggest packing and processing plant on the Island, which handles two-thirds of the potatoes grown for freezing, but they also operate, or farmers suspect they operate, the oil companies that sell the farmers fuel for their houses, cars and tractors, the chemical companies that dispense the precious fertilizers, pesticides, herbicides and fungicides to keep bugs and blight at bay, and heavy equipment dealerships.

"They got you going and coming," growls one old-timer. "Their oil salesman slides out here and insinuates that if we don't buy from him, we'll have problems with our processing contract. And you know what? I just smile and take it. I've got mouths to feed."

Most farmers believe that the Irvings, on top of everything else they own or control, are buying up farm land, and they lay the blame for the high price of potato land at the Irvings' feet.

"They're still buying," assures the old-timer, who won't even refer to the Irvings by name. "If a big farm comes on the market, they get it one way or another. They're the only ones who can buy the land at that price and still break even because of their other businesses. You watch: one day we'll wake up and they'll own most of the best land on the Island and just about every-thing else. Then you bet the price of potatoes will go up."

The man pauses in the manner of one who has a *coup de grâce* to deliver. "The other day, I went to fill up my truck. You know what they were selling at the gas station? At the goddamn Irving gas station? They were selling a ten-pound bag of goddamn Irving potatoes at the goddamn Irving gas station!"

Elmer, who has the Island way of pronouncing *Irving*, some-how making that short, simple name sound like a thorough throat clearing followed by the expulsion of a ripe wad, under-stands that it isn't just the Irvings who have their fingers on his throat and around his privates. "There's a half dozen whole-salers—Sobey's, IGA, McDonald's—who really exert a lot of control over the processing. McDonald's decides what price they're going to pay and that's the beginning and end of story. Even the Irvings can't push them around."

Potato farmers have a lot of people messing with their lives, from potato inspectors who arrive without notice to investigate the health of their plants to grocery chains, processors, fertilizer com-panies, wholesalers, dealers and other middlemen, not to mention environmentalists and developers. Short of what goes on under the bedcovers at night, all these people, companies and institutions leave a farmer little he can call his own. Independence is more an illusion than anything else.

Some merely bitch and moan but Elmer, who can work up an Irving or government rant with the best of them, has actually done something to elude their pervasive grasp. Mid-Isle Farms, owned by him, his brother and six other farm families, gives them a good deal more independence than the average potato farmer. "Before, we had to go to someone else and they didn't have the versatility to package things the way the market demanded," he starts off on the standard business explanation. Give him a moment and he will come up with the real reason.

"What it boils down to is we wanted some control of our destiny," he says flatly. "If you think about it, most of us are farmers because we don't want other people telling us what to do—controlling us. So what's the point of getting up at the crack of dawn, breaking your back, never knowing whether the crop you've put in the ground is even going to pay off next year's seed cost if you've sold your soul to some peckerwood?"

Mid-Isle is a free-standing company, not a co-op. The owners consciously took a very businesslike approach, hired a consultant and, like the cautious potato farmers they were, stretched their pennies every step of the way. They also made sure that they were educating themselves along with their paid hands. "When they said they wanted to travel to some exotic place to study their methods, we said fine, but one of us comes along with you, to see for ourselves. It was a major learning curve but it's allowed us to keep abreast of change. Particularly in marketing. You know marketing is still seen as something mystical by us farmers. And as a result, we really haven't done a good job selling our potatoes.

"We haven't even done a good job with varieties," Elmer laments, once again returning to his favourite subject. "There're dozens of them and most people can't tell one from another. Can you imagine that happening with apples? The farmer feels so far removed from the consumer. In the stores, potatoes are seen as loss leaders with no sex appeal," Elmer complains. "Potatoes have class!"

If anyone could have convinced William Tell to place a potato on his son's head, it would have been Elmer.

*   *   *

THERE AREN'T WORDS TO describe the smell. Neither chemical nor organic, rot nor excrement. It grabs at the throat, invades the eyes and somehow layers itself invisibly on clothing and hair. Driving east and skirting the postcard scenery of the north shore, Alison's delight in the vistas is interrupted by the growing olfactory assault that began as she turned inland at Brackley Beach.

Her memory struggles to connect the odour with something familiar as a way to diminish it. The best she can come up with is the eye-tearing smell of a large, half-thawed, very dead, partly decayed dog as it lay on a surgery table in the veterinary hospital where she worked thirty years ago. Stored in a meat locker for several weeks, it had been dumped there by the kennel boy to thaw sufficiently for autopsy. As the vet sliced into its belly, the stink of all stinks goosestepped into the room. Now that was a bad smell.

This one rivalled it.

Alison is looking for Barry Cudmore, a potato farmer. He's variously known as a bit of an activist, a bit of an environmentalist, a deadpan joker and a good farmer. He's also an educated man.

Alison arrives at the Cudmore farm to find him gone, having left instructions with his father and his father's brother-in-law, Bud, to send her along. "Up the hill, round the corner, along a piece and there he'll be, you can't miss 'im," says Bud, offering up directions the way one might toss a bunch of pick-up sticks on the table.

Asked for elaboration, Bud and the father confer for a moment, enjoying the puzzle of how to get Alison from the Brackley Beach farm to somewhere west, vaguely en route to Oyster Bed Bridge. Alison suggests a map but they'll have none of it. Despite their assurances that Barry and his tractor can't be missed—"it's a big un"—doubt lies bare in Alison's eyes. She envisages wandering lost in a maze of clay-packed roads with the odd portage, some fence jumping and many stops for further directions. Previous experience has taught her that the long strips of red furrows chasing down to the sea and separated by the occasional hedgerow all look more or less the same when you're navigating by Island directions.

As the two men chew over the problem, Alison takes in the surroundings. The Cudmore farmhouse, where Barry's father lives, is a modest white clapboard building lacking even a hint of pretension—just the solid, working home of three generations of farmers. Barry's home is a modern bungalow, set a few hundred metres farther along the road. Behind the houses a hulking pig barn squats. An acre of lawn stretches out in front of the farmhouse; the only decoration is a string of small white holiday cottages like rough pearls along one edge. The yard is immaculate, the surrounding grass neatly clipped and you just know that the tools in the work shed will be razor sharp, well oiled and hung up in their allotted places. Then a discordant note.

A Honda 250, polished up like a tart on the prowl, sitting there innocently, the fall sunlight bouncing off the shiny chrome gas tank and the deep black fenders. Even a person with no desire to have a throbbing machine between their thighs couldn't help but feel a twinge of yearning for the freedom of the road. This isn't just any old pig farmer.

Alison again suggests a map but Bud waves the idea aside, saying he'll "ride shotgun" to show her the way. Pure Island, like Bud himself, several generations, Alison guesses. A trim, seventyish man of average build, Bud is dressed like Barry's father—well broken-in clothes, feet clad in rubber boots trimmed by mud and manure. His most striking feature is the friendly open face of a man who always seems to be smiling. He hops into the car, slaps his knees mightily with his palms and nods westerly, "that way." He hums quietly to himself as they head off.

After a couple of miles, Alison discovers that Bud is a cheerful pretender; though born on the Island, he's an electrical engineer from Cambridge in southwestern Ontario. "You know, I'm blessed," he says with a long comfortable exhale of air. "I get to come here for a month every year and act like a farmer." Bud spends his days tinkering, jawing with his brother-in-law about this repair job or that improvement and lending a hand. Mostly he's soaking up PEI's aura and perfecting his Islandness.

Along the way, Bud has developed the Islander's knack of answering questions with one of his own—a particularly endearing aspect of PEI that makes one think Island people find you fascinating, so much so they want to explore you as much as you do them. A comforting trait in a hurry-around-the-next-corner world.

The façade of Island-ness isn't all that difficult to acquire because PEI stamps outsiders willingly with its personality. Anyone can be an Islander for a day or a week; it's one of the little liberties that PEI allows.

There are many special places around the world—the tiny, perfect alpine villages of Switzerland; the bleak, lava-covered hills of Hawaii's Kona coast; the bends and twists of the Bow River finding its way through the mountains of Banff—and PEI. Places where the spirit drags itself out of hibernation with heightened awareness and a feeling of being alive that gets lost in everyday life. In these rare places, visitors want to stay and grow into the landscape as if it had always been home. But such Shangri-Las come with a ticket for viewing only. You arrive as a visitor and leave as one. You absorb, extol and depart—your tenure being as insignificant as that of any of the hordes who preceded you. You can play native briefly, hope for it, but it can never be. In some places getting cosy with the local temperament is positively discouraged. You are an *Ausländer*, a "gorbie" as they say in Banff, and you must respect the boundaries that entails. Often it's a subtle message, rather than a sour rejection, but it's there nonetheless.

PEI is different, perhaps because it is, despite the Anne industry and the magical dunes of the north shore that draw summer tourists, a working island. You can't hang your hat on a few weeks of tourism every year. By September the visitors are mostly gone and all that's left is the Island, what it is and always has been. It doesn't give rise to feelings of superiority and aren't we lucky and don't you wish. As a result, there's no big deal in keeping people out of the club. If they want to play native, fine— there's always the howling winds of winter or the bleak grey chop of early spring to sober up a romantic spirit.

For Bud, the diversion of running Barry to ground is a fine adventure. Up and over one hill, around a corner, another hill and ten minutes later Bud is peering into the fields sloping toward the almost landlocked Rustico Bay. There isn't a hint of "can't miss 'im" Barry, though Alison slows the car when Bud mutters that he's "somewhere around here." They pull off onto a rough track and the smell, which had been building insidiously, hits full force. Bud doesn't blink or comment. Come to think of it, Alison recalls a much milder version emanating from Bud as he climbed into the car. She tentatively mentions the smell. "That'd be the manure," Bud drawls. "They're spraying pig manure around here. You get used to it."

No steaming pile cascading off the back end of horse, cow, sheep or even human kind ever gave off this kind of stench. Pig poop may be the only manure that smells worse when aged. It's not pigs' fault, they can't help their peculiar hindgut fermentation, which produces the 150-odd compounds responsible for the wrenching odour—3-methyl butanoic acid, skatole and 4-ethyl phenol, to mention a few. Pig pong is a huge problem for hog farmers who want to exist or expand within sniffing distance of the human population, especially of the tourist variety. Researchers from Guelph to Scandinavia have busied themselves messing about with pigs' feed, trying to fool their intestines into producing something less likely to burn the nose hairs off human beings. So far they've failed.

After a few turns, some of them quite invisible until you're actually on the road, the quality of which progressively deteriorates, Bud motions Alison into a field with a still rougher track ambling off into the distance. He points to a crude pull-off where they park the car and decamp. There's no sign of anyone, much less "can't miss 'im" Barry. Skirting a hedgerow, Bud resolutely tromps toward the sea. Suddenly a graveyard pops into view, right in the middle of the field. Greyed stones, some with mossy shoulders, overlook the bay. The tiny cemetery's sweet isolation pulls a little at the heart. A rumble of machinery drifts over the tangle of trees at the edge of the graveyard. Barry has been found.

He swings the big Ford tractor through a turn and heads back toward the pair standing at the top of the field. Introductions are made, and there is an awkward moment as they contemplate how to conduct the interview and what to do with Bud, who stands there, hands in pockets, leaning back on his heels, beaming. Finally Barry lifts an eyebrow and Bud gets the hint. "I love to walk around," he announces, then saunters off.

Despite the massiveness of Barry's tractor, there is little room in the cab for two. It's very cosy. He seems unperturbed by having a strange woman practically sitting in his lap and poking into his life. The bones of it are simple and fairly straightforward. Today there's an exotic allure to living in PEI, but when Barry was growing up in the fifties and sixties it was simply Canada's smallest province with not much of anything to recommend it but a few weeks' good swimming weather in the summer. By the early seventies, despite a small influx of back-to-the-landers and draft dodgers, it was still a backwater with farming stamped deeply on its psyche. Even the University of Prince Edward Island wasn't much of a draw and was considered a last resort by kids from off the Island. Barry was on fire to be out in the big wide world. As soon as he graduated in biology from the small campus of UPEI, he took himself about as far inland as you can get in this country —Edmonton—and a job with Amoco Petroleum.

Barry finds a small bit of irony in the fact that the Island caught up with him in Alberta. He met his Summerside-born wife, Ellen, in Edmonton and they married in 1975. It was around about then that the land began to call. "It seemed to me that agriculture allowed you to do the things you wanted to do," he recalls bemusedly. "There seemed to be more free time, more time to . . ." His voice trails off as the tractor lazily rounds another corner. Barry checks his line. Long, reddish brown sausages peel out from the blade of the harrow; the turf neatly folds over itself, burying the grassy hay to rot down over the long winter.

"More time to?" Alison prompts. He eyes her for a moment, considering. Time. For farmers time is a competitor in a two-person race and a partner in an uneasy but necessary alliance. A friend, an enemy, an implacable companion that forms the walls within which farmers must live. Barry provides no ending to the sentence.

There's a thoughtful side to Barry, as if a piece of him resides permanently somewhere else. He wouldn't be out of place as a philosophy professor, though his conversation is as concrete and

27

practical as the next farmer's. There's a sense that his brain is following a different path as his mouth forms the words of conversation. He talks about farming as a means to an end, merely the springboard to the kind of life he wants to live. That mythical life where time is always a friend and there is leisure to think and explore.

Though Barry Cudmore can be pensive and thoughtful, he's anything but languid. Over the past two decades he's flung himself into projects and causes in addition to building his farm, improving his land and raising his family with Ellen. In 1979, only three years after returning to agriculture and while carrying the staggering load of an eighteen per cent mortgage, Barry agreed to be one of twelve farmers hosting an international group visiting Canada to learn about North American farming. He assumed that those he met, also people involved in working the land, would be more or less like him.

"Our eyes were opened. I couldn't believe some of what I heard about, how little they had and how they farmed. There was so much they needed. We didn't know what we could do or even if we could do anything. "

Looking back, Barry is quietly amazed by what a small number of PEI farmers were indeed able to do. First came a proposal to the Canadian International Development Agency, then a month-long mission of twenty-two Islanders to Kenya and Tanzania and a return visit by the Africans to the Island. Farmers Helping Farmers was born—a low-key, almost completely unknown farming version of Doctors Without Borders.

"I guess some people thought we were just grabbing tax money," he says a little belligerently. "But we did things. We provided seed money—sometimes literally, money just so they could buy seed— to so many projects. There were lots of women's groups we helped out. It might just be a couple of hundred dollars, but it was enough to buy a piece of equipment or whatever they needed. Really, it wasn't about business, it was about self-sufficiency."

Over twenty years, Farmers Helping Farmers has handed out close to half a million dollars, tiny by foreign aid standards. And there's nothing that amounts to a monument to the group, no hydroelectric projects, no buildings, no burgeoning market for their products, just coins in the pockets of African farmers. But it is enough, it has made an impact. "That would be my legacy," Barry says, adding almost as an afterthought, "if I had one." Barry always seems to have an afterthought. Another slant or twist on something he'd already made perfectly clear.

By this time the ploughing is forgotten. Barry stops the tractor at the end of the field above a cliff leading down to a stony beach and the bay. The Gulf of St. Lawrence along the Island's north shore assumes many colours, but it seldom mimics the blue of the Caribbean. This day, the perfect combination of air and water temperature and sun imparts a rare azure cast to the sea. It dances across the eyes, mingling with the red soil and humps of land forming the far end of Rustico Bay. In the distance the glassy sea looks flat enough to skate on. Alison makes a ritual writer's apology for getting in the way of Barry's work and encourages him to continue ploughing. He'd told her a few days earlier that he would be catching up after a trip to Ottawa, "Mecca," he'd called it.

"No," he says, "that's okay, sometimes it's good just to stop for a minute." The view is stunning, mesmerizing. It occurs to Alison that this would be a wonderful spot for a cottage set at the edge of the cliff. A little playground, a barbecue pit, stairs to the beach —quiet, pastoral. Many Island farmers have severed sections of their farmland for such development.

Barry won't hear of it. With 250 acres of land near the major

29

tourist destination on PEI, 50 acres of it waterfront, he's sitting on a small fortune, several small fortunes. But he won't piece it off. He waves his hand at an unassuming little white clapboard cottage at the end of a neighbour's field. It stands all by itself and looks as if it's been there since the Island was settled. Only an electrical wire running into it gives a hint that it is of this century. "I don't want any more like that messing up the view." It's the closest he comes to obvious sentiment.

"C'mon," he says suddenly, jumping down from the tractor, "I want to show you something."

Off across the field, skirting the edge of the ploughed-under turf that will be in potatoes next year and plunging into a copse of trees, Barry strides purposely in front. Alison stumbles over a little ridge. It stretches all the way up to the top of the field; an old stone wall, long since overwhelmed by thatch and bramble. Barry walks out into the open and across an unploughed field, yellow-brown with stubble after the second cut of hay had been taken off weeks earlier. He simply stands for some minutes looking out at the water and a different aspect of the bay, the beach and the ocean beyond. "Nice, isn't it?" It is far beyond nice. Glorious, staggering—achingly beautiful.

"Agriculture's a high-stress occupation," Barry says unexpectedly. "Hard on your body, hard on your mind. I had lots of enthusiasm when I was younger. I'd sell this tomorrow if someone gave me the money. I put a high price on it, $2.3 million. If someone was foolish enough to give me that, they could have the whole thing, pigs 'n' all." He smiles at the notion of being a millionaire.

"I'll be fifty in the year 2000. I bought the bike a few years ago. Maybe I'm going through a midlife crisis." It seems a ridiculous statement. Midlife is the time when farmers' offspring begin to take the load off them, when young hands move in to grapple with the broken piece of machinery as a cold October rain sends a jolt of pain through joints that have been there too many times before. It's the time to watch a cocky teenager strip to the waist, clamber aboard a tractor and plough for hours under a sun that seems to come straight from the tropics. It's the time to take a half step back and watch the red dirt grind into the resilient pores of the children you had always hoped would find the land as irresistible as you once did. Midlife for a farmer can be the best of times.

But Barry's four children have no interest in farming and he's just as happy that they don't. So he now faces an Island quandary. Though he doesn't really want to sell, he knows that he could net far more on the interest from the sale than he does from the farming. And though he carefully doesn't say it, he'd rather not sell to the Irvings or any other large operator. But small or start-up farmers couldn't possibly afford to pay the price he wants. If he sold off half his land in order to take life easier, the remaining acreage wouldn't be sufficient to be viable. The cottages in front of his father's house are a way of pulling some cash out of the land without changing it much.

"Can you imagine messing this up with a bunch of cottages?" he asks, daring Alison to disagree. "You could never stand here and look out like this again. It would never be the same." Once you've owned land, it becomes a part of you—selling is a little like cutting off a body part.

But there's also a part of Barry Cudmore that said the vows but didn't marry the land. He can easily envision having travelled a different life path and he certainly wants one for his children. "For the most part agriculture's been good to me," he emphasizes as if concerned that showing the wandering side of his nature might be giving the wrong impression, presenting himself as being shaky or flighty. "We've had some good years."

One of them was 1997. Pork prices rose like the stock of a junior mining company after rumours of a positive assay. Pigs are far from Barry's favourite. "I only ever liked them on my plate. If I had to do it all over again, I wouldn't have a pig around the place." Less than twenty per cent of the farm's 250 acres can be in potatoes each year, so he needs the ballast of a second product. With a small land base, reliance on potatoes alone can strip a farmer naked financially with just one bad year, because you never make a big enough profit in fat times to carry you over the inevitable lean ones. With both pigs and potatoes, he hopes that when prices are soft in one they'll be better in the other.

In 1997 pork shot past Barry's $1.40-a-kilogram break-even point, soared to over $1.75 and kept right on going until hitting $2.18. That year he made $200,000. "Almost everybody could clear $50 a pig. It was great. Fantastic. You felt you were part of the middle class." But as in the stock market, no one can escape the tyranny of the average. By mid-1998, pork prices were hovering in the $1.76 range, teasing with the promise of yet another good year. Hogs began to look positively attractive. Then the Asian financial flu found its way to PEI and as the pork-loving Asian countries tightened their belts, they put the screws to pig prices, driving them down to twenty-five cents a kilo. Consumers didn't notice; pork prices hardly budged in the grocery stores, but farmers across the country were hammered to their knees.

"We'll ride the thing out," shrugs Barry. "January 2000. That's when things will turn around. But there's going to be a lot of bloodshed, a lot of pain." He fully expects some of his fellow hog farmers to be wiped out. It will be one of those years to be thankful for the potato crop.

Barry keeps potato growing as simple as possible. Unlike Elmer, he doesn't sell into the retail market. "I am a multiplier of seed," he says of his niche—growing seed potatoes. Barry's crop is purchased by other farmers to plant in the spring. He doesn't even get fancy with varieties, choosing to stay with the current most popular spud, Russet Burbank, the brick. "You can do anything with it—even sometimes make some money with it."

Barry is known throughout the industry as being environmentally sensitive. "He's got an environmental degree you know," we heard again and again, even though he's quick to tell you that it's actually a B.Sc. in biology. Several farmers awarded him a nonexistent M.A. and one even a Ph.D. All it takes to earn a sneer, or worse, from many farmers on this small island is to be known as an environmentalist.

Barry won't let you brand him anti-anything. "Crop protectants," the industry's euphemism for pesticides, herbicides and fungicides, have their risks and their benefits, he opines. "Until something better comes up, so far the benefits far outweigh the risks." Then the afterthought. "I'm happy to put my sprayer away in the winter."

The field is almost done. Last year's hay is cut, raised and turned. Next year potatoes will overlook the bay. Bud reappears, twigs and grass adorning his shirt and pants, having enjoyed a lie-down in a hedgerow beneath the dappled sun of Indian summer. His sated grin speaks of a man who has everything. Barry asks him to return at sundown to fetch him. "I'd rather not be driving this along the road at dark," he says, inclining his head at the big tractor and narrowing his eyes at Bud as if he expects a challenge to this point of view. "Oh no, no, no," nods Bud agreeably. "I can see why you wouldn't want to do that!"

In a few more days the potato work will be put to bed until next spring. There will be hogs to ship, over the fall and winter, and machinery to fix. But time, for a brief spell, will appear to stretch a bit. In that period of relative ease, Barry will head to southern Germany for an agriculture conference and "just to look and see." The group price was excellent, less than $800 for eight days. "I might have to show myself a tinge organic," he says wryly. "But I can do that."

SEED POTATOES AREN'T SEED at all but clones, like garden plants such as geraniums that are commonly propagated by cuttings or division. If you take the wrinkled pinhead-sized seed from a Yukon Gold and plant it, you'll almost certainly get another variety of spud entirely. And if you plant every seed in the whole pod you'll get 150 different varieties, most of which won't resemble anything you've ever seen before, let alone the parent potato. Potatoes don't breed true, perhaps nature's way of ensuring the survival of the species, maintenance of genetic strength, or some other perfectly good reason, but it adds a layer of mystery to the process of improving existing strains or developing new ones. Which might be one reason why there are so few people in the business of coming up with new varieties of potatoes.

In fact, there are only two on the Island who trouble themselves with the time-consuming and exasperating process of potato breeding, odd when you consider the Island's economic dependence on the potato. You'd think there would be backyard potato breeders in every little hamlet, eagerly competing to come up with the next Russet Burbank. One of the breeders is a buttoned-down scientist who works in a pristine lab with spotless test tubes, gleaming stainless steel equipment and a big corporation as his employer. The other is a little guy, actually two little guys who have laboured away for years before recently discovering their own brand new potato—Island Sunshine.

* * *

THE LOO FAMILY, pronounced "low," is well-known. Most farmers we spoke to are aware of their discovery and applaud it respectfully, but they have no intention of ever giving Island Sunshine a try. Few have the slightest inkling what motivates the Loos. "They're good people," one acquaintance told us, "but they're . . ."—he searched for the right adjective "characters, yes characters, that's the right word . . . real characters . . . that they are." Another warned, "They're different. Their place is kind of like a museum."

"It is," allows Raymond Loo to David over the phone, "a little untidy. But look for the church, you can't miss it." Raymond Loo navigates by church, as in "two churches past" or "turn three churches after" or "one church, then a field and two more churches." "Can't miss us," he says several times. "We've got a church right on the property!" Even so David still manages to pull into the wrong place, where the farmer is vastly amused that anyone might mistake his immaculate homestead for the Loos'. "It's over the hill." He gestures vaguely. "Can't miss it," he laughs.

Despite Raymond's directions, the church is the last thing that catches the attention approaching the Loos' farm. It isn't really ramshackle or rundown but rather full—full of things. There are things everywhere: farm things, equipment things, building things, antique things, unrecognizable things. They overflow from house, barn and shed, into the parking areas, invade the fields near the houses and mound up on each other where space is at a premium. The two houses sitting on a rise at the end of a long, pot-holed dirt driveway appeared to lean in opposite directions. (David thought they leaned toward each other and Alison was sure they leaned apart.) Neither building has seen paint in more than a few years, and they both look as if they grew out of the land itself. Beside and below the houses are several greenhouses, worn plastic sheeting stretched thin over their semi-circular frames.

But more remarkable than any of this glorious disarray are the birds. Hooting, squawking and clucking, they flow over the landscape. Hopping and flapping, they navigate the obstacle course of rusted machinery, bits of fencing and piles of just plain stuff.

David identifies the standard hen, rooster and goose. As for the rest, calling them chickens and geese is a little like labelling the British crown jewels trinkets. Some sport exotic head gear, towering feathered topknots; others are odd shapes—like basketballs on feet. Their colours are a dazzling mixture of deep rust, powder-puff grey, red, black and yellow.

David is barely out of his car when Raymond Loo, a thirtyish man with a round boyish mustachioed face, hustles out of the nearest house and introduces himself, saying that his father, Gerrit, will be out soon. "He doesn't move around as good as he used to," he confides conversationally, then asks if David had any trouble finding the place. David tells him he must have got the church count wrong. Raymond gives him a puzzled look. "I counted seven churches," David says. "Nah," responds Raymond, "you must have counted the Jehovah's Witness place down the road—we don't count that."

Farmers like to maintain the pretence that they go about their business not worrying what anyone else is doing. But Raymond, like all the others we met during the busy spring planting, is eager to know what stage the other farmers were at and what problems they were having. "We've got some in," he says, after receiving his progress report, "but the rain is slowing us down."

Gerrit Loo, 72, emerges from the nearest house and walks carefully toward them. Everything about the old man is creased and

36

wrinkled, his face cross-hatched by many lines. Raymond stays for a moment, but energy races around under his skin and he's unable to hang around for long when there are things to do. He jumps into an ancient truck shouting that he'll be back to take David on a tour. As he disappears over the hill, David notices for the first time the lushness of the 250 acres of the Loo farm. Other farms he'd seen were green after the ample rains. But the Loo farm is different, as different as a wild meadow with swaths of marguerites, milkweed and wild indigo is from a tended garden.

There's a sturdy, quiet dignity about Gerrit Loo. His life experiences, the good and the bad, lie on him like many subtle shades of the same colour. A writer's life is like a farmer's—you spend a lot of time digging. Often the people you interview are only spade deep. No matter how much prying, that's all there is. One spade and that's it. Some people throw themselves at you, anxious to show how rich are their lives, how broad is their knowledge, how interesting their history. But in the end there is still only a single shovelful of stuff. With Gerrit Loo you know the questions to be asked and the topics to be explored could be mined for days.

He's calm and obliging and it is a little surprising, a few minutes into the conversation, to sense his voracious intelligence. It's that rarest form—unassuming—and so takes a little while to identify. It is also the purest form, the self-made, self-educated, self-motivated variety. It only grows with a person who has done things, learned things and tried things because, and only because, he wanted to find out, to discover.

The slightly hunched figure of Gerrit shelters the soul of a scientist. Playing with nature, sifting through its ambiguous clues to find its shy secrets, then deciphering them, is something that comes as naturally to him as disorder does to his surroundings.

It was this omnivorous curiosity that led Gerrit and his brother

Evert to Island Sunshine, a white-skinned, yellow-fleshed potato with a rich flavour that has recently been registered as a variety. The process was simple but painstaking and fraught with setbacks. As Gerrit slowly leads David along the rows of planting tables in the greenhouse, describes the process and shows him the meticulous hand-printed records of trial and error, David begins to realize the magnitude of the accomplishment. A new potato. "It's a little like panning for gold," Gerrit says, picking up a slip just beginning to root. We've panned for gold and this is far harder.

First Gerrit plants potato seeds expecting, and getting, 150-odd varieties from those that grow. He estimates that he's planted a hundred thousand seeds since he started breeding potatoes nearly thirty years ago and he's still surprised by what comes up. Some of them are lovely, healthy plants with exuberant flowers and deep, rich colours. But just as easily the tuber might be a stunted acorn, a yam-sized monster or a nasty, misshapen lump. And some never come up at all.

The ones that look promising, and at this stage it's subjective because you've got the yield of only one plant, are noted in Gerrit's potato ledger and stored for the winter. In spring those that are still in good shape are destined for the test plots. Gerrit carefully cuts the potatoes up, ensuring each piece has an intact eye from which the new plant will grow, then sets them out in marked furrows. Throughout the summer the second generation is carefully scrutinized for size, general appearance, yield and resistance to bugs and blight. Whatever spuds are left are then subjected to the taste test.

"Take this one here," Gerrit says, pointing to a small pile of discards. "Beautiful flower, great brown skin, doesn't scab and beautiful firm, bluey-purple flesh. But when you cook it, it turns to mush."

Gerrit might find a lovely tasting spud that has sailed through the trials, but he knows that still won't make it commercially. "You have to test it for sugar because sugar turns French fries brown when they're cooked. McDonald's is death on brown." He makes no attempt to hide his disgust. The very idea that a potato, which may otherwise be perfect, won't make it to market because a French fry company pronounces it unacceptable offends him. He's also distressed that the fast-food industry dictates shape as well—the so-called brick. "If we developed another brick we'd be rich." Gerrit shrugs. "We'll take it if we find it, but we're looking for other things."

In 1998, the Loos planted 550 varieties, which they culled down to 50 worth trying again. In 1999 they put five thousand in the ground hoping to winnow the list down to at least a hundred for replanting. Gerrit estimates that he spent upwards of ten thousand dollars and five years, a lot of money and a lot of time for a small farmer, before he found Island Sunshine—blight resistant, a good producer and tasty. Raymond, if he's anywhere in hearing distance when his father describes the process, ups the figure to twenty thousand. "He never thinks the time he's spent is worth money."

The Loos paid a thousand dollars to the University of Michigan for a genetic fingerprint of Island Sunshine. "If we didn't, you could just up and walk away with my potato, put it into the ground and I could never prove it was mine." When other growers buy Island Sunshine seed stock, a small royalty goes to the Loos. They've just sold seed stock to Colorado and Idaho, a grower in Maine is heavily promoting it as a sexy alternative to other "yellows." Test plots are being grown in Germany, and growers in Manitoba are now interested. "We're not going to get rich on this, but there'll be something." Raymonds fingers a file of newspaper clippings about the new kid on the block. "But I couldn't sell a damn thing here on the Island! That would drive you crazy if you let it. They don't want anything different, no matter how good it is."

Gerrit gingerly walks out of the greenhouse and into the throng of birds. After breaking his back, "near everything else, too," his son adds, in a 1970 car accident, he couldn't do the planting or tend the herd of cattle. "I thought I'd get into chickens. Get me out of the house"—he smiles—"I didn't think I'd end up with four hundred of them, though." He says it as if he woke up one morning to find flocks of birds had taken over his yard.

"That one over there's a Silver Grey Dorking." He indicates a speckled bird as beautiful in its varying shades of cream, grey, black and white as a peacock is with its rainbow hues. "Caesar brought them to England." The Dorkings scatter as a white-crested duck, plumed topknot bobbing comically, runs them off. In their wake a crowd of deeper grey chickens rush about excitedly. There is a calliope of strenuous honking, some of which sounds like a klaxon horn, others more like a tuba. "Those are Scotch Greys. There are only two flocks of them on the Island," Gerrit says proudly. "I thought I'd just try a few to see how they'd do. Got more'n a few now though."

Gerrit watches the birds fondly, his lips twitching as they re-establish the yard hierarchy, put into disarray when he and David strolled out of the greenhouse. Raymond reappears. "Let's plant some potatoes!" He hustles David over to his truck, shovels a sizable pile of lost and found off the passenger seat and slams the old gear box protestingly into first. When his father broke his back, Raymond was called upon to pick up the slack. A butcher by trade, he's done a little of everything, including delivering milk and, when time has allowed, taken a few environmental courses.

The land he works belongs to his father and uncle—church, graveyard and all. When his uncle took sick in the mid-nineties, Raymond took over the whole farming operation.

Raymond inherited the family passion for discovery and experimentation. Bumping over the rutted ground toward one of his test fields behind the farmhouse, he points in the direction of what appears to be a weed patch. "My grandfather discovered white raspberries over there. They're beautiful. So pale they're almost white. Amazing. You buy those in the stores they cost a fortune."

Near the crest of another hill, Raymond stops again. The hill descends gently down to a valley just over half a kilometre away. Below them are two hayfields side by side, still in young grass, the bright, light green iridescent with the moisture of spring. "Did Dad mention we've been going organic?" he asks looking out over the valley.

"No," David answers.

"This is one of the reasons . . . a big reason." He nods toward the two fields. "Notice anything different between them?"

David stares hard at the seemingly identical fields, lovely with the flush of new growth. After a minute he detects subtle differences. The upper field seems slightly greener and the grass denser and longer. The lower field has considerably more weeds, not immediately apparent amid the early season lushness. Otherwise, both appear to be ordinary stretches of hay, still weeks away from the first cut.

But to Raymond the upper field is glowing with health while the lower field is merely getting along. As summer deepens they will diverge even more, he says. "The difference looks bigger to me, but then that's what I do. The bottom field is owned by the farmer over there, the top field is ours. The difference is our field's

41

been organic for three years, the farmer pours on the chemicals and pesticides on the other."

Raymond substituted natural products like copper sulfate and lots of manual labour, for pesticides, fungicides and chemical fertilizers, which leach vital nutrients out of the land. Potatoes are particularly heavy feeders, making the minimum three-year rotation essential to allow the land to recover and cut down the impact of blight and the many other diseases that prey on potatoes.

"Rotation! Ha! People around here call it potatoes and snow rotation," scoffs Raymond. It was a joke with a bitter undertone that we heard again and again. Every potato farmer we spoke to pointed to at least one other farmer who pays no attention to the one-in-three principle. There's no law against it, but farmers who cheat earn the quiet derision of their neighbours—quiet because many have done it themselves or at least have been tempted. Some violate the principle only occasionally when they think it's going to be a big price year. But Raymond knows a farmer who's had potatoes on the same field for twenty-six straight years.

And Elmer MacDonald knows several who've gone at least seven years. "There's so many farmers out there who are willing to find ways to cheat the system. Inevitably it kills the land. That's why we need legislation. Then again there's so many farmers with their backs to the wall. If it means the difference between your kids getting fed or not, what are you going to do?"

Raymond has no time for excuses, working himself into a fine lather at the "idiots" who ignore rotation, imperilling the crops of conscientious farmers in the process. "Hell, we take a lower standard of living rather than hurt the land," he growls. "Others can too. It'll pay off in the long run."

David's reaction to the differences between the two fields

apparently doesn't satisfy Raymond, because he immediately veers off on a ten-kilometre detour to a field where nature has simply given up. Cratered and criss-crossed by run-off fissures, some thirty centimetres deep, the dry clay is scaly and even the characteristic red has turned a sickly brown. It looks like it is suffering from psoriasis. David picks up some soil; it feels like sawdust. Raymond throws a handful into the air; it's so light it floats away.

"This is what you get when you use chemicals for an extended period. There's really nothing left alive in this soil. If you plant potatoes here they won't grow. The soil is dead, it's as simple as that. It's really like hydroponic gardening. If you add water and fertilizer—and you'll have to add more each year—potatoes will grow."

After an hour examining every nook and cranny of the ruined field, Raymond clanks the truck into gear and they rattle off again. This time he doesn't stop until he reaches the Loos' back fields in the shelter of a copse of tall evergreens. Once Raymond is out of the truck and onto the field, his earlier anger and restlessness are gone as if they never existed. He and David are there to plant potatoes, the survivors from last year's seed planting, and some new prospects.

"Now you'll see what real work is like!" Raymond announces, hauling buckets and bags out of the truck bed.

Almost no one plants by hand anymore, certainly no commercial growers. Mechanical planting is very fast and economical, even though there's waste because the machine can't tell if a piece of potato contains an eye or not. The Loos plant by hand in order to rigidly control what goes into their test plots.

The ideal technique is to move along the furrow as you're cutting and dropping, making sure that each piece contains at least one eye that will be the beginning of a new plant. Every thirty to forty centimetres another chunk drops into the furrow. David falters quickly, discovering that it's hard to cut and move at the same time. He develops a system, cut first, move second, plant third. Even so, the potato pieces never fall where they should and have to be constantly adjusted in the furrow.

"Good thing I'm not trying to chew gum too," David quips when he sees Raymond critically appraising his work.

"You said it!" Raymond is ostentatiously holding, cutting and dropping the potatoes using only one hand. As David watches, he adds a flourish with his wrist to demonstrate just how easy it really is.

Eventually a rhythm of sorts catches David up and he begins rolling from one task to the next, a quick step with the feet, a snap of the wrist and the potato piece in its place—more or less. He even manages to keep pace with Raymond, never mind that he's planting one row to Raymond's two. Raymond enjoys talking almost as much as breathing and he has a habit of stopping work whenever he gets to a key point. David encourages this—for professional reasons, not the sweat trickling down his back.

"Maybe you've just planted the perfect brick," jokes Raymond, eyeing David's ragged line. "My chance to go down in French fry history." David stretches his back.

Then Raymond performs what David comes to refer to as the "organic stoop and grab," because each organic farmer he meets performs some version of it. "Get a handful of this and see if there's a difference between it and that crap up the hill," Raymond instructs. The soil is different, moist and cohesive and obviously brimming with life. David says so. Raymond is finally satisfied. He bends down for more spuds. "You know, this is what it's all about. A guy working on his land. You know farming isn't any great way to put food on the table . . . but it sure beats anything else I tried." Raymond turns back to his potatoes.

"See if you can plant 'em a little more evenly this time."

The Loos send David on his way with a five-pound bag of first-generation Island Sunshine seed potatoes. He feels like he is carrying a poke of gold back to southern Ontario. Somehow the potatoes seem infinitely more precious than the lobsters he purchases at the Summerside pound. The lobsters go baggage. The potatoes ride in the cabin.

The night David returned, we ate steamed lobster with drawn butter, warm sourdough bread and boiled Island Sunshine napped with garlic and olive oil. We felt a little guilty consuming the potatoes, knowing with each bite we'd reduced our seed stock. But we couldn't wait for September. Without a stretch, the potatoes were as good as the crustacean and certainly far better than the industry sex appeal leader Yukon Gold, which, in comparison, was so much pyrite.

With an effort of will, we didn't eat every single one, planting the remainder on our little farm in what had been an old rhubarb patch. Into the dark, heavy clay they went, lined up in more or less straight three-metre furrows and marked by rusted pieces of T-bar we'd salvaged from the fence lines when we'd moved in. David became mildly obsessive about their health and well-being. He phoned several times from Yellowknife later in the summer, interrogating Alison and the girls about how many were up and how big the leaves were.

We've always had vegetable gardens, seething briefly over our failures and then forgetting them. But the potato patch was something else. As Ontario's longest dry spell in decades browned everything, the hose was endlessly hauled from house to patch. PEI farmers, also experiencing unprecedented dryness, had to wait and pray. Only a few—almost exclusively the big corporate potato farms—have irrigation; the rest are at the mercy of nature. If there were bugs on the leaves, David plucked them off one by one. But even just six metres of furrows took several hours of work, hard on a back nearing its fiftieth year. It gave us new insight into what the potato farmer faces.

IN EARLY OCTOBER ALISON leaves for PEI to check on David's success as a planter. Raymond Loo obligingly saved that section of field for her. The roads are, for the Island at any rate, busy with tractors, harvesters and trucks moving briskly between field and barn and plant in a last burst of frantic activity to get the crop out of the ground before hard frost. Several early morning frosts have farmers fretting until nearly lunch, waiting for the air and soil to warm enough to begin harvesting. Even the lightest freeze on the surface of the ground spells ruin if potatoes are exposed to it. You often can't tell if damage has been done until they've been stored a while and the frost-bitten spuds turn into something resembling the Wicked Witch of the West when Dorothy threw water on her.

"I'm glad you came," greets Raymond with a worried look on his face. "I don't think David quite understood everything. He just didn't seem clear on the potato business. He's not a farmer type, I'd guess. You look like you'll get it right." Raymond is eager to get to the plot. Weather is one reason, the mystery in the ground is another. Almost as long as he can remember, Raymond has been plunging his fork into the soil in early fall to see what their latest efforts have produced. Each time is like the first.

Up the same bumpy track, Raymond drives with Alison in the cab of his old truck, after shifting around what is apparently the same pile of items as the last time. He stops briefly at a pothole big enough to swim in and kicks the truck into four-wheel drive. "I keep filling that in," he muses, "but it doesn't make any difference. Must be a spring there or something."

Some bits of machinery lie near the field David had helped plant. One of them is an antique beater digger used to get potatoes out of the ground. Its age and working past are reason enough for Raymond to hang on to it. "You've also got your bagger digger and your elevator digger. Kind of interesting, these old things, don't you think? Still works too. Friggin' annoyed me, though, I paid eighty-five dollars for a universal joint for it." It doesn't seem much money for an essential part but to Raymond it's an outrage worth several minutes of grumbling.

He walks along a row looking for a marker, M19, the pinkish-yellow potato David planted. Raymond has forgotten his fork and gloves. "Hmmmm, I should go back and get 'em," he says, whapping his pockets, hoping a pair of gloves will materialize, "but I won't." He plunges his bare hands into the cold soil. "Let's see what we got here." A few puny spuds are exposed. "Ooooh, not too promising." He moves to the next plant and unearths a soggy mass. "Ugh, not lookin' too good for David here." Each plant is the same—there are too few potatoes, they're too small and many are diseased. Raymond straightens up. "Well, I guess we won't be planting that one again." It doesn't even rank as a disappointment (except to David, who was already imagining a plaque in his honour at the potato museum). The odds against a new variety battling all that nature throws at it and then producing itself in a colour, shape, quantity and size that is pleasing and profitable to the market are long.

Raymond strides over a few more rows before finding David's second planting, Blue Splash. The first plant teases with three good-sized spuds. Raymond's fingers scrabble around, digging hopefully, heedless of the freezing soil. Three more. "Those are good-sized fellas. Not enough though." Third plant. Five lovely potatoes, medium-sized, perfectly formed, not a blemish anywhere. Raymond straightens up and studies one in his hand. "That's what we want!" He brushes the dirt off gently. "People won't go for 'em, though."

All this work and a flat rejection? The potatoes look wonderful. Raymond cuts one open, showing Alison the streaky lines of blue running through the creamy flesh. It looks like a wall that's been ragged with a rich indigo colour over an ivory base coat. How could anyone not want to buy, or at least sample, such a delightfully variegated veg?

"People'll think they're diseased or something," Raymond explains, unperturbed by the cruelty of the marketplace. Alison asks why he bothered planting them in the first place knowing he couldn't sell them. "I guess I just like to see what comes up. You never know what kind of surprise you're going to get. Sometimes when I'm sitting back working in the fields, I get to thinking about different varieties—there's lots of time for thinking, nothing else to do."

Last row. The sun is sliding down the sky and the cold deepens. "I'd better bring a fork next time," Raymond mutters, shaking warmth into his battered hands. "Let's just take a look over there and then we'll pack it in." He has some potatoes already dug and lying on the ground in one of the fields near the house. With freezing temperatures in the forecast, he must get them inside before nightfall. C21 is a pale yellow variety. He barely teases the soil before he shakes his head and points to tiny spudlets growing up the stem of the plant. It's a condition called rhizatonia; there will be no potatoes in the ground. The second plant is the same and Raymond doesn't bother to go any farther.

Not a single potato from the afternoon's work will go into next year's breeding program. If Raymond is discouraged, there's no sign. There are more rows to dig and perhaps one or two will be worth carrying forward. If not, he'll spend the winter studying his logs, thinking about the thousands of possibilities the next batch will present, discussing them with his father and, every now and then, allowing himself to dream about finding another new potato.

WITH THE EXCEPTION of the Loo family, whom many already consider peculiar, most organic potato farmers keep a low profile. John Hardy is no exception. It's not that he fears being set upon by his fellow growers, smeared with Diquat from head to toe, then fed into a manure spreader, but he recognizes that making holier-than-thou noises within the powerful Island potato culture might start others "looking at you funny."

The Hardys' farm, where John lives with his wife, Louise, two sons, daughter and father, is nearly an hour northeast of Summerside, smack in the middle of, by all accounts, the reddest collection of necks in the whole province. As a small-acreage farmer with a still growing family to raise and educate, John Hardy would just as soon go about his business and change what he can by quietly doing things his way.

John's grandfather bought 134 acres in the 1920s. Now the Hardy spread is 220 acres, 50 of it leased. Each year John's goal is to put fifty acres into potatoes and the rest into carrots, turnips, and hay and silage for their dairy cattle. On the face of it there's nothing in particular to distinguish the Hardy farm from its neighbours—except size. Though he's by far the largest organic grower on the Island—two or three acres being the norm—he's small potatoes compared to his neighbours. There are six corporate farms nearby, all around three thousand acres and all, in Hardy's words, "well-oiled machines" with fleets of new or near-new tractors, huge equipment sheds and barns, refrigerated storage facilities and full-time employees. The Hardys store potatoes in the traditional manner, on the cool clay floor of their shed, and their tractors, though as big as their neighbours', are much older.

The big farmers are more executives than toilers on the land, men who might not see the inside of a tractor from one year to the next. "They're great farmers," John says with open admiration. "They're wonderfully organized and very wealthy . . . but we do things differently."

The Hardys started doing things differently about ten years ago when they noticed that their organic kitchen garden out-produced their neighbours' gardens. "Everything seemed to taste better," explains John's wife. At the time their farmland was eating up fifteen to twenty thousand dollars in fertilizer, pesticides and other chemicals annually. "We're inclined that way anyway," adds John, "but when you add together the costs of doing things the chemical way, you've got an added incentive. We also noticed that food stores were starting to sell organic products at a premium. In the end we thought it would be a way for our small farm to support our family."

Becoming organic isn't just a matter of exchanging chemicals for poop, and the knowledge gleaned from the garden wasn't necessarily transferable to the larger scale. Years of traditional farming had depleted the Hardys' soil, reducing its capability to grow crops and its capacity to hold water. "It took us three or four years to build the soil back up," explains John. "Fortunately, we had a ready supply of manure thanks to the cattle."

Sydney, John's father, is amused that his son is returning to how he farmed half a century ago because there was no other way. He recalls the drudgery of hauling wagonloads of mussel manure from the processing plants in pre–chemical fertilizer days. "They'd give it away," he laughs. Now what's available is quickly scooped up by home organic gardeners who have been tutored over the last few decades by hundreds of books and magazine articles.

But planting a few dozen tomato plants, a stand of corn and a couple of rows of beans and peas isn't the same as farming 220 acres. "We couldn't find out anything about how to do it, how to get started. Government was useless.

"You'd ask them a question. They didn't know anything and you could tell from their answers that they thought you were crazy for wanting to know. They still don't know anything but now they send people with questions about organic farming to me." He shakes his head. "As if I have time to answer questions!"

John Hardy, forty-five, red haired and bearded, is a slender quiet man who carefully thinks things through. He's not given to quick criticism, but he, like many organic farmers, is intensely frustrated by the government's lack of interest in alternative practices. There is a Job-like quality about him, the sense of a man who perseveres. If the government wasn't going to help him out, he'd find another way.

"Finally I asked my dad how they controlled blight before pesticides," he says a little sheepishly. "Copper sulfate was his answer." Weeds are another problem with no easy natural answer. John resurrected another artifact from the past, a finger weeder, a device that looks like a Mixmaster with prongs. It's pulled through the field just before the weeds are established, disrupting them enough to give the potatoes a head start.

"Everything is timing," John emphasizes. "If you hit the field with copper sulfate before the blight comes, it's great. After, not so good. If you hit the bugs with Bt [*Bacillus thuringiensis*] when they're soft, it works like a charm. Same with the finger weeder. If you weed at the right time, the potatoes will dominate the weeds."

Some traditional farmers claim that copper sulfate and Bt are just as dangerous as pesticides. Bt is a naturally occurring bacteria which kills many different noxious insects, especially the potato beetle, but isn't toxic to animals or bees. It is now licensed for use on cotton, corn and potatoes in the United States.

As John explains his methods, Sydney, a distinguished-looking man with white hair, whose fifty years of farm labour haven't dulled his sense of fun, doesn't hesitate to let you know he happily abandoned these very techniques the minute science offered improvements.

While anyone can call themselves an organic farmer, John wanted to be *certified* organic, which meant farming for five years free of chemicals using a number of provable farming practices to ensure that the product was in fact organic. The period of transition, like an addict coming off drugs, is miserable, marked by meagre yields and wretched crops devastated by pests, as the soil is built back up and the farmer learns to battle bugs and blight naturally.

Most people go organic for environmental reasons. The carrots on our little farm fed the carrot rust fly larvae last year, but we felt virtuous about pulling the stunted, invaded roots out of the ground just before we went to the supermarket to replace them with perfect, non-organic ones. The Hardys had similar feelings, but the deciding factor was the possibility that organic might also be a cheaper way to farm. Along the way they got religion. "Once you get into organic, you don't want to cheat. When I've had a bad field, it's made me even more determined to get it right. And I have had beautiful organic crops. There's nothing like looking at a field, seeing a beautiful crop and knowing it's clean—really clean."

John and David walk across one of his favourite fields, a little oasis surrounded by thick hedgerows. John stops abruptly and performs the organic "stoop and grab." He massages the dirt sensuously then holds it out for David's inspection. "Just looking at it and knowing it's alive makes me feel alive."

One of the problems with going organic is the other farmers. "The organic farmer definitely has to tread lightly," John says with a long sigh. Nineteen ninety-six was a terrible year for blight on the Island—fields were razed left and right as the virus attacked and no amount of spraying seemed able to bring it under control. If blight is spotted by a farmer or the potato inspector, the usual cure is to torch the whole field unless it is only a small patch that can be destroyed before it spreads.

That year one of the Hardys' neighbours reported them as a suspected source of blight, reasoning that because the Hardy's don't use today's typical arsenal of chemicals, their fields are a breeding ground for disease. In fact they had none, but that didn't stop a small army of inspectors from descending and examining every plant on the farm. "Ironically, we think the guy who reported us was the source of the blight himself and they eventually caught him," says John.

It's something every organic potato farmer has experienced. "We've been accused of spreading blight," grumps Raymond Loo. "They came here and took a leaf from every plant for sampling. Then they came back a week later. They didn't find anything. Everybody else they take one leaf from every hundred plants. Not us. Figure it out."

In some quarters the enmity toward organic farmers makes it almost impossible for the two groups to converse. "Some farmers are almost hysterical about it," admits a non-organic potato farmer. "I've been to meetings where people have stood up and said that natural home gardens are causing blight. They wanted to ban natural home gardens, for God's sake!" A few years ago John was a member of the farmers' soils and crop committee, but when he became organic the atmosphere changed. "They didn't want nothing to do with me after that," he says with little rancour. Time has passed, people protect their livelihood, he understands that. "The bottom line is you've got to pay your bills."

John Hardy's reluctance to slam his neighbours isn't political—he genuinely appreciates the farmers around him even if they do things differently. Like the farmer across the road. "He's got a beautiful spread. Everybody has a job and they do it well."

Those from off the Island have a hard time understanding John's tolerance—his go-along, get-along attitude—and wonder how he can live next to those whose practices he believes are ultimately destructive. In a life crammed with causes and vocal proponents, you're almost taken for a coward if you don't defend your point of view by attacking others.

In 1997 an earnest urban crew from CBC was researching a story on genetic alteration of crops and farm animals. They figured that the largest organic farmer on the Island would have something negative to say about genetic manipulation. Hardy, in his quiet way, was indignant. It wasn't so much their desire to record a verbal harangue against his neighbours that bothered him but the reporter's failure to understand that, for the sake of a twenty-second sound bite, he was being asked to turn on the people he'd been living beside all his life and beside whom his sons and their children would live—the people he would turn to if some disaster struck.

"I told them on the telephone that I wasn't going to criticize other farmers—my neighbours. They said fine, we just wanted to talk about the issue. Then they got here and got right in my face—kept at me, trying to get me to say something negative. I think what I'm doing is right, but also happen to think there's plenty of room for all of us."

The Hardys had a treat in store for David the day he visited. They purchased a load of expensive organic seed potatoes and after a great deal of discussion concluded there would be less waste if they planted them by hand.

The furrows had all been ploughed the day before, leaving the pungent smell unique to freshly turned earth hanging in the air. They seem straight as a rule to David's eye, but Sydney frowns, asking if John is having trouble with the tractor. "Nooo," retorts John slowly with the air of one who knows full well what's coming, "why'd you ask?"

"A little crooked, aren't they? Maybe I should have done the ploughing."

John looks to the heavens. "Fathers never change, do they?" Then he adds, "I think you were busy having a nap at the time." Sydney's habitual smile fades slightly.

John, his father and his oldest son, John Jr., 19, a taller and slightly heavier set version of John, and David suit up together. With Raymond Loo, getting ready was only a matter of picking up a sack of potatoes and some plastic buckets and dragging them with you as you moved along the row. The Hardys have the full regalia: burlap aprons sewn by Sydney, with a big kangaroo pouch in front to hold the potatoes and reduce the bending. Bags of seed potatoes are dumped strategically around the field and upended into the pouch as the planter empties it. When fully togged up, the four look like a collection of bindlestiffs.

"You'll need this," says John Jr., tossing David a commercial bug cream. He'd already slathered it on with the abandon of one laying on cologne before a hot date.

"Organic, right?" David asks ingenuously, looking at the label. The four men guffaw at the incongruity of drenching their bodies with a chemical mosquito repellent while going to great lengths not to do the same to the potatoes.

There was none of Raymond Loo's "see what you're made of" challenge, however kindly meant, about this planting. The Hardys are genuinely glad to have a helping hand no matter how inexperienced. David doesn't let on that he's already had some practice. A good thing, because he is little improved—still having to come to a complete stop each time he drops a cutting and more often than not having to bend over and correct the spacing. Even so he feels he's keeping up a fair pace, about a quarter of the way along his first furrow—sweating, but not profusely.

Then he spots Sydney rounding the corner on his first furrow and heading back on the second. The old boy looks for all the world like a riverboat gambler shuffling and dealing cards as each potato chunk flies out of his hand into the precisely perfect spot, exactly equidistant from the last and the next. About twenty yards to his rear is John Jr., also moving steadily but, David is pleased to see, dripping sweat. Sydney looks as arid as the desert.

When Sydney passes David going the other way, a slight smirk cranks the corner of his face—it brings to mind the quote attributed, with many variations, to Ty Cobb. "I doubt that I could hit for a three hundred average against today's pitching. Mind, I am seventy." As David stands admiring his skill, the old boy shoots him a wink and speeds up.

John Sr., a paragon of Island hospitality, keeps pace with David by covertly slipping potatoes into his line. David calculates his planting rate—if you subtract the handicap of surreptitiously helping his visitor—to be about three quarters that of his father and roughly the same as his son's. Quality of job: not as good as Sydney but, fittingly, a little better than the son.

"Don't worry," laughs John when David curses yet another spud that rolls too close to the one before. "Mine aren't very even either."

"Supper!" yells John Jr. from one end of the field. "I'm hungry!" He walks quickly back to join the other three, bouncing on his toes like an athlete heading into the locker room for half time. As he draws closer, David is startled to see blood streaming down his face. Horseflies apparently liked the bug spray so much they called on their neighbours to come for a taste test. David explores his exposed skin and finds two huge welts swelling like an extra collar on his neck. Funnily, no one had noticed while the flies were feasting. John Sr. is similarly wounded. But the old boy seems unaffected; at least, if he'd been bitten he isn't letting on. And if he hadn't been bitten, he wasn't about to pass on his secret. They'd spent three hard hours on the job. After supper the Hardys will return for another two-hour stint. David escapes to another interview.

"WE'RE NOT GOING TO BE too sociable today," John Hardy explains as Alison arrives at harvest four months later to check out David's work. His fingers are dark with grease and dirt, and frustration lies heavily on his features. John Jr. wrestles with a piece of equipment. "This here's a digger bed chain," explains John. "We call 'em all kinds of things . . . some things you don't want to hear either."

It is a farmer's powwow, a pleasurable tradition. Everybody is standing around jawing and everybody, including Gerrard, a family friend and temporary hired hand, is freely ladling out advice to John Jr., who is fiddling around under the device and is, incidentally, the only one actually doing anything. They were delayed by a slight frost in the ground and then had to stop for an hour when a piece of the conveyor belt chain broke. "What do you expect," says John with a shrug. "We work with leftover machinery and equipment. I never know from one day to the next what's going to work." Finally the thing is fixed, and everyone piles into trucks and heads out to the field. John turns into a rough track. On a neighbour's field a massive harvester works its way to the end of a fifty-acre section.

John inclines his head. "These guys are big time." His youngest son, Matthew, fifteen and quiet spoken, looks over at the field and guesses at the price of the machine: "One hundred?" His father smiles. "More like $120,000." The truck bumps through an opening in a stand of trees. "This is my land here. Me and the bank—the bank and I."

These days they don't empty out the schools for able-bodied children to help with the harvest. Giant machines called windrowers can do in five minutes what it once took an army of hands an hour to accomplish. But Matthew can help because he is home-schooled. He's a diabetic, subject to periods of high and low energy, which makes traditional schooling difficult. "I find they're better behaved . . . happier too," his father says, glancing at his son. "They don't learn to curse as quickly."

"I'm teachin' him quick as I can," informs Gerrard helpfully. John's other two children—his eighteen-year-old daughter Melissa and John Jr.—attended public school. Matthew looks like a boy who would choose a music major in university. He seems too delicate to spend days and weeks at hard labour in the fields but his lanky frame is surprisingly resilient and he handles a tractor with the special *joie de vivre* that you see only when you watch teenage boys on farm equipment. Still, he's a sharp contrast to his older brother, John Jr., who swings himself onto and under machinery like a man born to the task. There's an energy and efficiency about him that is so pure and easy you want to capture it, put it in a bottle and study it with envy and wonder. When you ask if he's ever considered a life other than farming, he looks at you like you're crazy. But his words are as polite as his father's. "No, I've pretty much known all along that farming's for me."

Sydney pulls up in his truck. Three generations of Hardys focus on getting the digger chain reattached in the belly of the rusting harvester.

"Got her!" hollers John Jr. He scrambles out from beneath the machine and jumps into the cab of the tractor.

Away he goes, the windrower scooping into the furrows and driving the potatoes onto the chain belt where they bounce up to the top of the machine, then cascade down onto another belt before being disgorged into the truck being driven slowly alongside by Sydney. There's a little platform at the top, just enough room for the sorters. Matthew stands guard as the potatoes come spewing out. He grabs at the bigger rocks, chunks of weed and grass and flings them out of the way. Gerrard and Alison also pick rocks and whatever debris Matthew misses.

Every stone removed at this stage means one less that will have to be taken out in the warehouse. The activity goes in fits and starts. A sudden burst as a bunch of potatoes come charging up the belt, then a respite. It is a beautiful day, sharp with fall's chill but comfortable. Sorting is often a version of hell with a cold, driving, pre-winter rain, leavened by the Island's ever-present "wee bit o' wind." But on this day there is no better place in the world to be than with a family doing its job.

Rounding the corner at the bottom of the field, the conveyor belt is suddenly throwing up more rocks than potatoes, then mostly rocks. "Here we go!" shouts Matthew, throwing a clod of dirt at Gerrard to prod him into action. Gerrard has hands like catcher's mitts and they envelop great piles of rocks. "You're not bad," he says to Alison, who's pecking away at whatever he misses.

"Beats driving cab, huh?" comments Matthew to Gerrard after the harvester moves along and rocks give way to potatoes.

"Oh, I dunno," the big man answers. "But good thing I'm here or you'd be out here another week just getting this here field done."

Matthew's response is another clod of dirt.

"What's under this land is more valuable than what we grow on top," John Sr. observes. As potato land the 170 acres he owns is worth, given the day and who's asking, in the neighbourhood of $750,000. A while back the Hardys got curious about the number of rocks in the lower part of this field, which never seemed to decrease no matter how much rock picking they did. To their surprise, they discovered a gravel pit bordering most of the acreage, courtesy of an ancient glacial stream. The deposited gravel is likely worth at least a quarter of a million dollars.

It's nice to know it's sitting there for a rainy day, but it would have to be very rainy—Noah, the ark and all—for the Hardys to consider turning the field into a gravel pit. " It would make a mess of a perfectly good potato field. And the noise," he adds wryly. "All that machinery. And the trucks going back and forth. We'd never be able to stand the noise."

Like all the potato farmers we met, John knows he could sell out or develop his land and, with the money placed in conservative investments, net far more than he does at farming. But at the heart of men like him is the knowledge that they are farmers.

That's all they are. And all they want to be. There is no sense of the diminutive in the word "all." On PEI, farming for three or four generations is common. The Hardys and others have learned through the example of others that once land is sold it's impossible to retrieve. Everyone has a story of a farmer who sold his land—forlorn caricatures, never the same afterwards. Though John might have an easier life, once the land is gone, he could never be a farmer again. And worse, his boys would never have the opportunity.

The contraption breaks again. Pow-wow time. They study the feckless digger bed chain. In places the metal rollers it moves along are as thin as paper and cracked. John leans against one of the bald tires and peers. "Guess we need a replacement"—a statement you know he makes every year about this time.

Sydney offers to drive into town and see if the local equipment dealer has some spare parts. John Jr. is doubtful, it's an old machine. "Near ancient," Matthew pipes up cheerfully. They decide to have a go at surgery on the spot, which is what they all really knew they were going to do from the beginning.

John Jr. once more wiggles into the dirt, his reddish-blond hair mashed into the reddish-brown soil. One of the metal bars has twisted and snapped, leaving the entire chain sagging loosely like the belly of an old man. Proper repair is impossible, at least in the middle of a field with no welding equipment. John Jr. thinks they can simply remove the broken bar and take up the slack; hardly the manufacturer's recommended solution, but with less than half the field dug and the day wearing down, getting it working is all that counts. The bar comes out easily enough but pulling the now tight chain back together is a formidable job. John Jr. manages one end, lying flat on his back and grunting with the effort. His father quickly rams the metal rod through to pin the chain together. "Hey, Dad!" squawks John Jr. "You near put it through my jugular!"

The other end of the chain is harder now that one side has been brought together. "We need a muscleman. C'mere, Gerrard." John waves him over. "See what you can do." Gerrard is surely capable of ploughing an entire field with the fingers of one hand. He grins and flexes an arm, which Matthew punches disparagingly. "Outta my way, boy," he growls, wrapping two beefy fists around the resisting pieces of chain and, three or four heaves later, has them pulled close enough to accept the metal rod.

"She's coming," coaches Sydney. "Give her a tap."

"Keep going," urges John as the rod waggles a little before meeting the female end of the chain. "Got her!"

"Cross your fingers and say your prayers."

"She'll last a day," observes John Jr.

"That's all we want," his father says with a smile. "She can break down tomorrow." He stands back and watches as John Jr. fires up the tractor and begins to pull. "We plan on breakdowns two or three times a day."

Matthew sings out, "Yeah, and then we're doin' good!"

The thin warmth of the day has vanished. The field David helped plant is almost harvested. Digger bed chain willing, it'll be done before supper. It's a good crop but not great. They'd hoped for a slightly better take after all the work of hand planting, and a slightly better take in the potato business is the difference between steak and hamburger. The Hardy men agree that next year, if they use the same potatoes, they will plant by machine. The time saved will more than compensate for any waste.

It's been a hard ten years for the Hardys as they've toiled to master organic farming. They've tried other things either as sidelines or to add value to their crops. John drove a milk truck, they're part of an organic marketing co-op and for a time he was working on becoming the roasted soy bean treat king of Atlantic Canada. "They tasted really good," he says a little defensively, pointing out a large pile in the garage. "We've got some more in a warehouse somewhere."

Nineteen ninety-six was to have been their breakout year. They had fifty acres of certified organic potatoes, ten times more than any other grower on the Island. "It was a wonderful crop. We were so proud of it." John sold it at an excellent price to a wholesaler, who was going to promote it and sell into upscale retail markets in Quebec and Ontario. With no warning the wholesaler went out of business, leaving the Hardys with thousands of pounds of unsold potatoes. In desperation they were forced to unload their crop at less than market prices. The next year, John had a serious heart attack. Despite the Herculean efforts of Sydney, Matthew, and John Jr., who left school to help out, they were able to harvest only a partial crop. By 1998 they were back on track.

"We've done enough experimenting, we'd like to make some money now," John says quietly. It's a vow.

John asks if he can send Alison on her way with a couple of bags of organic potatoes. Back at the farm he fills two heavy paper sacks with unwashed Kennebecs, a long, pale, symmetrical variety, still gritty with dirt from the field. "I'd never go back," he says, answering the unasked question. As he ties the bags with heavy wire, he tries to explain himself.

"It's a great feeling, if we can make a living at it. I like it. The soil likes it. I've gone to some fields where there's only a few inches of soil." He scrapes up some of the dirt on the rough table in the warehouse. "It really is a living organism. Maybe people will come by and say, 'If he's doing it, why can't we do it?'"

Alison loads herself and two large bags of potatoes into the rental car, and John Hardy waves as she backs into the road. "Hey, I should have fired up the soybean roaster!" he calls. "Oh well, next time."

SHARON LABCHUK, A SINGLE parent who was born on the Island, is a small, slender, almost fragile-looking woman in her mid-forties. Soft-spoken and articulate, she rarely raises her voice. She's attractive, but wears no make-up on her slightly angular face and dresses plainly in sweaters and jeans. Her single most striking feature is thick, hip-length dark hair slightly streaked with grey. Twenty years ago she would have been called an earth mother, and indeed she lives in a solar-powered home that she built herself, preserves her own fruits and vegetables and believes in self-sufficiency. If one had to sum up Sharon Labchuk in a single word it would be inoffensive.

Yet to the PEI potato industry, Sharon Labchuk is the personification of evil.

"They call me a terrorist," she says, genuinely perplexed, though she's heard and read it hundreds of times. "I'm an environmentalist, sure, but a terrorist!" She laughs at the incongruity of it while sitting at her dining-room table in her still unfinished house, surrounded by piles of flyers and brochures. By the time David met Sharon, he'd seen otherwise sane farmers flush with rage at the mere mention of her name. Elmer MacDonald solemnly warned him not to tell other farmers that he was going to see her. "Sharon Labchuk's poison," cautions one grower, oblivious to the irony.

Sharon's first act of "eco-terrorism" occurred in 1996 just before construction began on the Confederation Bridge, which now links PEI to New Brunswick. She and a couple of supporters crossed by ferry from Borden to Tormentine, N.B., to distribute flyers to people waiting for the boat to PEI. The flyers were cheaply made photocopies—no colour, no jazzing up with CD-ROM clip art, no fancy borders or backgrounds, just a few stark pictures and reproduced snippets from newspaper stories. But Sharon Labchuk has a wicked touch with words, crafting them into ice picks and knuckledusters. It's a talent that could earn a rich living on Madison Avenue.

"Come get sprayed on our Island," is the heading, playing off the official tourism slogan, "Come play on our Island." PEI becomes Pesticide Exposure Island. "Summer Pesticide Drift—An Island Tradition" jabs at the Island's promotion of itself as a folksy place.

TOURISTS BEWARE!
Pesticides are a product of the post World War II boom, based extensively on NAZI research for nerve gas. At small doses, they kill people, at even smaller doses, they kill everything else; songbirds, waterfowl, animals, fish, trees, plants and even the family pet.

The pamphlet reels off discomforting statistics. That lovely fat baked potato smeared with butter and sour cream endures about twenty applications of various pesticides before it reaches your fork. Sharon cites evidence that pesticides cause behavioural and learning problems in children and in the past three years have killed hundreds of thousands of salmon and trout, not to mention a number of Islanders. She points out that the majority of potatoes are sprayed with endocrine-disrupting pesticides every four days. These chemicals mimic natural hormones in humans and animals. Males can be affected in a broad number of ways including impotence, undescended testicles and a smaller penis at puberty. Women can look forward to an increase in breast cancer.

It's a sharp, shocking contrast to the warm, welcoming and glossy official tourist literature—a clever tactic. Potatoes are far and away the number one industry on the Island, but tourism is number two and closing. There's no number three. Get the people who run the bed and breakfasts, the resorts and the restaurants that depend on tourists concerned about what potato farming is doing to the environment and, as a consequence, their business, and you have a powerful group of allies.

Sharon provides tourists with a list of survival tips.

- When driving, if you see a tractor hauling a sprayer, immediately wind up your windows, turn off the fan and leave the area.
- Select accommodations *away* from potato fields. If you don't know what a potato field looks like, be sure to ask someone!
- Don't pick berries or flowers from ditches or hedgerows near potato fields.
- If you're camping on PEI never erect a tent in an agricultural area.
- If near a potato field, keep your window closed at night. Spraying occurs around the clock.
- If near a potato field, don't hang out your clothes or leave your belongings outside unless you know the spray schedule.

Even paying attention to one per cent of the warnings, a tourist couldn't safely eat, drink, sleep or wash on PEI.

Sharon and her cohorts lasted barely half an hour at the ferry terminal before horrified ferry officials hustled them away. Faced with the threat of arrest on trespassing charges, their only option was to move outside the enclosure and try flagging down cars as they arrived and left. They elected to return home to fight another day. It was a small, quiet event; fewer than a hundred pamphlets were handed out, nothing was broken, no blood was spilled and there wasn't even a confrontation. The only people inconvenienced were the environmentalists themselves. Yet Sharon Labchuk's first stand has grown to mythical proportions. "A cannon shot into the potato industry," in the words of one observer.

That single burst of pamphleting has swollen in popular lore into dozens of bold and outrageous provocations. Islanders authoritatively told us that Sharon Labchuk set sail like Captain Blood waylaying visitors coming by boat; others had her blockading Confederation Bridge itself; still others told of her returning to the car ferries time after time and rampaging through the passenger decks. No one we met had actually seen any of these incidents but they knew them to be true.

What Sharon Labchuk has done is stick a shiv into the tender sensitivities of Island potato farmers, their workers and the host of people employed throughout the industry. In the 1998 publication *Portraits*, a calendar/diary celebrating Canadian women activists, Sharon is featured in the month of September. All through the booklet are women who do good deeds captured in nice but unexceptional portraits.

Not Sharon Labchuk. She sits smack in the middle of a denuded PEI potato field, naked save for a World War II gas mask and her abundant hair. It's just a picture. The potato industry would have been better off ignoring it or laughing it off. But the industry is not accustomed to being mocked. Labchuk's picture was denounced in the *Guardian,* the Island's daily newspaper, which naturally reprinted the picture, making it into an even bigger outrage. Since then the photo has hung in a Charlottetown gallery and been made into a poster and a postcard.

"I've shown it to some guys who laughed at it," says a clearly unamused Ivan Noonan, general manager of the PEI Potato Board. "I think it's pretty bizarre and I don't know if it's going to help her cause. Sharon won't gain any respect in the industry by doing extreme things like this."

But Sharon is past looking for farmers' respect. Her response to the charges of extremism and publicity hounding is a shrug of resignation—she's come to accept what she has become to farmers as her fate, her karma. She left the Island as a young woman, vowing never to return. But a yearning for the quiet pastoral setting she recalled from childhood drew her back with her two children in 1988. "I spent five years looking for the land to build my house on. It had to be rocky and steep on the approaches so the potato farmers wouldn't be tempted to plant nearby.

"I was always interested in the environment but I had no intention of getting into this fight. I just got worried about what these sprays were doing to my kids. I started asking questions. The chemical industry types are very slick, and as far as they're concerned everything is good about their chemicals. The government scientists were useless, they didn't know anything. So I started reading and reading. And I started getting more and more afraid. I felt I had to tell people what I was finding out—to tell the farmers. I thought they'd want to know. I thought anyone who handled something this dangerous would want to know about it." Her voice trails off. "I really thought they'd want to know.

"We did all the right democratic things. Spoke to pesticide committees. Wrote briefs. Wrote letters. Made phone calls." Instead of meeting with customary Island politeness, she was rebuffed and more. "They wouldn't listen. Didn't care. And they called us liars and fear-mongers to boot. And that was the least of what they called me."

Underlying many of the criticisms is the insinuation that Sharon has something to gain from her actions, something hidden from public view. "I don't have any money and I'm not making any," she scoffs. "I suppose what I do has become an avocation." Sharon hesitates over the last word, uncomfortable with the idea of holding herself out as a paragon. "At one point I got some funding from government, little bits of work—that's dried up. But lots of people call me. They're scared about what's happening and they expect me to do something about it. They have nowhere else to turn. I don't have any money. But I do what I can."

At first Sharon diligently attended meetings, anxious to open communication with the farmers, to discuss changing to safer, more environmentally sensitive techniques. She was shouted down and vilified, even threatened. "It's a very intimidating industry. I've been accosted on the street. Harangued on the phone. People are intimidated from speaking out. If you speak out, you'll be punished. That's the message." Two years ago, she showed up at an agricultural fair to hand out material. It was cheeky and provocative. She was quickly recognized and hemmed in by three potato farmers.

"Three big farmers," she recalls, still visibly shaken. "They were huge and very angry. They trapped me. Went on a rant. Voices raised. Arms waving. I don't know who they were. I don't even remember what they looked like but their faces were all red."

After the confrontation, Sharon gathered up her kids and fled the Island. "I was very frightened. I just had to get away and I was thinking of never coming back." One farmer loudly denounced Sharon in church in front of his whole congregation.

"I think Labchuk goes too far, way too far," said another farmer who was at the service, "but this guy was out of hand. A bunch of us had a word with him—set him straight."

Sharon Labchuk came back punching. A recent brochure features a man wearing a gas mask with the caption "Dying for Fries." Another depicts the Grim Reaper hosing down birds in flight with a hand sprayer, one bird already dead in the background. And she's developed a guide for visitors entitled "Prince Edward Island, Toxic Playground?" It explains how tourists can protect themselves while on the island and reads like the primers given to troops facing possible poison gas exposure in the Gulf War.

Whether it's Sharon Labchuk's pamphleteering or raised environmental consciousness, virtually everyone on the Island worries about the sprays and chemicals used in potato farming. We sat down for dinner with a friend in Charlottetown and the topic of health came up. "The Island has the highest asthma rates in North America," he stated. "Now why do you think that is? We don't have any smokestack industries." Another acquaintance told us authoritatively that cancer, not asthma, was the problem. Still another pointed to genetic irregularities. They all suspect that the source of the problems, real or imagined, can be traced back to the chemical coddling of the potato. Urgency was added to the situation in the summer of 1999 by a number of fish kills, several of them devastating, in PEI rivers.

Aside from two small concentrations in Charlottetown and Summerside, most Islanders live in villages, hamlets, at the intersection of country roads and, increasingly, on chunks of land severed from farms. Tourists and inhabitants alike don't need to get out of their cars, let alone wander through the back roads, to come face to face with agriculture. Farming on PEI is an intimate, always visible fact of life. The potato is a neighbour, and not the kind politely standing on the other side of a stone wall. It's the pushy, in-your-face kind of neighbour. Potato fields are ploughed as close as one and a half metres from houses. Routinely, especially on the smaller country roads, the fields run right to the edge of streams, drainage ditches and roads—and often closely surround schools on three sides.

For six months of the year, the fields are full of activity. In late April or early May, weather permitting—which it often doesn't—the harrows and cultivators come out to turn and loosen the soil. Planting is guided by the Queen, or rather her birthday, May 24. Sometimes farmers beat it by a few days or a week, but that's the average and over time it has held. As urban Canada gets into its summer mentality with the May long weekend, farmers on the Island fire up their tractors, curse themselves for a repair not made during the winter and pray that blight and half a dozen other potato ailments will leave them alone.

Spraying doesn't begin in earnest until July. Masked and swathed in protective clothing, farmers pilot their huge tractors towing Rube Goldberg spraying machines with clouds of chemicals billowing out in all directions. Every four or five days, the various bugs and diseases must be hit, so during the summer you can't drive far without seeing spraying. Then there's the Island's "wee bit o' wind." There always seems to be a wee bit o' wind. The legal spraying limit is twenty-five kilometres per hour, hardly more than a faint breeze, to combat "pesticide drift." But farmers can't wait on the breezes for long—they must spray at precisely the right moment for the chemicals to be effective.

During our two-week vacation in 1997 on the north shore

near Darnley, the spraying issue edged into our consciousness. During a dawn walk along the beach with the rising sun at our backs and the long lip of dunes ahead of us, we strolled into the fairy-tale mist shrouding land and sea. As we walked, inhaling the salty miasma of the surf, we caught a subtle scent, acrid yet also sweet. The nearest approximation is the whiff of cheap perfume masking, not completely successfully, poor sanitary habits.

We heard a low rumble in the distance, and being inquisitive holidayers with time on our hands, we climbed up the bank toward it, only to be almost mowed down by a rig spurting red-tinged clouds that mixed with the fog to form a nightmarish pink-out.

Farmers, chemical salesmen and scientists all proclaim the harmless nature of potato sprays "when handled properly," and they emphasize that each person using pesticides must take a one-day handling course with a written exam at the end. Sceptics, Sharon Labchuk chief among them, question who actually does the spraying—the farmers who take the course or hired hands who are relegated the dirty jobs? And even if the farmers take charge of the spraying, there are problems. "The illiteracy rate among farmers is shocking," she emphasizes. "Lots of them can't even read the fine print on the cans, so how do you expect them to mix up the pesticide correctly, even if it were safe to use, in the correct quantities?"

A veterinarian told us of watching a farmer preparing his brew. The man sat perched on the side of the sprayer tank pouring in the chemical. "Then he started looking around for something to mix it with. He couldn't find anything. You could see what was going through his mind. Finally he rolled up his sleeve, stuck his arm in as far as it would go and started stirring." The vet pauses for a minute. "You wonder what that did to his gene pool."

Farmers would be surprised to hear it and would likely reject the idea out of hand, but they share some common ground with Sharon Labchuk. She fears for the future and health of the Island and they, in their own way, do too. Much has changed since the days of mixed farms, not long in the past, and no one is really sure of the impact. Farmers fret about their livelihood and their ability to keep their farms in the family, and they fear for the future of their children.

Those farmers who think about it, and many do, deep in their souls, also fear that what they are doing is wrong. And that is one of the reasons many have overreacted to Sharon.

Farmers feel they are riding on the back of a tiger and can't get off. They wonder if they have reached a point where there's no turning back. Much as chemical fertilizers and pesticides have revolutionized farming, the next wave of advances in bio-technological engineering threatens to transform it into something no one can envision or control. Anyone who follows the stock market knows that bio-tech is big business, getting bigger by the second. The colour of trout is being altered to make them more visible to anglers, and crops are being genetically altered to become more resistant to disease. The British media have taken to calling the products of these bio-tech advances "Frankenstein Food."

Greenpeace claims that in the process of trying to patch traits from the brazil nut onto soybeans, scientists have created soybeans that trigger nut allergies. The industry counters by calling such allegations "bogus," "inflammatory" and "metaphysical." A toxicologist in Scotland added insect-resistant genes to potatoes, then fed them to rats. In the summer of 1999, he went public, claiming that the rats had growth problems, damaged immune systems and shrunken brains. His employer denounced his findings as "muddled" and "misleading" and fired him.

73

All the usual charges and countercharges are flying about, but farmers know that there's more at stake than the battles over pesticides, chemicals and genetic engineering. Each advance or development is one more loss of control over their livelihood. Working the land represents freedom—farmers said that to us again and again. But the pace of change is starting to overwhelm them. "There's something new every day. I've got more ways to screw up than my father ever dreamt of," Elmer MacDonald sighs. "But then again, who'd want to do anything else? It's been one hell of a good life."

WHILE TEMPERS ARE FLARING and blood pressures rising elsewhere on the Island, Phil Corsi has taken it upon himself to turn the clock back or ahead, depending on your point of view. With his gangly appendages and a dreamy, distracted way of talking and moving, Phil could be a cousin to Ichabod Crane. His numerous careers have spanned everything from computers to neurosciences and now the land. He came to the Island looking for solitude and serenity. Somewhere along the way he found his cause, a quiet one. The potato's ever-growing demand for *Lebensraum* offends him. Not only is the tuber claiming more land by the hour, but it is more intensely using land it already occupied.

Once farms had hedgerows and trees surrounding each field to reduce erosion and provide a habitat for wildlife that would consume its share of bugs and other farming miscreants. And a woodlot was an essential part of each farm. Now, if they exist at all, trees and hedgerows are relegated to small clumps in the rocky periphery of the potato fields. The silhouette of the land, its aesthetic dimension, is every bit as important to Phil as its function. He decided he ought to do something, so he has bought one hundred acres of prime rolling potato land alongside the Dunk River and has been planting trees—as many as his money and other people's help allowed.

It's been slow work, but twenty-seven years later his land is fifty per cent reforested, and the areas where the spud once dominated are receding. Phil is a contented man as he happily guides us around his land prior to a lunch of his specialty, Three Sisters' Soup, a hearty, savoury bean and herb concoction. He points out deer scat and other signs of nature returning while describing when and how each stand of trees was planted. "Don't tell the farmers, but I got a government grant to plant those beauties," he chuckles, gesturing to a lovely group of three-year-old pine. Then his brow wrinkles at the thought of an unpleasantness. "I'm going to have to thin them soon."

Phil isn't evangelical; he doesn't give speeches. "The farmers around here—the ones who know what I'm doing—think I'm nuts," he says with a quiet laugh. "Maybe I am, but I feel like I'm accomplishing something. I feel good. It's all about balance, you know. Balance is important."

CHAPTER TWO

NORTH

A MASTERPIECE OF A mid-August northern day. Temperature warmed nicely into the seventies by a friendly sun, a sapphire sky and just the right dab of cotton-puff clouds for contrast. Undulating terrain stretches into the distance: rock and tundra and bush. The sameness of colour and shape is soothing; there's little to disturb the eye or distract from thought. No tiring, riotous growth, rushing water or busy panorama of mountain, wood or valley.

Some call it harsh, and it is that, inhospitable too. Life struggles here on the barrens 230 kilometres northeast of Yellowknife, 200 kilometres south of the Arctic Circle. Tough grasses cluster on the shoreline of an unnamed lake, and small wiry shrubs with iron constitutions and leathery, grey-green leaves find nourishment in scant soil. But this morning in August there isn't a more welcoming place on the planet. No wind intrudes and not a single fly, nor even a mosquito, normally the north's summer bane, is evident. There isn't a hint that winter lurks just a few weeks away. When it comes, the transformation will be swift and violent.

Moments earlier, a bawling caribou calf thundered by looking for its mother. Small herds of a dozen or so flit by on the ridges, led by males with antler racks so big the animals seem about to topple forward at every movement of their majestic heads. A bear has recently come to drink or fish; its scat lies warm and moist at the lake's margin.

A man sits on a rock in the shallows of the small lake. Low bald hills, grey and olive green, frame him gently. Stone-washed green shirt, worn jeans almost white at the knees, neatly trimmed greying beard and faded blue baseball cap, he's at one with the setting. The only spot of divergent colour is a pair of extra-heavy orange rubber gloves tossed onto the shoreline. The man is handsome and rugged with sharp, curious, blue eyes and a wide, generous mouth made for laughing and talking. His hands are big and rough—hands that can do things. David perches on a nearby rock watching the silent rhythm of his movements.

In the background, there's quiet singing, the words unintelligible. A slender woman, on a rock of her own, feet in the water, croons as she works. She could be weaving a blanket of gold in an enchanted forest. Her legs are spread wide with long rubber waders pulled up to mid-thigh. Dark, straight hair is pushed up into a summery white straw hat with a red ribbon tied around the brim. It's a dramatic face with broad planes and a fine chin, a face of character and emotion. Black jeans, now pale grey with wear, fit her body snugly. A bulky navy turtleneck sweater is tucked into her pants, making her slender waist and hips look boyish. Head bent and bobbing from time to time, her melodious song continues. Every now and then a grunt from the man serves as her accompaniment.

There isn't another soul for at least seventy-five kilometres.

The couple are concentrating fiercely. They could be ancients, so powerful is their focus. No one has spoken a word in more than an hour. Back and forth they swish rectangular wooden pans of water: sand, pebbles and dirt sifting from side to side. The pans look preindustrial, like long, shallow wooden serving dishes from another century. Side to side. Side to side. Then back and forth, a practised flick of the wrists sends a puff of silt away into the water. Back and forth, side to side.

Occasionally one of them stops and peers intently into the pan. Somewhere in the soupy mixture may be a clue to a great secret. Occasionally, but rarely, it will be visible to the naked eye; more often it is found only through the lens of a microscope. But it's there, if not in this pan then the next or the one after that. A secret worth billions.

Nick and Lucy Pokhilenko are the pros from Dover, or rather Siberia. They have spent their entire adult lives searching for that most legendary of gems, diamonds. Nick, now fifty-one, has been in the field every year since he was twenty-two, never a season missed. From the Sahara to the Mekong Delta to the wilds of his own country, there is little about the world's cruellest and most desolate lands that he doesn't know, hasn't trod upon. He's the top gun of geology, considered to be one of the two or three best diamond finders in the world. Lucy is also a geologist. Once

Nick's student and now his wife, partner and mother of their twelve-year-old son, she shares his passion.

This particular chase was sparked in 1991 by an obscure junior mining company based on the west coast and listed on the frequently notorious Vancouver Stock Exchange. The company, Dia Met Minerals Ltd., along with its partner, the giant Australian multinational mining company BHP Diamonds Inc, announced it had discovered a gem-quality, diamond-bearing kimberlite pipe at Lac de Gras, 300 kilometres northeast of Yellowknife in the Northwest Territories. The discoverer, Chuck Fipke, was an equally obscure Canadian geologist. "We thought he was just another rumpled asshole like the rest of us, out looking for gold," observes one prospector. The news touched off a staking boom in the north unlike any ever seen before—anywhere. It made the Klondike gold rush seem like rush hour in a very small town. Just seven years later, in October 1998, the Ekati diamond mine opened, turning Canada into the fourth-largest diamond producer in the world with an expected revenue of $800 million annually.

Still the hardest known natural substance, the diamond is created by heat and pressure deep within the belly of the earth, 120 to 250 kilometres below the surface. Molten material, under terrific pressure, picks up the diamonds on its way to the surface. The liquid explodes to the surface, creating fissures in the earth's mantle and crust. The cooled liquid is called kimberlite, and the so-called pipes are formed on the explosive journey to the surface. The pipes vary from carrot to funnel shape and tend to cluster together in groups, some as wide as two kilometres across, but in the Territories far less.

There are more than five thousand different types of diamonds, but only the scarce transparent ones become gems. Ancient Greeks, believing the stones were splinters of falling stars, called them *adamas*, meaning invincible. Others thought they were the tears of gods. One legend traces the source of all diamonds to an inaccessible central Asian valley where they lie openly, a blinding carpet of brilliance protected from above by birds of prey and guarded on land by snakes "of murderous gaze."

Diamonds symbolized strength, courage and invincibility to the Chinese, who used them to ward off evil spirits. They also believed that ground into a powder diamonds made wonderful aphrodisiacs. Pliny, a Roman naturalist, recommended swallowing diamonds, presumably small ones, to counteract poison and to prevent insanity.

Diamond fanciers extol the gems' flash and fire, but there are many beautiful things available on this planet for far less money. It is the mythology of love that keeps us buying them. With diamonds, size counts. Aficionados adore talking size when they get together and compare rocks, sounding like a bunch of jocks in a locker room. At more than two kilograms, the Cullinan is the largest ever found. We owe the jewellers' unit of weight, the carat, to the carob tree—*keration* in Greek. It was common in the ancient Middle East and handy as a benchmark for weight because its seeds are remarkably uniform. By the early twentieth century, the weight of a single diamond carat had been standardized at 0.2 grams.

The highest-quality cut and polished stones are called "polished goods" in the diamond trade. The most expensive have deep colour and are flawless. When they are magnified, illuminated and viewed against a black background, not a single blemish can be seen. In 1987 a purplish-red diamond, slightly less than a carat, was hammered down for US$926,315. The highest price ever paid for a colourless diamond was US$142,232 per carat for a 52.59-carat stone in 1988. The Maouawad Splendor, a 101.84-carat cut and polished gem, sold for nearly US$13 million in 1990.

Rarely is something so exquisite also practical. It's akin to discovering that a beautiful model with an hourglass figure, a mane of spun gold and lips like ripe strawberries is also a Rhodes Scholar who dabbles in astrophysics. No other natural substance conducts heat better or has a higher melting point than diamonds. From abrasive grits and powders to drilling tips and cutting edges, diamonds are everywhere. But the "forever" part of their legend is what happens when the fire of that cold stone touches flesh. Nothing else can refract light and separate it into all colours of the spectrum in quite the way diamonds can.

Sexy, exotic and objects of lustful and criminal desire, diamonds seem, well, un-Canadian. Even though this country is a notable gold producer, base metals define us. Solid stuff like iron, zinc and copper. In our sprawling Great Lone Land, granite, not Elizabeth Taylor's favourite bauble and Cleopatra's aphrodisiac, is our style.

RANDY TURNER IS PRESIDENT of Winspear Resources Ltd., the junior exploration company that has managed to bag some of the best diamond finders in the world. Some VSE company presidents are honest, others would like to be and a few flaunt their sleaze. David wasn't quite sure what to expect when he met Randy for coffee in a downtown Toronto hotel. There isn't a trace of flamboyance about the small, dapper man. No hint of bucket shop promoting clings to him. He's from the old school of rock bangers, the kind who believe, modern gizmos notwithstanding, that there's no substitute for shank's mare and the physical, often tedious, business of messing around on the land if you're looking for clues to precious secrets below the surface. Randy spent his early years exploring for Esso until the giant corporation summarily closed its exploration wing. He then formed his own series of companies, exploring for everything from silver to molybdenum, until he was lured by the rumour of diamonds in the north.

David asked about visiting the Winspear camp and Randy thought it over for a moment before mentioning that he had a load of seven or eight analysts going up to the camp in August for a "show and tell"; perhaps David would like to tag along. The idea of going to camp with a group of mostly young, very urban number crunchers and bean counters had all the appeal of a sightseeing bus trip. Still, there didn't seem to be any alternative.

Mercifully, Randy called a few weeks later. The analysts' trip was off. "Most of them were fired," he told us. "The brokerages are cutting back and they killed off half the analysts in town in one pass." At the time, the Vancouver Stock Exchange was mired in a deep slump caused by low world commodity prices and the exodus of panicky speculators after TSE-listed Bre-X flamed out. "Name your date," Randy told him, "we'll get you up there. You can hop on the regular float plane from Yellowknife to the camp."

YELLOWKNIFE IS AN INTIMATE town of twenty thousand, most of whom know each other or at least know of each other. There are hundreds of smaller places in the country, but after a day or two Yellowknife feels more like a village of only two hundred. Though the residents are probably better travelled per capita than anywhere else in Canada, once you're in the town it is as if you've walked into a room and shut the door. The vast Great Slave Lake hems in Old Town and the even vaster land mass beyond corrals downtown, creating a rare sense of intimacy not only among residents but between them and their elected officials. "The guy getting shit-faced in the bar next to you is just as likely to be a cabinet minister as your next door neighbour, and maybe he's both," emphasizes one Yellowknife old-timer.

The cab driver who picks David up at the airport is a burly, dishevelled man—mid-thirties, hair shorn almost flat on his head but irregular, as if he'd done it himself—a few fast passes with a pair of dull clippers. He could have been provided by central casting for a bit part as a prospector, hunter or backwoods hermit. At first Chet is gruffly distant, popping the trunk with the cab's interior latch, making no move to get out of the car and help with David's bag. His manner changes radically when he learns that David is a first-time visitor to Yellowknife.

With an expansive grin, Chet flicks off the cab's meter and sets out on an impromptu tour of the town. On the left is the local swimming hole. "Never been there but people say it's good. Clean." On the right, Max Ward's plane is parked, a monument to the former bush pilot who fought a David and Goliath battle to create his airline, Wardair, and carve out a piece of the highly regulated Canadian skies in the 1970s. It's the kind of tale northerners love, but Chet is a little vague on the details. "Had something to do with planes," he explains. "People think a lot of old Max."

The tour continues. "Yonder's our Ford dealership." Chet slows so David can fully take in its grandeur. "Now that there's the museum," he indicates a little farther on. "Good one I hear. Never been in it but people say it's good. Back there you got the government buildings. And over this way's the Kentucky Fried." As they wheel slowly by, David gets a lungful of the Colonel's patented, oily, secret ingredient odour. "We got ourselves a brand new RCMP headquarters too. You can't see it but it's over there."

Chet burns up twenty minutes showing off the hospital, the Canadian Tire store and virtually every other building in town before he hits his specialty, bars. At each one Chet offers an animated commentary on the environment, whether there are strippers, the esthetic quality of their performances (how far they can shoot ping-pong balls from various orifices), which bars the natives frequent and, importantly, if a guy might get clouted for looking at the wrong girl. David guesses, after a quick survey of indentations and protrusions on Chet's face that a clout or two might have been aimed his way. Chet eyes David. "You'll be fine. Just don't start any fights."

At the Bayside Bed and Breakfast, Chet fairly leaps out of the cab and sprints round to snatch up David's bag, which he carries inside and deposits carefully on the carpet. He grandly refuses a tip. David asks where in the Territories he was born and what his family connections are. Chet is amused. "Oh no! I'm not from here, not me. I was born in Ontario." David asks how long he's been up north. "Two years. Love it. Here now. Not going anywhere else."

Wayne and Mary Bryant own the bed and breakfast, a three-storey west-coast design smack on the harbour, a curvaceous protected bay of Great Slave Lake. Wayne, a short, dark, tightly wound man with a two-day-old five o'clock shadow, greets David with the information that he hasn't slept for thirty-six hours. There's a trace of accusation in his voice as if somehow David is to blame. Wayne quickly blurts out that, in addition to the bed and breakfast, he runs an engineering firm in downtown Yellowknife—Bryant, McIntyre Inc. He's been losing sleep preparing a bid on a big project for one of the many diamond mining companies and his firm has just won another competition to clean up the debris left behind at the site of the very first diamond find in the Territories, the strike that brought the name Yellowknife to the lips of the diamond trade in Capetown, Amsterdam and New York. "When they finished work, everyone just went. Nobody thought about what they were doing, they just up and left. It's an awful mess."

Most northerners do more than one thing—Wayne and Mary are perfect examples. Part of it is financial pressures; there aren't a lot of jobs up north and those who are passionate about the Territories will do anything in order to stay. It might be three jobs one year and none the year after.

Many feel less constrained here—they're comfortable pursuing their dreams even if the dreams are a little odd and the pursuit leads nowhere. The difference between the north and the south has something to do with the air and something to do with the people, but it's mostly to do with the land, the endlessness and harshness of it. The hard beauty of the Northwest Territories somehow undresses the soul, cleans it out and offers a second or a third chance. There's a sense of possibilities, which makes you feel things can be done, people can accomplish the unexpected, can reinvent themselves. It's one of the reasons some can't stay: the north also demands something in return. If you shirk the opportunity, you are lessened.

In addition to doing all the basic work at the bed and breakfast—Mary apologizes profusely for offering "only" eggs benedict, wild cranberry pancakes and fruit cocktail that first morning—she works full-time as a nurse at the Yellowknife hospital. For years she ran a tea house every Sunday at the old Hudson's Bay depot about a hundred metres from the inn. Her dreams include another tea house at her own establishment and perhaps a full-service restaurant.

A few weeks before David arrived, Mary staged a play in her

backyard. The script was written by a local, a long-time newspaperman with a fascination for bush pilots. "I'll see your pony express types, your mountain climbers *and* your big game hunters and I'll raise ya ten times!" an old-timer stated one night to David at a nearby bar, crashing his beer mug to the bar for emphasis. "There ain't no one, not one single goddamn person who can match our bush pilots. Those bastards got balls that'd make an elephant faint."

The Bryants' bed and breakfast is in Old Town, the original settlement with the rugged aspect of an eastern fishing village. But there's no sleepy, picturesque demeanour to the small industrial harbour that surrounds most of it. This is a harbour with a job to do and there's little attempt to prettify. The bustle and activity are inviting, even more so than postcard bays that have long lost any connection to the work of the sea and now exist for tourists alone. An engine orchestra serenades from dawn to twilight, the straining whine as seaplane pilots race toward take-off and the deeper, thumping growl after touchdown. The air is the north's highway. David can see a half dozen different firms from the inn and there's a government seaplane base just next door. Adding to the tumult are fishing boats, mid-sized cargo ships and the MS *Norweta*, a large cargo hauler refurbished as a tourist boat, one of the few concessions to visitors visible in the harbour.

A stone's throw from the shores of Old Town, an island, connected to the mainland by a small bridge, houses the Dogrib village of Dettah. Down the lake is Lutselk'e, home of the Snowdrift band. As David stands absorbing the rich canvas of a harbour at work, a water-skier improbably slices through the chaos, sending a rooster tail of spray into the air, nearly drenching the deck of a houseboat of sorts moored at the shore. The float homes are mostly barges or made-over boats rather than the full-fledged houses that just happen to be on the water in the trendy float-home communities in Vancouver. When someone complains to a town official about their being illegally moored on their foreshore, the owner simply moves farther along the shore.

There isn't much housing in Old Town but what exists makes for odd neighbours. Sweeping west coast–style houses sit cheek by jowl with shabby warehouses and broken down buildings. Single-storey plywood structures lean haphazardly; one stretch seems to have countervailing leans like a row of dominos all tilted in different directions. Bare plywood is the siding of choice, sometimes covered by the remains of decades-old paint or occasionally peeling asphalt roofing strips nailed horizontally.

Old Town sits largely on rock, which lends considerable challenge to architects. One house is perched in an inverted V on a large outcropping, while another straddles the rock in several places, looking a little like a clipper ship under full sail. Yet another resembles a giant angular boomerang laid on its side against a cliff.

Old Town rock presents more than just architectural difficulties. Most of the houses aren't hooked up to water or sewer because surface pipes freeze in the 40-plus below winters, and no one has yet figured out how to drill lines through solid granite at anything approaching reasonable cost. So water is trucked in and waste is trucked out.

"Bunch of idiots," sniffs Hal LeBlanc, who worked in Yellowknife as an architectural student. "I got a summer job through an uncle of mine who said I'd learn more about building in four months in Yellowknife than I would pussyfooting around with a firm in Toronto or Vancouver. I felt quite superior to my classmates, who all got soft jobs sharpening pencils and carrying maps around for the big windbags. Then I get up here and I'm thinking, what the heck are they thinking about? Working up here isn't about designing things, it's about fighting Mother Nature. You build on solid rock in Victoria, well okay; in Halifax, a bit tougher but okay again, the view's worth it. But up here? Solid rock, minus 60? Then again, you've got to admire anybody crazy enough to give it a try."

Many of Old Town's buildings look like they have historical significance, or at least ought to, and sure enough, a few of them boast fading historical plaques. Up on the rock behind the bed and breakfast there's a boarded-up twenty-by-twenty clapboard shack, with a fading sign announcing that it was once known as the House of Horrors or the Snake House because of wild card parties held inside during the 1940s. At tourist information David inquires about the intriguingly named Snake House. "There's no historical plaques in town that I know of," responds the young woman, shaking her head. David assures her that he saw several in Old Town. "And one says this building was called the Snake House or House of Horrors." The woman again shakes her head in puzzlement. "Never heard of it. Have you heard of something called a snake house?" she bellows to another older woman, who shrugs helplessly.

The first evening in Yellowknife, David rejuvenates his jet-lagged legs by walking around Old Town and stumbles across a real find, Bullocks' Bistro, located in the unprepossessing former headquarters of Weaver and Devore Trading Ltd.—bush orders, dry goods, grocers, hardware—now moved across the street to more spacious quarters. At first David is a little put off by the shanty-like exterior, but the people on the patio overlooking the lake seem to be having fun and there's a wonderful smell enveloping the place. Inside he finds about thirty people seated in the long, low-ceilinged narrow interior dominated by a huge stainless steel gas range with four or five stools in front of it. This is the source of the smell and now it's almost orgasmic. There's only one stool left in front of the grill. David dives for it.

David sits at the long narrow bar almost on top of the cook. She offers a running commentary on the food, the patrons, the owners and anything else David cares to inquire about, while she flips, flops, seasons and deep-fries.

The patrons are about half locals who "always complain about the prices—too high they say. But I notice they always finish every scrap," she hoots. The rest are tourists who "complain less and tip better—a lot better." David scans the menu. "Get the Fisherman's Platter," she commands. "You'll be happy."

After several minutes of listening to the cook and waiting patiently for someone to offer him a drink, David finally asks for a beer. "We just help ourselves around here," she says, gesturing expansively toward a large cooler.

As promised, the Fisherman's Platter, $14.95, is excellent. Fresh lake cod—not as firm as its saltwater cousin but tasty; trout; arctic char—very rich and flavourful; whitefish—delicate flesh belies an almost but not quite gamey flavour.

Right next to the grill, where these wonderful platters find life, is a thick-sided, workmanlike deep-fat fryer redolent of fish and chips, for those needing heavier ballast. And for anyone requiring even fuller loading, the caribou poutine beckons. David watches a stray dog tackle a half-eaten plate of the French fries laden with gooey, cheesy gravy, but even the hungry hound trots away unable to finish it.

Bullocks' "award-winning wine list" consists of one word—Gato—red and white. David assumes it's a joke, but there is an enormous bottle of wine in the cooler. For cooking perhaps. Sure enough it's labelled Gato. The wine is also self-serve so David, in the interests of research, pours a glass—drinkable, as long as it's plenty cold, which it is. When Gato warms a little, there's a lingering taste of something David can't quite identify and isn't sure he wants to. It does have a cork, which he takes to be the bottler's inside joke. To finish the meal, David expects large thick mugs of your basic tin can coffee, ubiquitous in the north—people drink more of it than water. But alongside caribou poutine, Bullocks serves a fine cup of espresso.

Downtown, about a kilometre and a half inland, a cluster of two- and three-storey buildings, several small malls and a couple of eight-storey high-rises spread out to form the main intersection, which is anchored by a Canadian Tire store.

There's no rock downtown, and the surrounding modern subdivisions enjoy the amenities of water and sewerage. But frost jacking makes architectural life even more interesting than attaching structures to solid rock. Though you can't tell just by looking, you don't have to dig very far to hit permanent ice, permafrost. In the winter, heat from the houses slowly melts the ice supporting the buildings, causing them to sink as if a herd of voracious subterranean termites had been munching away at the foundations. Some buildings have metre-wide gaps in the basement. David spots one alarming example of a house tilted almost thirty degrees. He assumes it has been condemned. "Oh no," a passerby assures him, "it's good for a few more years yet. Not near bad enough to tear down. You just get used to walking funny while you're inside, that's all."

Over the years innumerable remedies have been tried: wooden pilings, thirty-centimetre–thick Styrofoam slabs designed to insulate the structures from the ground, elaborate cantilevered affairs making the house look like it's standing on stilts and, more recently, refrigerator coils to freeze the ground in winter so that the ice won't melt. "Can you believe it?" Hal shakes his head. "We're freezing the goddamn ground north of the 60th parallel. You say that out loud and you'll hear this tinny sound. That's the ghosts of the early settlers laughing their heads off. God, I love the north." Hal abandoned architecture to go diamond prospecting.

WHISPER THE WORD *MINING* anywhere in Yellowknife and one name pops up—Brian Weir. Even those who don't know him personally or know exactly what he's done know "for a fact" that he's the guy to see.

Brian is a Renaissance man, northern style, and he's always happy to talk prospecting, or anything else for that matter. Now semi-retired, he does a little of this and a little of that and by the by has made himself rich. But you'd never know. He and his wife, Penny, live quietly in a mobile home across from the Bayside Bed and Breakfast. In contrast, Brian's partner built a $700,000 house, the biggest in Yellowknife.

A handsome, greying man of sixty, Brian looks a little like a wise coyote wearing spectacles. He speaks learnedly and sometimes angrily about every subject affecting the north, from politics to the environment. There's no need for paint or paper in the Weirs' mobile home, as the walls are literally covered with books, mostly history, and northern history at that—all carefully catalogued by Penny, a former librarian. When David comments on what surely is the largest collection of books about the north in private hands, Brian and Penny exchange looks as if this is a family talking point.

"I've actually got a few more books here and there," he says. "Truth is, I've got a lot of things stored away here and there." David wonders about the comment until a few days later when

Brian shows David his "warehouses and worksheds." Five of them, scattered over the city, all meticulously organized but jammed with "things," including a lot more books.

As David browses among Brian's things—really a catalogue of mining implements used in the last fifty years in the north—he comes across several strange-looking contraptions. One of them is brand new and resembles a gleaming, stainless steel clothes washer. It is used for separating soil samples of different specific gravities and during the staking frenzy had been purchased by one outfit that left town before the thing was even out of its box.

"I can't even remember exactly where that came from. Somebody ordered it and never picked it up," Brian says. "It was crazy back then." Brian and a bunch of his cronies have various types of mining equipment stashed all over town, hoping one day a mining museum will become a reality. "They've got stuff in their warehouses too," Brian laughs. "Between the lot of us we've got fifteen or twenty warehouses. And a lot of the stuff just sitting outside. Too big for anyone to steal." Recently Brian's group got permission to display their old mining apparatus on the three-metre–wide grass border in front of the airport.

You couldn't ask for a more affable individual than Brian Weir, but when he looks hard in your direction you know he's a man you'd never want to cross. Which is why and how he's survived as long as he has staking claims in the north. "He's a go-to kind of guy, no question about it," another geologist sums him up. "When De Beers wants claims staked who the hell do they call? They call Brian."

The spring of 1991 was a slow period. Gold exploration, then the lifeblood of the mining industry in the Territories, had slipped into one of its periodic ebbs as the days of eight-hundred-dollar-an-ounce gold were falling farther and farther back into memory. Brian was using the time to clean up a little paperwork when he got a "fact-finding" call from Monopros Limited, the Canadian subsidiary of Cape Town–based De Beers Consolidated Mines, the largest and most secretive diamond concern in the world, with powerful tentacles plunged deeply into every aspect of the industry worldwide. In addition to owning all or part of several diamond mines, De Beers runs the fabled Central Sales Organisation, which buys roughly 90 per cent of the raw diamonds mined in the world, stockpiles them, then doles the gems out through their London offices in order to "stabilize" the market.

Many believe the company has had agents in diamond hot spots for half a century, keeping track of things and reporting back to Cape Town. Old-timers in the Territories are convinced that De Beers found strong indications of diamonds up north many years ago, before anyone else was even looking, but kept the information quiet until they were ready to move. "You buy a little rock for your girl in Moose Jaw, and some asshole in South Africa who gets X-rayed before he can even open his office door is recording it before you even get it on her finger," Sam Johnson, a Toronto diamond buyer, observes. "Nothing happens without De Beers knowing."

Brian was intrigued when Monopros called again in the fall and told him to get ready to do some staking. "A lot of staking was all he'd say," he recalls. "Wouldn't tell me where, how much land or anything—just said get ready."

Shortly after, Dia Met announced it had found a kimberlite pipe with gem-quality diamonds in it, near Lac De Gras. Almost immediately Monopros faxed Brian a map. As the machine spit out the details moments later, Brian boggled. "It was stupendous. They wanted a million acres! For gold miners a claim of a thousand acres is considered large. The most I'd ever staked was ten thousand acres. And gold miners mostly stake *after* they've found something, not before." Still, it was De Beers and if ever there were deep pockets in the mining industry, De Beers had them. Drawings and co-ordinates arrived soon after. "When they said go, I just started spending."

Diamonds are found in kimberlite pipes, but only one in a thousand has stones of sufficient grade and quantity to mine. But one pipe can be the basis of a mine worth billions. The Dia Met find touched off the biggest staking rush in the history of mining. That summer the Territories was like a toy liquidator on Christmas Eve. Everyone wanted a piece of land and didn't care how they got it. De Beers had beaten everybody to it except for the Dia Met boys, who found the original pipe, which did eventually lead to the Ekati diamond mine.

De Beers got the jump on other prospectors and explorers, but the rest weren't far behind. "Word gets around fast in this town. When we found out that Brian Weir bought every fucking stake in town, we knew something was going on," says geologist Walt Humphries. "One helicopter heading north, no one thinks twice about. A dozen heading north is another matter." In addition to every stake in town, Brian had purchased every bit of fluorescent marking tape, every single heavy-duty stapler and all the freeze-dried food available.

During the frenzy Brian didn't stake anything less than a forty thousand–acre parcel, a hundred thousand being the norm. "I'd get calls from people I didn't know, from companies I didn't know, wanting me to stake a million acres. I'd ask them what geology they were working on. They'd say no geology, just get me some land near the mine. You'd tell them there was no mine. Didn't matter. You'd tell them that all the land near the discovery was taken. Didn't matter. Just get them some land. We were just grabbing acres. It was crazy."

On one occasion, a company wired him cash on Monday, then called him on Wednesday cancelling the job. "You can't cancel the fucking job, it's already done!" barked Brian. Some companies were slightly more scientific, staking land showing anomalies, magnetic patterns that didn't conform to the norm that had been identified by the federal government's airborne geophysical survey, hoping the anomalies might be clues to the existence of kimberlite pipes. "The damn survey was done way back in the fifties or sixties," snorts Brian. "And anyway no one, me included, knew anything about finding diamonds, so how did we know what anomalies to look for and what they meant once we found them?"

Most were simply looking for land somewhere near where Dia Met had found the diamond-bearing pipe. In stock market parlance it's called a "location play," and one has to understand a little about the Vancouver Stock Exchange to understand what happened in the NWT. Dia Met was listed on the VSE. When the find broke, its stock catapulted from pennies to dollars in hours. Overnight, VSE-listed gold, oil and base metal exploration companies, as well as juniors in the biotech field, fish farming and computers, began transforming themselves into diamond mining outfits. At the peak of the rush, there were more than 150 junior companies actively staking land in the north.

"We didn't know anything. Not a thing. Nobody knew anything," recalls Randy Turner of Winspear, one of the few junior companies that's still exploring. "The guys like me running the companies didn't know anything. The geologists didn't know anything. The investors didn't know anything. And most importantly, the analysts working for the brokerages didn't know anything. Any news, no matter how irrelevant, produced a stock spike. At first it was if you had any land near Dia Met, then it was if you found a kimberlite, then it was if you found a kimberlite near a lake. It was ridiculous in retrospect. Today you have to find the Hope diamond before anyone's going to get excited. Hell, we've got better results than that original find and no one gives a damn."

Brian wouldn't lace up his boots unless he had $50,000 in cash or certified cheque in hand. Bona fide junior exploration companies, let alone those who wouldn't know a vein of ore from a gusher of oil, are notorious for melting away, bills unpaid, when the rumours of a find turn out to be just that. In the pell mell intensity of the staking rush, cash became king. Sometimes, if Brian didn't actually have the dollars in his pocket, he'd take stock in the company. Occasionally, he swapped some or all of his work for an overriding royalty on the land, which would give him a piece of the action if anything was ever found.

Brian did everything on cost-plus. And the pluses were astronomical. He had three helicopters flying virtually non-stop, with two twin-engine Otter planes feeding them fuel. Helicopters went for $800 an hour, and it cost $13 for every mile flown by the Otters. Staking can be done by helicopter in the barrens but not below the tree line, which stretches about 160 kilometres north of Yellowknife. There the lines have to be laboriously blazed by hand. One company hired Brian to stake 1.5 million acres, mostly in the tree line. To do it, he set up a twenty-three–man camp. It cost nearly half a million dollars just to pay his crew over the ninety-three days of staking that summer.

Like a treasure hunt gone wild, there were maps on napkins, sketched on the back of matchbooks, pencilled over other crumpled maps. Brian had one man working full time redrawing the rough maps into "pretty" ones for the government when the claims were registered.

Everything was done in secrecy, at least as much secrecy as you can manage in a small town where everybody associated with mining knows everybody else's business. Sampling results were carefully guarded, and the location of exploration camps was top security with false place names being used for all communications. Some outfits even used high-tech devices to foul up other companies' magnetic surveys.

The indiscriminate staking leapfrogged north so quickly that it threatened to overtake conventional mining. Geologists with Noranda were exploring for base metals that summer. They were going at it systematically, unconcerned about whether or not they had staked the land they were exploring. There would be plenty of time for that if any of the samples looked promising. Then the rush began. Within a matter of days, it looked as if the land they were on would be staked right out from under them. "We watched the staking come north so fast that we finally had to take out permits just to work," recalls one of Noranda's junior geologists.

In the midst of turbo-charged helicopters, satellite reconnaissance and ground positioning systems, the stakes themselves are wonderfully low-tech. They're made out of wood, just as they were during the Klondike rush. But there the similarity to the old days ends. Instead of compasses and magnetic north, Brian and the other stakers use ground positioning systems, portable locating devices that calculate triangulations from earth to satellites, getting a precise location in less than a minute. They speed everything up, and when you're staking a few hundred thousand acres with a bunch of other stakers stepping on your heels, every hour counts.

Claims are supposed to be staked every five hundred metres with claim tags and posts secured by a concrete footing or a cairn of rocks at the corners of every block. "Have you ever tried to pull together a pile of rocks at 40 below on the tundra?" Brian asks when David queries the process. "In the first place they're frozen to the ground. In the second place," he adds with finality, "there's no time." No time ruled over the winter of 1991 and spring of 1992. Stakes were sometimes just flung out of helicopters willy-nilly. "They all said they'd go back later and do the job properly but I don't think anyone did," says one pilot with a grin. "It didn't matter much, so many of the claims lapsed anyway."

Dia Met and its partner, BHP, quickly increased their acreage to over one million. Even so, the companies "got caught with their mental pants down," says Brian. "They'd expanded their original claims, but they never dreamt that over one million acres weren't enough to fully protect their claim." When the dust cleared in the fall of 1993, 60 million acres of the Northwest Territories had been claimed by the diamond seekers. Brian Weir was personally responsible for staking about a quarter of it all.

Money flowed in and out of Yellowknife like the massive tides of Fundy. But despite the fortunes involved and the furiously competitive pace of staking, there was a congenial, almost clubby atmosphere among the four principal stakers. Sometimes, even in the vastness of the north, they'd bump into each other while laying a line of overlapping stakes. During the gold rush days, beatings, killings and ambushes were common when men setting out claims happened upon each other. In the heat of the diamond staking rush they'd set the helicopter down, or if they were in the tree line, they'd head back to the nearest camp and thrash out their differences. Instead of trading blows, they'd trade this bit of land for that, rejig the claims so the people who were paying the bills would be happy.

One day Brian's helicopter almost flew into another carrying a geologist; their two lines had overlapped. Later they met back at Brian's, "drank a bottle of rum and solved the problem. Basically we traded our staking. It was better to sit down individually and informally work it out. Everybody did it. We had to. We were staking 60 million acres. Only one legal problem came out of the whole mess."

ONE EVENING BRIAN TAKES David to meet a dozen or so geologists having a drink at the Explorer Hotel. They're an interesting collection, men and women, young and middle-aged, with plenty of stories and laughter. When you get together with people who work in the bush, the yarns revolve around cooks, drinking and snafus about camp. When those tales peter out, they move on to the south, as good a punching bag as exists for exorcizing frustration and an excellent way to refine the northern sense of superiority, a lovely, rough version of disdain—it doesn't matter that most of them are from the south: they're here, they're working, they belong. One favourite story is about a young newspaper writer from one of the faceless, soulless cities down south who came north to get a "feel for the country."

The writer duly absorbed, asked questions, took notes and tried to imbue her writing with authenticity. "Each day before we left camp," she wrote earnestly in the ensuing article, "we were careful to bring our rifles lest we run into any lurking caribou." The last two words elicit howls from the youngsters and old salts alike. "Lurking caribou!" they yell, convulsing each time. "Lurking caribou!" The phrase has become a fond password among this

99

group of geologists, and the bush-bound will often be cautioned, with great solemnity, to watch out for lurking caribou.

Once everyone has calmed down, happy sighs and the odd hiccup being the only remnant of the tale, one of the women hands around some photographs taken during a field trip with the high school class she teaches. She took her grade 10 students out to the bush as part of their environmental studies. She guides David through the pictures, explaining what the teenagers were doing. They could be kids from anywhere in Canada on an outing to a provincial park or wilderness sanctuary—boys and girls examining flora and fauna, pools of water and natural formations. There's a striking shot of a giant boulder—a scratching post for many generations of bears, worn smooth in places and darkened by the oil from their hides.

It's the final group of pictures that tell the story of the north, blood-drenched images of Dogrib Indians slaughtering, butchering, and then cooking three caribou. The contrast with the earlier photos gives David a start. He doesn't react physically, but there must be some psychological clue because the group quiets almost as one and when he looks up they are watching him intently. Though not a hunter, he's been hunting, helped drag carcasses out of the woods, cleaned game and buried too many of our own livestock. It's not the slaughter that gave him pause, it's the contrast between what is acceptable and ordinary in the north and what falls into that same category in the south.

David tells them that if anything even remotely resembling the slaughter of the caribou happened in one of his daughters' school outings, it would be a front-page newspaper story that would likely end up with some kind of official inquiry. Heads would roll. Psychologists would be called in. Here it is a fact of life worthy of no more attention than any other everyday activity.

The environment has a different meaning north. It's not that people north of 60 don't care about the environment, it's just that they have an entirely unique take on it. Yellowknife pumps untreated sewage into a nearby lake. If that fills up, the town will simply move on to another one. There are lots of lakes, it's a small town, the land can handle it. "People down south simply don't understand," says one long-time resident. "We've got millions of lakes up here. What does it matter if we spoil a few?"

Diamond mining is rapidly becoming the lifeblood of the north, but the mines are horribly intrusive on lakes and waterways. Digging often tunnels right underneath lakes, which entails diking, draining or relocation. There is a rigorous environmental approval process that every mine must go through and, as a matter of rote, that every mining company grumps about. It's almost like a script, and everyone from Native groups to green lobbyists and miners read their lines. They've seen the play before, they know how it ends.

BHP Diamonds, operator of the Ekati diamond mine, talks the talk and even walks the walk of a concerned corporate citizen, but the company is fully aware of what the mine will do for the community and officials aren't slow to point it out. During the build-up to the mine opening, the company complained about costs and slowdowns and took a few expected shots at those who would suffocate free enterprise. "We're not bottomless wallets," said Graham Nicholls, head of public relations, in the face of demands from native and environmental groups. When all was said and done, there was no question that the mine would be going ahead; approval was taken for granted by everyone. With commodity prices spiralling down and unemployment in the north spiralling up, no one doubted there would be a mine.

*   *   *

GEOLOGIST WALT HUMPHRIES is the kind of guy Farley Mowat would like to have been. Fiftyish and burly with a greying, bushy beard, long pony-tailed hair, booming voice and hearty laugh, he's every inch the prospector and backwoods/tundra man that he appears to be. He's still too young to be thoroughly grizzled, but he's working on it. Walt's a trained geologist who has earned his looks and mien having prospected all over the north since 1969. He also teaches a highly sought-after course on prospecting. At the same time, he's an artist, raconteur, amateur historian and a self-described "man about town."

Walt's paintings take a few minutes to fully absorb. They're part satire, part social statement and all whimsical tributes to the north. Though the characters are finely drawn, there's a purposeful crudeness about them that sharply contrasts with the intricate detail. In style they are a cross between Hogarth and Ralph Stedman with a dash of Rube Goldberg thrown in. Averaging $80 a signed print, they are the best art deal in the country.

Walt's pretty laid back about life and his art, but still, he insists David inspect the picture he's proudest of—an eight and a half by two and a half metre mural of Whitehorse he painted on a giant billboard outside the Yellowknife hospital. "You've got to see it," he urges. "You've got to see it." Beer in hand, he offers to drive David there on the spot. It's quite a sight, so full of character, humour and just plain stuff you can look at it for an hour and still not see it all. Every satirical jab has a punch line, but they aren't all easy to spot, especially for southerners.

In the foreground looms Great Slave Lake, a Viking galley plying its waters, and at the other end is a sea monster with her brood. There haven't been any reports of sea monsters lately, but Walt thought it only fitting that it have one anyway. In the air a biplane tootles by, and on the boardwalk around the lake strut a variety of northerners, including natives and an environmentalist with what looks like an ocelot on a leash. It's a riotous scene, gloriously alive. In the far background is an Inuit jumble of rocks. Those intriguing piles of rocks, dotted here and there near Inuit communities, are interpreted differently depending on whom you talk to. They are either sculptures honouring the animals and elements, spiritual cairns or simply just landmarks on the endless tundra.

Walt also pens "Tales from the Dump" for the weekly *Yellowknifer* newspaper. His prose is simple with a hint of Hemingway's muscularity, but it isn't fishing, hunting, war or love he's writing about but the local dump, as rich a vein of material as Hemingway found in Spain. The columns are funny and nostalgic on the surface, but even an outsider can see they provide Walt with a platform to launch blistering attacks on the government and anyone else who falls short in preserving the history and way of life of his beloved north. In one series of columns, he embarrassed the northern government so badly by detailing what they were discarding that they rewrote their policies on getting rid of surplus items.

In another column Walt describes a treasured find—an item of machinery he took to be of 1920s farming vintage. He ponders where it might have come from and how it might have been used, in the process gently informing readers about the north's little known farming history and the brief period when horses were used to work the land. One week he lamented about the many abandoned gold mines being lost to forest fires. "They're a big part of our heritage. Every time there's a big fire we lose one. And nobody seems to care."

Walt doesn't just write about the dump, he lives it. "I like hanging around the dump. How else can you find out what's really going on? All the secrets are there." Walt's house is furnished with discarded items. Often, after turning up a particularly interesting artifact, he works to find a new home for it.

Secrets are the last refuge of the geologist. No matter how down and out a prospector is, no matter how many samples have turned up diddly, he's still got his secrets. The wife may have left, the partner died in a white-out and other prospectors won't front him for a cup of coffee, but he's got his secrets to cherish. Chief among them is where he's currently exploring and what he's looking for— questions that are impolite to ask and equally impolite not to ask. He wants you to ask just so he can tell you nothing. "In the Gordon Lake area," the normally forthcoming Walt responds vaguely when David wonders where he's been spending his time, describing a piece of geography roughly comparable in size to Vancouver Island. "Gold," he replies at the second question, the *what*.

BRIAN WEIR INSISTS THAT David needs one further experience before he heads up to the Winspear exploration camp. "You've got to play a round of golf," he says simply. "If you haven't played a round in Yellowknife, you don't understand anything."

David protests that he hasn't been on the fairways since he was a teenager sneaking onto the Uplands golf course in Victoria after hours.

"Doesn't matter," responds Brian with a distinct twinkle in his eye.

"But I don't have any golf shoes or clubs or anything."

Brian chuckles as if at some private joke. "Your running shoes are perfect. I've got a spare set of clubs or two . . . in a warehouse somewhere. Or you can share mine." Then Brian turns his steely gaze on David and announces, "It's settled then. You'll play."

Brian picks up David and Wayne Bryant from the Bayside Bed and Breakfast and the three of them head to the nine-hole Yellow-knife Golf Club course, now expanded to eighteen holes. There's nothing unusual about what David sees from the parking lot. The first hint that there's something different comes when they start unloading the equipment from Brian's trunk. After hauling out the clubs, Brian hands David two fistfuls of golf balls. "You may need these," he says dryly. "And this," he adds, dangling a scungy, deeply pitted piece of plastic carpet measuring fifteen centimetres square. Brian's piece, David noticed, was pristine, looking as if it had just been snipped off a roll.

"AstroTurf?" asks David.

"AstroTurf," Brian responds firmly.

The Midnight Sun's fairways are sand and the rough truly warrants the title, consisting of rock and plenty of it, trees and more sand. You don't get much bounce on the fairways and far too much in the rough. Obstacles are such that some players have become specialists in carom shots off various impediments—a fresh-air version of billiards. You carry the piece of AstroTurf around with you so you can hit off the fairway; otherwise you'd spend all your time with a sand wedge, hip-hopping your way to the greens.

The pièce de résistance is the greens—which are, unlike the fairways, green—very green, AstroTurf green, though sprinkled with sand for a more realistic look. They're also hard as concrete. Divots are unheard of and unimaginable anywhere on the course from tee-off to last hole. "If you think you're too far to putt, you can chip to the hole. Hell, you can use your driver on the greens if you want. Nobody cares."

At the first hole, David again mentions that he hasn't played golf in thirty years. Brain and Wayne almost in unison assure him there's nothing to worry about, but David takes their quick disclaimers to be the words of a couple of sharpies setting up a mark. Brian is unruffled as David smashes a 220-yard drive down the fairway, but Wayne explodes in a flurry of curses—he's already shanked his ball a paltry 30 yards into the bush.

"You brought a ringer into the game," he accuses.

Brian plays a solid, no-nonsense game, keeping his shots safely on the sand fairways. Not great distances, but he always sets himself up perfectly for the next shot. And he's all business. Normally voluble, with a golf club in his hand he's terse and to the point, answering questions but not initiating conversation. Golf brings out the emotion in the more excitable Wayne, who talks nonstop. His odd excellent shots are bracketed by erratic salvos punctuated by furious outbursts. Usually he's playing from deep in the trees, and from time to time David hears the distinct sound of club head hitting wood. There is much talk of a far better round shot last week.

David birdies the first hole, one under par, then settles down to a game more befitting his long absence—two or three shots over par for most holes. He's playing well enough to enjoy it and manages to overcome any latent sense of competitiveness as Brian methodically knocks down par after par. Wayne tallies about the same as David, but seems to take a lot of strokes to do it.

About halfway through the game, David fires a soaring drive that lands at the end of the fairway. When he strides up to whack it onto the green, his feet begin to sink into a glutinous hole. "Ooops, sorry about that," Brian laughs a little apologetically, eyeing David's nice new hiking boots, which are now covered in a gucky coat of sticky sand. "That was where the green was. We used to oil 'em to keep the sand from flying all over when you're putting, but the environmentalists made us stop."

After a few holes, David is feeling a little hot, though the temperature is only in the low 70s. A golf cart pulls into view, driven by a couple of young boys and, to David's delight, bearing a load of beer. He gives the lads a generous tip and thereafter they are very attentive. At first David is hesitant about walking down the fairways beer in hand, but after observing other golfers quaffing merrily he relaxes. Some regulars have adapted their golf bags to hold their beer bottles.

The players wear everything from sneakers to cowboy boots and jeans to loud Bermuda shorts. Some are excellent, others are duffers. Everybody seems to be having a very good time. David fully gets into the spirit of the thing, intentionally hitting shots off the rocks as if he were playing pool and chatting with passing golfers.

AT EIGHT O'CLOCK THE next morning David and John McDonald, Winspear's vice president of exploration, board a twin-engine Otter float plane, the workhorse of the north. John, medium height with thinning hair, wears a natty suit, which is a little out of sync with everyone else's garb. Smiling and open-faced, he has a pleasant, sincere manner. If David hadn't read his résumé, he'd guess salesman—a good one. Despite the suit, you can see signs of the outdoors—he has the well-worn oak burnish to his skin that only comes from the wear of sun and wind, and he still has the easy roll in his walk of one who's scrambled over a rock or two.

Just before the Otter takes off, the co-pilot hands out wax earplugs. They knock only a few decibels off the machine's considerable noise. Nonetheless, David and John manage to carry on a conversation of sorts during the little over one-hour flight to Winspear's Snap Lake exploration camp.

Just north of Yellowknife, the ground is surprisingly green and forested, at least the part that isn't burned to a crisp. Here and there are great blackened swathes where fire has spent itself, and grey, rolling clouds where the forest is still burning. "Do something!" you want to yell. But the fires just burn until they run into a lake too big to jump over or go around or are snuffed out when the wind turns and chases the flames back over their charred trail, eventually starving the blaze.

Pushing north, trees become scarcer and the terrain evolves into rock and bush leavened by strips of gorgeous sand. Yes, sand—lakeside sand just sitting there as if a truck had dropped a load by mistake. There are beaches to make Maui jealous—the gracious leavings of glacier eskers, rivers of sand and gravel.

Finally the trees give way, petering out into little blotches here and there, then suddenly disappearing entirely only to reappear just as suddenly in a lonely, gnarled, stunted copse, a far north bonsai tucked into a little microclimate, usually a depression protected by a large rock face or a nearby lake—just a fraction more hospitable. If you squint into the far horizon, the blotches of trees occasionally move and become caribou—little herds of a dozen or so.

There is water everywhere, which seems strange because the land in late summer is parched, the tough shrubbery looking as if its last drink was an epoch ago. Minnesota may be the land of a thousand lakes, but the Territories is the land of a billion lakes. Every shape and size imaginable, everywhere you look a Rorschach test of lakes. "I'm still amazed every time I see all the water," says John, reading David's mind. "It's glacier melt. Snow melt and rain. But aside from the big rivers, there's little running water. It's all just lakes."

Despite the power of nature over their lives, people in the

north feel they're more in control of their destiny. Once you've been out in the bush a while and acquired the skills and the rhythm of living there, you begin to understand it. There are certain things you can change but most you can't, so you don't even try. And once you stop fighting the land and the weather and do what they allow, the sense of freedom is as startling as the first plunge into icy water on a blistering day.

About 120 kilometres from Yellowknife, you hit the barrens. The trees are largely gone, except in sheltered spots near the lakes, and the country is mainly rock and water. The untouched vastness is astonishing. A glint off a steel roof, presumably a seasonal hunting lodge, is the only hint of civilization that David sees during the entire trip. Amid great stretches of nothing, Winspear's exploration camp jumps out. The plane lands and suddenly it's like *M*A*S*H* with incoming wounded. The entire crew hurries to unload, and hardly is the final box on the ground before the plane is airborne again. At over $2,000 a round trip, you don't keep a twin Otter hanging around.

The Winspear camp is a tidy little oasis set in the tundra— nineteen people in nine cabins plus a large headquarters, a sprawling building for cooking, eating and washing, a sample sorting cabin and a single outhouse, all set on a rise overlooking Snap Lake. It's a brand new camp, roughly knocked together with forest-green–stained plywood—built to be torn down.

David is immediately struck by the neatness and order. He's been in plenty of logging camps over the years and in comparison they were a shambling mess—slashed out of the woods and then abandoned. The laws in the NWT demand that camps like this be dismantled so that there's no trace of their existence. "The problem is that they apply the same rules to small cabins used by trappers, hunters and prospectors," grumbles Walt Humphries.

"Most of us old-timers know where they are and they can be the difference between life and death. Now we're supposed to destroy them to protect the environment. What are they hurting?" Brian Weir, who's had contracts from the government to clean up old sites, agrees. There's a suggestion, the merest hint in his voice that he might have left the odd one standing despite the government edict.

At the camp David is immediately taken in hand by Greg Burroughs, a short, somewhat sombre young man. Camp life is ordered and unvaried—cook gets up at 5:30, breakfast at 7:00, the sampling teams are helicoptered out at 8:00—they pack their own lunch—pick up 5:00 to 5:30, back to camp 6:00 to 6:30, dinner at 7:00. Then again the next day and every one after that till freeze-up.

Twelve of the nineteen camp residents are geologists—of those, five are Russian. There's a cook, a cook's helper called a bull, a handyman called a jack, and a helicopter pilot as well as three women diamond sorters. In all there are five women in camp. "Adds a little gentility to the place," comments Greg, "unless there's drillers around," he adds cryptically.

Moments after David and Greg start talking and less than five minutes after he got off the plane, a new John McDonald strides by with a huge smile on his face. No one, short of a quick-change artist, could have shucked a suit and donned bush pants, a red checked lumberman's shirt and work boots so quickly. He looks—well, born again. "It's great to be alive," he calls cheerily in passing. "Come and find me when you want to talk some more."

At thirty-one Greg is a seasoned geologist. He graduated from the University of Saskatchewan and took a job in the far north with Noranda as a field geologist, looking for base metals. After a few years of that, he worked for a variety of junior exploration companies in the early days of the diamond hunt. For the past two years he's been with Winspear, from mid-June to mid-September working on the sampling program, then back in January until mid-May on the drilling program.

With more than four months off, salary in the $55,000 to $60,000 range and nothing to spend it on when you're working, plus stock options that give you the opportunity to buy the stock at a fixed price even if it goes up, the life of a geologist seems enviable.

"Nice setup," David comments.

"Not really," says Greg, scrunching up his face earnestly. "Either you don't have enough money to enjoy your free time or you have lots of money and no time. It takes me a long time to get acclimatized to being back in town. I'm thirty-one. I want to start a family. I want to have children. I own a computer and a desk, which is in storage. That's it. I want to have some things of my own. Geology isn't really compatible with that."

It is an odd note, David thinks, on this beautifully sunny, optimistic day, where it seems to be the best place in the world on the best day ever.

This camp has all the mod cons to while away the long nights. In July the sun is still going strong near midnight, and many have trouble sleeping during their first few weeks. There is satellite TV, hot showers, laundry and a satellite phone, though the workers are restricted to one call a week. The crews aren't crowded, no more than three to a cabin, and there's all the fishing and hiking one could want. It's like a luxurious summer camp, but one that comes with a fat paycheque at the end of the season.

Underlying everything is an atmosphere of barely controlled excitement in camp, particularly among those directly in the hunt for diamonds. It's a feeling of momentum gathering, of something imminent.

Finding diamonds is like solving a complex murder mystery—only here, in the north, the clues have been shaken up in a cement mixer, spread over hundreds and sometimes thousands of square kilometres and then, to add complexity, often buried underground or hundreds of metres below the surface of a lake.

Nature isn't about to give up her treasures without making the searchers work. Glaciers, which once scoured the north, cleaved off the kimberlite pipes' soft tops like a voracious child munching the rim of an ice-cream cone. The ice scraped and scored and then moved on, leaving the pipes buried by rubble or filled in by melt water, which formed the region's uncountable lakes. As the ice advanced, it deposited bits of the sheared-off kimberlite across a huge territory, adding a little extra twist to an already complex game.

Geologists follow these clues back to their source like Hansel and Gretel following bread crumbs. Finding a mine is a matter of following the trail of indicator minerals—pyrope garnets, chrome diopsides and ilmenites. Bits of kimberlite and indicator minerals can be scattered many kilometres from the pipe itself. The whole thing makes lottery odds look like sure bets.

It all comes down to a bag of dirt—twenty-five kilograms of sand, pebbles and rocks. The contents of the bag are distilled down to a handful of sand-sized particles, which skilled eyes examine for the indicators. The sampling results are collated with the geophysical, topographical and bathymetric surveys. The results are plotted on maps and charts; in time a pattern starts to emerge, a pattern that can be followed back to the hidden prize—at least in theory.

Kimberlite gives up its secrets reluctantly. Sometimes geophysics uncovers a pipe that emits a clarion call of distinct properties. Other times the pipes are mute—the geologists at the Lac de Gras find uncovered some of their kimberlite pipes by actually looking for a complete *lack* of geophysical response.

When a pattern emerges, the heavy guns—the drilling crews— are brought in to find the pipe itself. Drillers are the prima donnas of the exploration set. Their work is dirty, uncomfortable, dangerous and expensive. Winter drilling usually begins in January when the lake ice is thick enough, over a metre and a half, to support the ten-ton rigs as they probe for the pipes resting beneath the water. The season lasts until mid-May, when the ice finally relinquishes its hold. A standard drill hole is about two hundred metres deep and every metre costs about $200.

Winspear had been conducting intensive sampling along with geophysical analysis since 1991, after the Dia Met find, without turning up a single kimberlite pipe. Randy Turner and John McDonald began to suspect that there was something wrong with their exploration program. That's where the Russians come in.

It was John McDonald who found the Russians, or more specifically the Russian, in 1994. He and Randy Turner were looking for someone to come in and evaluate their exploration program—basically tell them why they weren't finding any diamonds. John used his many contacts in the academic world and called friends in the big diamond companies, canvassing them for a shortlist of the world's top diamond finders. Every single person put Russian Nikolai Pokhilenko at the top of the list. John also knew Nick Sobolev, the top diamond scientist in Russia, who happened to be Nick's boss. Before you could say Elizabeth Taylor, Nick was climbing out of the twin Otter, ready for a summer with Winspear.

Nick has returned every summer, this year bringing with him

four other Russians, including his wife, Lucy. All are former students and they lead three of four sampling teams. The fifth Russian, Lada, the most recent arrival and now a landed immigrant, prefers picking to sampling. David is scheduled to spend the next day, Sunday, taking samples with Nick and Lucy.

DAVID SNAPS AWAKE AT 5:00 a.m. to find the windowless cabin flooded with sunlight. As he becomes unfuddled, he realizes that shafts of light are coming up through the floor. He's pretty sure the sun doesn't belong under the cabin. Over in the next bunk John McDonald snores peacefully, oblivious to the strange play of light. It's like a siren call David must obey—in any case he has to go to the bathroom. He opens the door and there hanging in the east is a great roiling ball of fire—twice normal size. Like a living, sentient being it shimmers and throbs, seeming to throw off huge solar flares, a different galactic orb than the dispassionate sun lurking over the 49th parallel.

David stands on the cabin step staring for several minutes before turning to study the cabin. It's built on stilts and the fierce sunlight is forcing its way up through substantial gaps in the floor. Half an hour passes as David communes with the sun and fills himself up with the morning air, so calm, clean and fresh it seems to have a bouquet like a fine wine.

At 5:30 David hears Darren the cook, a hefty lad of twenty-two, thrashing around in the kitchen, beginning breakfast preparations for twenty-one people that day. David ambles over for a cup of coffee, thoroughly content. No one else stirs for another thirty minutes. The early morning communion with the fiery sun is a happy ritual he continues for the five days he spends at camp.

David isn't sure what to expect from the Russians. He met them the day before, and while they were polite enough, none were particularly talkative. Though they were friendly with the non-Russian camp members, he saw that they didn't initiate many conversations and stuck pretty much to themselves. One of them, Mikhail, spoke little, emerging from his cabin only to eat and take samples.

Each evening after dinner, the Russians and the exploration leaders, Greg Burroughs and Jennifer Irwin, and John McDonald when he's there, gather to discuss the day's sampling, any lab or picking results that are in and where the samples will be taken the next day. In last night's meeting the Russians were relaxed and friendly. Still, there was an aloofness to them, and they think nothing of carrying on separate conversations in vehement Russian, leaving the English speakers standing mutely waiting for them to finish. In the morning, when Jennifer assigns them their sampling area, they invariably discuss the matter in Russian. After the evening meeting, the Russians left together and convened in Nick and Lucy's cabin. In a different time, a few decades ago, it would have been sinister; now it is just curious.

As it is, Nick starts talking the minute the four-passenger helicopter drops him, Lucy and David, and doesn't stop until the three return for dinner. "Pretty terrible place to take samples," he says, looking around the rock-strewn area. "This place looks a lot like Siberia, but it doesn't work like Siberia. The terrain is very similar. But there it's sedimentary rock. Here it's much older, harder rock, many more trace minerals, many more indicators. Plays hell with geophysics. At first I didn't know what to make of it." As Nick talks, he's shouldering his backpack, doing a radio check and consulting his map for the first sample target area about a kilometre away.

"Everything is different. In Siberia, at the start of the season, we'd be taken out into the field in a huge military helicopter. One big enough to hold a tank. Sometimes there'd be a tank in there with us. I've been in three or four crashes. Once I didn't even know I'd been in a crash; I woke up hanging upside down in the cabin. The pilot was badly injured."

"These helicopters," he says, gesturing to what is now a dot in the sky, "they're wonderful. There the helicopter maybe came back halfway through the season. Maybe not at all. Everything you had you carried on your back. We had two big guys just to carry samples. Here you don't need that. The camp moved just about every day. In the evening we shot a caribou, or caught fish and roasted them on an open fire. Sometimes we found wild vegetables."

David interjects that it sounds like a lot of fun, a comment prompted by the obvious pleasure in Nick's voice. "Yes! Yes!" he booms. "We had great fun then but it was hard, hard work. We were younger then." Lucy interrupts with a harsh burst of Russian that prompts a laugh from Nick. "She says that *some* of us are a *lot* older than we were."

Nick spent most of his first summer in Canada testing his techniques to determine if they were applicable in the Territories. He was bemused by the Canadian methods. "Wrong, all wrong." With equipment and machinery at their disposal, the kind of support he could only dream of in Siberia, they were going at things—to be charitable—inefficiently. The helicopters set down at the most convenient spots, the sampling crews jumped out, rammed their shovels into the softest place on the ground and took a sample. Some crews routinely took less than twenty minutes to get a sample and were knocking down more than twenty samples a day.

Long ago Nick concluded that poor sampling was Winspear's main problem, that much of what they'd collected was meaningless at best, at worst misleading. A bad sample is worse than no sample at all, because it can, and did, lead to wild goose chases. Having accepted that truth, Winspear has painstakingly re-examined the old data and, where it's in question, taken fresh samples. And they've added a new job to the Russians' résumés: teaching the young Canadians how to take a proper sample—something they would never learn in school.

"It was definitely a setback," John McDonald confirms. "When you're spending $2,000 to get a single sample, when you count up all the costs, and you get back garbage, that's a setback." But John likes to see a silver lining. "We've been able to pick up some good property that other companies dropped because they didn't find anything. They didn't find anything because they were sampling the way we used to."

Nick has been known to take half a day to find a single good sample. This morning he and Lucy range over nearly half a square kilometre, covering every centimetre, up steep inclines and into little gulches in their quest for the perfect spot. They are tenacious. "If you don't have a good sample," Nick explains simply, "you have nothing." Finally, after nearly an hour, they find an area that might be suitable. The ideal place is undisturbed, exactly the same as the day a few millennia ago a glacier ground on by, depositing tantalizing hints as it went. It should be free from organic material, with no clay and containing rock of varying size throughout.

Lucy finds the first site. About four metres across and encircled by boulders, it would have been easy to miss altogether. Even close up it looks like a pile of large rocks. Nick pronounces the first shovelful adequate—still, they spend another fifteen minutes searching for a better place to dig. They collect nearly thirty kilograms of material, log it in, rate it as good, adequate or poor. Then they tag the site with a red or blue plastic identification ribbon and pinpoint it using a portable ground positioning system.

The next step, the Russians' specialty, requires water, which is never far away in this part of the NWT. Nick and Lucy divide the till sample into white plastic buckets, adding equal parts water. Then they don elbow-length rubber gloves and mix it by hand to remove fine sand and clay particles before pouring the mixture through a wire screen to eliminate the bigger pieces. What's left is a sample about a quarter of the original size.

Now comes the art, the panning. In shape the pans resemble two small coal shovels welded together open end to open end. Unlike smooth gold pans, these wooden ones have ridges that help retain the particles. The pans are very personal items. You never pick one up without asking. Lucy's is only a couple of years old, but Nick's is a battered and cherished veteran of ten seasons, held together by screws and fibreglass on the back. "Careful, that's a Stradivarius," Nick cautions as he hands it over for David's inspection.

Nick and Lucy pick out rocks to sit on while they pan, their bums protected by thirty-centimetre-square pieces of plywood they carry everywhere. The motion is mesmerizing. First several minutes of side to side swishing to bring the lighter material to the surface, then they slowly sink the pan under the water, and a quick kiss forward sends a puff of sand billowing out of the pan into the lake. Side to side again and back and forth, the turbulence created by the movement and the ridges sending more and more material out. No gloves for this job; you need the fine touch of bare hands no matter how cold the water.

Nick is all grunts and guffaws and conversation. Lucy pans in silence but when she thinks David isn't close enough to hear she sings in Russian. David can't hear the words distinctly but the musical undertone lends a magical feel to the place. He doesn't ask what she's singing, fearing that she'll stop.

Nick and David hit it off right away. Nick enjoys talking and David enjoys listening. Nick is vastly amused when David tells him that Randy Turner and John McDonald had been concerned about how the Russians would react to having a writer following them around. "In Siberia, in the summer, I had a KGB man with me, always. We knew who he was. He knew we knew who he was. He was a good guy, but still he was KGB. Later he came with us on his vacations to go hunting.

"You're probably wondering why us Russians are here," he says suddenly, the question unasked. "We are on vacation! One thing we have in Russia is lots of vacations. I've saved up three hundred days. We all have good jobs in Moscow, we just don't get paid. Here we have good work. We get paid and I've got stock options, thousands of them. Seven years ago we found a mine in Siberia worth $15 billion. I was given the President's Medal of Honour with a cash prize of $600—barely enough to take friends to dinner in Moscow."

Nick is by turns serious, funny, sarcastic and witty but when he speaks of Mother Russia, it's all emotion, all from the heart. "Six hundred dollars for finding a diamond mine!" he roars. "While those criminals in Moscow are stealing all the diamonds in the national treasury. I have it on good authority that all the good diamonds are gone. I won't find another mine for those criminals." Even so neither he, Lucy nor any of the other Russians have any thought of not returning home.

At home Nick is chief research geologist of the Russian diamond mining company Almazy Rossii-Sakha, which controls the second most important diamond deposit in the world. He's also head of minerology and petrology at the Siberian branch of the Russian Academy of Sciences in Novosibirsk. Except for Lucy, who has a Master's degree, the Russians are all Doctors of Science in various branches of geology, a title above a Ph.D., and they're all seasoned in original research and fieldwork.

Panning has distilled this particular sample down from twenty-eight kilograms to fifty grams, about a fistful of material. The panning is a Russian trademark born of necessity. In Siberia the samplers must carry everything, and they simply can't hoist around the full-sized samples accumulated over a summer as the Canadians were doing with the luxury of helicopters. In Canada, the panning shortens the time from taking the sample to getting it back from the lab by three weeks, allowing Winspear to get results quickly and alter the sampling schedule to pursue a red-hot lead or abandon a dead end. It's an important edge considering the costs of exploration and the eight-to-ten-week-long season.

Nick spent most of his first summer in Canada watching, listening, absorbing. Then, "One day he just went at things his way," recalls John McDonald with ready admiration. "He gathered up all our maps and our all geophysics and shut himself up. Within three days he found us our first kimberlite pipe. We'd been looking for three years. Told us exactly where it would be. There were diamonds in it but it turned out to be uneconomic. That didn't matter. He found us a pipe in three days!"

Nick isn't the least bit modest about his accomplishments. "I've been doing this for twenty-nine years, every summer. The fieldwork is very important. That's why I'm here. You've got to be very motivated to be good at it. I go back to Russia and study and teach. All the Russians here do the same. Once they were my students, now they teach. The fieldwork is critical but there must be a balance. In Russia we have an advantage. We have diamond mines. We can use them to backtrack, to try to find out what the clues really mean—to look for better indicators. . . . And of course there's this," he says, patting his nonexistent gut.

Nick hasn't found another pipe—yet—but in 1996 and 1997, he focused on the Snap Lake area, finding diamonds in the till samples and also kimberlite boulders. When they drilled they hit an unusual dike formation. Dikes are vein-like intrusions in the earth's crust created as the molten material drives laterally through seams or weakness. This one could be as long as two thousand metres. In 1998, the summer David was there, a bulk sample of two hundred tonnes was taken, yielding 226 carats of high-quality diamonds averaging US$301 a carat. If they found the same quantity in a bigger sample, they'd have a mine. This sample was very small. Still, there's a strong sense of imminence among the geologists. "The diamonds are excellent," John McDonald says. "We just don't know how big the dike is. We could have gotten all there is. On the other hand it could be massive. And we still can't find the damn pipe." The dike suggests that the pipe is near but they still haven't been able to pinpoint it. Likely it is underneath Snap Lake.

Nick is a real charmer, funny and glib, with a thousand wonderful anecdotes related in a heavy Russian accent overlying perfectly intelligible English. He's the most western appearing of the Russians, with little hint in his face of his Slavic heritage. He's about 5' 10" and 175 pounds but he looks bigger. When he moves across the land, he's so erect he appears to be marching. The cadence looks slow and deliberate from afar, but David follows across the tundra one morning and tarries for a few moments to examine a shrub. When he looks up, Nick is striding off far in the distance.

Before they set out John McDonald fretted about David being gone all day, worried that his visitor might be bored or find the activity too taxing. So he arranges to have the helicopter pick David up at noon, just in case. David politely declines, assuring him he'll be fine. Nick thinks this is hilarious. After the first hour, he alludes to the helicopter bail-out. "You're doing okay, huh?" David nods. "Thought so," Nick chuckles.

While David and Nick are talking and ambling around looking for the next sample, Lucy is hiking circles around them. Tall, slender and sylph-like, she ranges far and wide with none of the slight hesitancy she shows in social situations. Moving across the terrain she is like a graceful bloodhound following a scent—picking up her pace at some invisible sign as the geological scent freshens. Most of the time she is out of sight, over a rise, burrowing into a depression, and most of the time she finds the best sample. "Lucy has a real flair for the sampling. What's more she really likes to get out in the bush," says Nick admiringly.

"She is your student?" David asks. "No! No! No!" Nick responds hurriedly, jumping on the verb. "*Isn't* my student. *Was!* Was." He adds more quietly with a smile, "A man has to be careful what he says."

Lucy is faster than Nick mainly because he's distractable. When there's someone around to talk to, Nick's work pace slows as his word pace quickens. David can only imagine how wonderfully voluble he might be with a bellyful of good old country vodka—unfortunately, the camp is dry.

Around camp Lucy is shy and retiring—she always looks as if her mind is busy in some other place. Like all the Russians—except Nick—she apologizes for her poor English. And, like all the Russians but one, her English is excellent; she doesn't trip over the longest words and is at home discussing the most esoteric subjects. But Lucy is wary, the least willing of her compatriots to share feelings and opinions, language notwithstanding. David begins to think he will never draw her out. When they take a break, he plies her with questions about panning, diamonds and how exploration differs between Russia and Canada. He finds out that Lucy's father was a metallurgist in Russia and she grew up in the culture of mining. Nick and Lucy have a twelve-year-old son, who she misses. She offers the information with a fatalistic shrug. He is with family, a stone's throw from his own home, and—another shrug—you do what you have to do. She likes it here in Canada but Russia is home and she'd never leave.

Unexpectedly, during one afternoon break Lucy volunteers a small, proud boast. For three years running she was champion panner in the Siberian diamond fields.

For all Lucy's shyness and reticence, she's plenty quick to give Nick the sharp of her tongue when she thinks he's wasting too much time. She speaks rapidly in low-toned, cross-sounding Russian. Nick won't translate but body language and facial expression are easy to decipher between mates. Out in the field, if Nick finds a boulder balanced on another, he can't resist toppling it over like a kid who spots a can and absolutely must give it a boot. The large ones he levers over with his shovel. When Lucy catches him at it, she delivers a sharp rebuke. If she can put the rock back she will, giving it a gentle pat. Once, after she replaces two small rocks Nick has kicked over, she glances at David. "It's our little thing," her eyes say.

David, Nick and Lucy fall into a routine. David hoofs along with one or the other while they look for a sample. When one is found, he sits on a nearby rock making notes and asking the occasional question while they pan. It gives him time to look around and reflect. The landscape is a chaos of stone, from boulders as big as cars to grains of sand, all strewn about as if some god had tired of a complicated game and brushed all the pieces off a table. Yet sometimes there appears to be a careful hand at work. Perfectly balanced piles of various sized rocks are mounded on top of each other, supported—surely contrary to the laws of nature—by a single little rock at the bottom. Occasionally, long lines of almost identical stones, oddly symmetrical, appear in flawless order as if arranged along the edge of a ruler.

When you fly over the land north of Yellowknife, what is encompassed by the horizon is hard to grasp. No matter how many times the vastness up here is described, no matter how much you pore over maps, there's no way to really comprehend the reach of this land except by flying over it or, better yet, walking on it. You can believe, as you set out across the tundra, that there are 3.38 million square kilometres here—or at least there were until the creation of Nunavut.

In our corner of Ontario, walks, outside the parks, involve roads and fences and other people's property that must be skirted. David has the sudden desire for a horse, a squat, hard-hooved creature to take him farther than he can see.

At 5:30 the helicopter comes for a pick-up. Nick, Lucy and David are back in camp within fifteen minutes and having hot showers within twenty, though David has to dry himself with paper towels because he's forgotten his towel. In less than an hour, they are tucking into the cook's specialty—shrimp creole, thick, flavourful and gloriously filling. Not Paul Prud'homme perhaps, but close to the Arctic Circle it tastes as good as any in the French Quarter. Between mouthfuls Nick observes that in Russia the crew would just be starting to set up camp and build a fire.

He doesn't sound unhappy to be here with his stock options and a stomach warmed by someone's excellent cooking. The two evenings David has been in camp, John McDonald has talked for hours in their cabin, going over what David has seen and explaining the subtleties of diamond mining.

That night John, after their nightly conversation, announces that he'll be heading out tomorrow. "I've talked to everybody I can talk to—twice. Now I'm just getting in the way. Making people nervous." David thinks he senses a trace of wistfulness about the man who once was a rock banger and is now a "suit," as he calls himself.

John must have noticed that David had forgotten to bring a towel. The next day when he returns from the field, he finds John's neatly folded up on his pillow. A nice man.

In successive days David tags along with the two other Russian-led sampling teams. Sergei is an exotic-looking man, medium height and lean. Blue-steel oval glasses frame his face, and a thick drooping moustache lends him a Far Eastern air. He was born in Siberia. "I studied math and physics but when it came time to think of an occupation—it's no life sitting in an office all the time. I talked a lot with friends about this. Came up with geology. I'm in the office thinking when it's cold, then three or four months in the field. Like a holiday. Leave everything else behind." Sergei doesn't say it but his face makes it clear that he's leaving plenty behind. He, like Nick, speaks angrily about the political and economic situation back home, but there's a strong undertone of resignation. "It's home," he says simply.

Outgoing and friendly, Sergei suggests David have a try at panning, exactly what he's been waiting for. Unfortunately, his first step into the lake is a slip and an undignified face-first landing in a half metre of water. Water dripping from every part of his body, but unhurt, with laughter ringing in his ears, David sets about swishing and rocking and sifting. It is surprisingly difficult. He's hunched over the pan, which gains weight with every movement; the jerk forward taxes his stomach muscles and the side to side motion has his arms screaming after a few minutes. In order to control the pan and not send too much material scooting out, you must tense and lock your back. It too begs for mercy in short order. The gentle, almost languid work of Lucy is impossible to duplicate.

"Little" Matt, Sergei's Canadian assistant for the summer, is getting quite good at panning but Sergei still finishes off the last three or four critical minutes. Matt, twenty-one, is Randy Turner's nephew. The short, dark-haired and talkative young man never intended to become a rock banger, but this summer's experience is changing that. "What's not to love about this?" he asks expansively. The Russians like him, his easy give and take, but most importantly they like what he does in the field. "He's got fire," notes Sergei. "You've got to have passion to be good at it. He likes it out here, he's got a good eye and he's determined. Now all he needs is experience."

The sheer depth of the Russians' experience and their obvious competence are daunting. Sometimes the younger and less experienced Canadians are reluctant to push themselves forward in the face of these masters. Matt, rooting happily about early in the morning, finds what appears, to David's rookie eyes, to be a better sample than the one Sergei has settled on. But Matt doesn't draw it to the Russian's attention for comparison.

Though Sergei is the youngest of the Russians at thirty-seven, he still has seventeen years in the field taking till samples. He's every bit as exacting as Nick. He searches for thirty minutes after the helicopter drops them off before declaring a sample satisfactory. He stands and looks around, studying the ground, then sets off and hunts for another half an hour, hoping to turn up a better one. Once he determines he's got the best he's going to get in the vicinity, he rewards himself with a cigarette before he digs. His panning is slower than Nick's but more deliberate and emphatic. And his plywood bum protector is a classier model, customized with padding and wrapped with duct tape.

David's third day in camp is spent following around Mikhail (Mike) and "Big" Matt, another Canadian. Mike is forty-one and looks like a young Charles Bronson, except with muscles and height. In the field he's a force of nature, striding straight up the side of hills others surmount by zigzagging. Though Nick and Sergei are hardly leisurely, Mike puts them to shame. Stalking about the tundra, he's more like a hunter on the prowl than a rock hound. The terrain is harsh, though mostly gentle topographically. But every now and then the land throws an unexpected curve ball. Shortly after David sets out with Mike, they find themselves at the bottom of a very steep ravine left by some long-ago river. David doesn't even try to climb it. He traces his footsteps back until he finds an easier route and plods uneventfully to the top. Mike stares at the cliff for a few moments, then charges. Looking down, David can see Mike halfway up the ravine and seemingly stalled. Just as Mike appears certain to topple over backward, he goes into overdrive, arms and legs churning furiously, dust flying, teeth bared. Up he pops beside David, breathing deeply, a smile of satisfaction playing at the corners of his mouth.

Mike pans as vigorously as he covers the territory. He finishes faster than his compatriots, somehow managing to pan side to side, backward and forward at the same time. When he's done, he strides over and pours the contents of Matt's pan into his own to finish that off too. Mike has also embellished the basic bum protector with padding and duct tape and added a refinement—a strap across the hips to hold it in place. When he stands up, the plywood stays attached to his backside. On anyone else it would look comical, but Mike doesn't invite that kind of laughter.

He's aloof and a little brusque and David thinks it is going to be a long day. But after a few hours, Mike explains to David that he's embarrassed by his English. He stumbles more than the others and struggles to put his thoughts into words. Mike's wife is also a geologist and, like Nick and Lucy, they've worked together in the field. He unleashes a warm, happy grin at the mention of his wife. But this summer she's 9,500 kilometres away in northern Siberia pursuing the same hunt for the national diamond company. "We'd like to be together but . . ." Another Russian shrug.

Geology is starting to look close to perfect, as professions go—separations from loved ones notwithstanding. Endless fresh air, plenty of time off, decent money. It's also a job that combines the physical and mental. David voices his thoughts to Big Matt, twenty-eight, who has his master's in geology and has been in the field every summer since 1992. They've stopped for a break and both of them are perched on a comfortable flat rock on a little rise, which gives them a lovely panorama. Many of the stones in the distance are tilted slightly upright. It looks like a rundown graveyard. "I think I could trade writing for this," says David.

"It's okay," Matt responds, though his expression says otherwise. "The real thrill for me comes from doing the analysis on the data." He doesn't exactly say it, but David has the distinct impression that Matt would never go into the field again if it was up to him.

After three days in the field, David can tell the difference between a bad sample and a satisfactory one, but actually finding the right spot to take the sample is still a mystery. Big Matt confesses the same thing. "I'm pressed all the time to tell the difference. Maybe it's the language difficulty combined with my own lack of knowledge. But I'm baffled. I can tell the very bad spots to sample, but not the good ones. I think they can't explain it themselves . . . after thousands and thousands of samples, it's intuitive, not something that can be precisely explained. For the Russians it's something you just know."

DAVID IS GOING TO explore the intricacies of diamond "picking" on his final day in camp. His guide is Jennifer Irwin, the slender, twenty-nine-year-old redhead who's the camp exploration boss or, more correctly, the Project Geologist. A pixieish air wafts around her; she could be mistaken for a lightweight, a happy-go-lucky girl, with the emphasis on girl. But Jennifer handles with aplomb the considerable responsibility of keeping the daily work of sampling moving along efficiently. And it doesn't take too long in her presence to discover that she is plenty quick to tell people the error of their ways if they aren't doing what she wants. "I think part of my success is that I worked my way up and earned my spurs and everybody knows it."

Being a female geologist is "the best and worst of times. The worst are the drillers. They've got a crappy job, hot or cold, uncomfortable and they're always pushing their rigs to the limit." In the world of mining, drillers are a species apart—and they know it. They're essential, they get paid more and they get away with more. Just about everyone agrees many of them have a wee bit of an attitude toward women. "Oh yeah, that's a big problem," Jennifer rolls her eyes. "It's hard enough to run this camp without that. Sure, lots of them are chauvinists. Some of them cover their cabins with pin-ups of naked women. But I don't really care about that. I just want them to do their job when I tell them to do it."

Jennifer offers to introduce David to the marvels of picking, something she has done for six years. "The concentration required is terrific. You can't afford to miss anything." Each sample, whether the twenty-five-kilogram bags the Canadians were hauling out of the field or the Russians' handkerchief-sized ones, is sent to a lab for processing and chemically reduced to a handful of pinhead-sized grains that are then "picked" or examined for the so-called indicator minerals. This part of the process is every bit as critical as the sampling itself. When the diamond rush began in 1991, it took six months to get a sample analyzed. Companies explored all summer long not knowing until winter whether they'd wasted an entire precious season.

Usually mining companies locate picking facilities in small secure buildings in Yellowknife or farther south. Jennifer worked in one early in her career and didn't care for it. "You never felt you were part of anything and there always seemed to be someone looking over your shoulder." Picking results are company secrets and guarded like the formula for Coca-Cola.

With one mine in the Territories opened in October 1998, a few months after David's visit, and another expected to begin construction early in 2001, security is looming issue. Together, the two mines could throw off revenue topping $1.25 billion annually—not quite drug money but enough to attract a certain element, to David's way of thinking.

"No one's in from the Diamond Squad but they'll be back soon," he's told when he phones the RCMP in Yellowknife to find out how they're tackling what could turn into a huge problem.

The Diamond Squad. It has a reassuring ring: a crack team of no-nonsense crime fighters; steely-eyed, hard-edged cops ready to get down and dirty with miscreants.

In fact the Diamond Squad consists of two well-groomed and perfectly nice young corporals, Sue Munn and Ray Halwas, each with less than ten years on the force and both trying to cram a lifetime of diamond experience into a few years.

It had occurred to the force back in 1992, a year after the staking rush started, that there might well be some small problem or two associated with a brand new billion-dollar business in the Territories. Chief Superintendent Bill Watts wrote a still secret report on the federal law enforcement implications of the new industry, based on his extensive tour of overseas mines. After many rounds of "strategizing" and more trips to exotic diamond sites, the force developed what they call a "comprehensive pro-active" strategy. The Diamond Squad was born in 1996.

Munn and Halwas promptly embarked on their own tours of all the diamond hot spots, as well as the cutting and distribution centres of London and Antwerp. They see their job as primarily educational—a reassuringly Canadian approach. They're concentrating on "updating" their colleagues and "liaising" with the diamond mines, while suggesting changes in legislation that one day might produce a Canadian law equivalent to the draconian act in South Africa that makes it illegal for individuals to own raw or rough diamonds unless they can prove the stones were acquired legally.

Many of the world's diamond mines are located in countries with stone-cold dictatorships where security measures Canada would find abhorrent are routine—and unquestioned. At De Beers' Orapa mine in Botswana, a 3.2-kilometre fenced "no man's land" surrounds the site—locals call it a "shoot to kill zone." The entrance to the mine is divided and cross-fenced into gated security zones controlled by armed guards. Anyone entering or leaving the mine is subject to a strip search and full-body X-ray. There are two white footprints in the middle of an otherwise empty room where you stand waiting for the flash of bright light.

Much of the diamond processing is automated, but when humans become involved they touch and sort the stones through "glove boxes" as if they were handling the Ebola virus. It's all designed to separate temptation from the temptee. A 1996 geologist and media group visited the Orapa mine, and though they managed to bypass the strip search they were all X-rayed. On the train ride into the mine, they were stopped just inside the border by police who seized their passports. Everyone sat fuming for several hours while security checked them out. Finally three journalists were manhandled off the train because their identities couldn't be confirmed. "Never saw them again and no one would tell us what happened," related one bemused geologist who was on the tour. "To this day I don't know if they were real journalists, smugglers, terrorists or what."

Actual loss figures from diamond mines are impossible to come by. But experts in the field estimate that, despite security and a police presence that would be impossible in Canada, the criminal element relieves mining companies of between ten and thirty per cent of all the diamonds taken out of the ground. "The RCMP is slow to identify crime anyway," scoffs one former officer in the north. "And the commercial crime section has had their budget cut several times. But when the first big heist takes place, the resources will suddenly appear."

*　　*　　*

A GOOD PICKER CAN HANDLE only three or four samples a day, sorting through the grains with a fine paint brush. Sometimes companies will salt samples by placing indicators in them to keep pickers on their toes, which adds considerably to the stress. Picking can be mind-numbingly boring, days and weeks of nothing but eyestrain, the microscope an intimate companion. Then exhilaration. "I've seen a diamond on the slide. It just jumped out at me!" Jennifer enthuses. "A perfect little diamond right there in front of me."

David looks in the microscope, expecting an enlarged view of sand grains. Colourful boulders assault his eyes—orange, ruby, black, emerald. Luminescent, metallic and one as clear as glass yet with the fire of hell in it. David knows for sure he's spotted a diamond. Jennifer takes a look. "That's nothing," she snorts. "Just flash. It's beautiful but not what we're looking for." Jennifer does isolate one of the things they are looking for. It's disappointingly matte black with no gloss. "That's a chromapont. One of the indicator minerals." After nearly an hour poking around the boulder field on the tray, David's whole face aches—he can hardly imagine doing this all day, seven days a week.

Winspear's pickers, four women including Jennifer, who picks when she has time, are lucky. They work right on the Snap Lake site in a small cabin. It gives the company a security edge—leaks are difficult when your only contact with the outside world is a once-a-week satellite phone call that's easily monitored. At the same time the interaction between the pickers and samplers is motivating. Each evening after dinner, the Russians check into the picking cabin and examine the results, looking for clues about where the diamond trail is leading.

Jennifer is at the top of her game. Whether staring into a microscope, organizing the camp or striding across the tundra she has come to love, she exudes the kind of confidence that arrives after years of work. It comes with the rich warm feeling of "I can" instead of "I wonder if." Most never reach that point— Jennifer has. Though she doesn't have the experience of the Russians, there isn't an aspect of diamond exploration she doesn't know. She has a rare eye picking indicator minerals, she's capable and determined in the field and she has a great capacity to learn. She also likes the work. On top of it all, Jennifer has the people skills and the toughness to boss a camp. And she has rocks in her blood. Her grandfather worked with Falconbridge and her father was a metallurgist.

But just as she has arrived, Jennifer Irwin is leaving.

Family, or the prospect of one, is pulling her away. She's leaving the profession to take a nursing degree because, like Greg, she doesn't think the life of a geologist in the field is a good match. In a typical year she might spend 150 to 175 days away from home.

Her decision puzzles the Russians. To them the land and its secrets are an avocation, and the hunt for diamonds gives them a satisfaction they can't imagine getting anywhere else, despite leaving family and friends for much of the year. They could no more abandon their life work than shed their own skin.

The loss of young, nearly world-class geologists is a big one for Winspear, which has been nurturing its young talent for years, knowing the pros from Siberia will be gone one day. "People with the experience and skill of Jennifer and Greg, and trained by the Russians, are hard to come by," John McDonald acknowledges sadly. "We've got a lot invested in them—particularly Jennifer. And she could just about write her own ticket, anywhere."

John believes that it's possible to be a geologist and have a family. "I've always felt that the separation builds relationships. It leads to strong men and strong women, thus strong families.

Reuniting can be difficult but it can also be exhilarating . . . a sense of newness and renewal that few have the opportunity to enjoy." He concedes it doesn't always work that way. "There's no in between. The alternative is divorce. There's a personality of you and your wife together, and when one is away for a time the other's personality moves in their own direction." But John is from another generation when the roles of men and women were more sharply delineated, particularly in childraising.

Just before David leaves camp, Greg approaches shyly with a request. He wants David to tell Jennifer what the Russians think of her, "not as a person but as a geologist," he hastens. "It would mean a lot to her."

"Why me?" David asks curiously.

"Well, you probably know them better than anyone."

David's eyebrows shoot up. "Me? I've only been here a few days." After thinking about it for a bit, it starts to make sense. Despite their willingness to teach and share their expertise, the Russians are a little cultural island up here on the tundra. They divulge very little personal information or opinions. Though Jennifer has been working with them for years, the relationship is strictly dictated by the land, the work and the rigid schedule of the short season. The Russians' conclaves, meetings and quick departures into their own language aren't sinister to the Canadians but distancing. Why are they meeting? What are they saying? What are they really thinking? Even Mike's nightly disappearances into his cabin make them wonder.

David respects no boundaries, cheerfully wading into subject areas the Canadians in camp would never think of broaching. None of them would have pressed Lucy for information about her life, her home and her son. In camp it is easy to forget their differences because everyone shares one goal—all else is superfluous.

They congregate for the summer at the oasis on the tundra and there is a camaraderie naturally born of that. But it doesn't run very deep. Aside from the huge cultural gulf, the Russians have known one another for decades; they learned together, teach together and have travelled the world together. In the face of all that, everyone else is an outsider.

After some consideration, David pulls Nick over for a chat when he arrives on the evening helicopter and cautiously explains the situation to him, without mentioning names. At first the Russian is nonplussed, then a little chagrined. "I never thought about this before. I never thought they would want to know how we feel. But of course! Of course! It makes sense. Sometimes people are stupid, you know . . . us, not them. Yes please. Tell them what you know. I'm happy for you to tell them."

David spends a poignant hour with Jennifer just before he leaves for Yellowknife, explaining what he knows and what he surmises. Nick had used the term "gifted" several times when he spoke of her. Her face lights up.

The meetings that Nick has with his countrymen are reviews and critiques of the day's work, often leading to far-ranging discussions of geology, particulary theoretical matters. Nick is working on a hypothesis that diamonds were created more recently than has been assumed. Millions of years ago rather than billions. If he's right, the idea will have enormous ramifications for diamond hunting worldwide. "We are all students at heart," Nick says. "And each one of us has a different discipline. It makes for interesting discussion. We speak Russian to each other when we're speaking of geology. I suppose it's a little rude, now that you mention it. But it is our first language and it's easier for us to be exact using it."

And Mike, the mysterious Mike. Each night he disappears into his cabin for several hours with the dictionary, doggedly improving his English. His diligence is the source of some amusement among the other Russians.

Early the next morning, David regretfully flies out of camp before the sampling crews board their helicopters. The last tinge of dawn is fading, and as he looks down the grey rock is bathed with rosy warmth. What secrets there. The chase has caught him up. He'd like to be here when they run the next pipe to ground.

CHAPTER THREE

SOUTH

A BIG OLD MACKEREL SKY yawns up from the horizon, pinking the stubble of the cornfields and warming the purplish glower of the Niagara Escarpment. After a bitter cold spring, followed by a dry, suffocating summer then a sodden fall, such a day means work will be missed, school cut and babies conceived.

Even dour farmers, still grouchy after being cheated out of their second hay cut by rain that refused to come until too late, then came in torrents, find something good to say about the morning and the land that has held them willing prisoners since the day they took up arms in their battle with nature. They all could have done something else—they will assure you of that. But you can see the lie in their eyes.

There was only ever the land.

In rural pockets still hanging on at the edge of the spreading megalopolis that begins at the Rouge River east of Toronto and barges past Hamilton, farmers cling tenaciously, sometimes stupidly with an unreason that grows out of chores never finished and weather that never, ever does what it should. They expect the worst and wear their pessimism like a comfortable pair of slippers, husbanding joy and praise for those rare times when they can't possibly be disappointed.

But on this perfect morning, those men and women of the land offer up a grudging blessing to a passably fine day, which, they quickly warn, surely won't last.

Beth couldn't care less about a sky dressed up like a girl aiming to get lucky and leaving nothing to chance. Slender to the point of emaciation, but not tall enough to be called lanky, she seems impossibly fragile with fine, blue-veined wrists and fingers you'd be worried about breaking with a vigorous handshake. Not exactly beautiful, not exactly sexy, not exactly bountifully built— but there's something about Beth that draws men.

She is bent almost double, head cocked slightly to one side, fine, long red hair hanging down, its gentle waves bobbing dangerously close to the cigarette crammed in one corner of her mouth.

Her buttocks move back and forth rhythmically. Every now and then her head snaps back as the odd grunt or gasp escapes her lips. Alison can't see her lower half, which is partially screened by the corner of a shed. Mesmerized, Alison approaches cautiously. What is she doing? Alison clears her throat. Beth is too engrossed to notice. She moans, a long hollow sound.

"What are you doing?" Alison asks carefully.

Startled, Beth almost loses her grip. "Ahhhh! Oh, it's you." Her head drops suddenly, nearly to crotch level. The cigarette wobbles wildly. "There! Got her again."

"What are you doing?" Alison persists.

"Fucking the dog."

And she is.

The shed and fence hid what is pulsating and writhing between her legs. A Rottweiler. An unhappy Rottweiler bitch. Duct tape is wrapped around her muzzle; great furious bubbles of spit balloon and pop in regular succession out of the sides of her mouth and there's a steady undercurrent of growling.

"Shit! Can't get 'em locked," Beth curses, struggling to keep the dog immobile. "I've got to get this bitch bred and she'd rather rip him to hamburger." In the waning of a heave, she inclines her head toward her rear end. Mounted on the back of the animal clamped between her thighs is the stud dog, banging away like an out-of-control jackhammer. Tongue waving and flapping from one side of his face to the other, he humps blissfully.

Alison sidles closer. "You know, he looks a little like Roger Rabbit when he's doing that."

Beth grunts, her words choppy with the staccato of the dog. "Yeah, uh! If the, uh!, bastard'd breed, uh!, like one I'd, uh!, be one happy lady."

Finally it's over. They lock, the gene pool is deposited where it belongs. Beth unbends stiffly. The suddenly freed Rottweiler bitch races around the enclosure. Despite the duct-taped muzzle, she manages to click her teeth together in a semblance of a bite, a promise to the sated stud of what she will do to him once the damn stuff is peeled away.

Rottweilers are Beth's bread and butter, Quarter Horses are her jam. Her short lifetime of twenty-three years has been filled with horses. Early on it was versatile hunters, then hot-blooded jumpers and courageous but often half-crazed eventers who fling themselves over courses severe enough to make a Navy Seal blanch. There have been stately dressage mounts and innumerable coiffed, cosseted and pedigreed steeds.

Now she has turned to Quarter Horses. On the surface it's an odd pairing. She seems a thoroughly thoroughbred girl and Quarter Horses are, well, elemental, earthy. They make you think of cattle, hot, dry plains, beans and hard men with crinkly blue eyes, pointy boots and huge belt buckles, not ribbons and show rings and braided manes.

Quarter horses used to be everything from simple transportation to herders, cutters and a cowpoke's best friend. Big-bummed, small and often just short of stumpy, utility defined them. Those were the foundation horses who could look a dogie in the eye and make it drop in its tracks just begging for the brand. Men who walked as if they carried two pairs of balls between their legs and women who talked tough but could put on the girl when it suited them rode Quarter Horses.

Beth dabbled in the breed for a few years. Scrounging a stallion here and a mare there. Nothing special, nothing to make anyone think about selling their first-born to acquire. Just horses. But Beth has aspirations. She wants to be a Quarter Horse breeder. Super Horse prances in her future, she's sure of it.

Super Horse is a coveted title, awarded every November at the World Championships in Oklahoma. Only horses that have accumulated sufficient points during the previous show season are qualified to enter, and only animals that can perform well in many different events have any chance at the title. Often disparaged by those who have never won it, Super Horse defines the most versatile Quarter Horse in North America—in the world, insist the Americans, who can't imagine their own horse ever being produced in quality anywhere else.

Before the American Quarter Horse registry was begun in 1940, Quarter Horses were called Steeldusts or Billys, after two influential racing sires. Today, the best of that group can cover 440 yards in under twenty-one seconds. Early working Quarter Horses had names like Leo, Wimpy and King, solid no-nonsense animals bred for cow sense and athleticism. The Quarter Horse doesn't enjoy the historical cachet of breeds like Arabians but it can trace its ancestors back to the 1600s and the first horses brought to North America by the Spanish Conquistadors. Called Big Dogs by the Indians, some of them escaped or were let loose and over time bred with various other imported horses, most of them brought over by the French and English. There's even a suggestion that the thick-necked, hardy Canadian horse lent some of its genes to establish the breed.

With today's specialization, Super Horse is the decathlon gold medal of the equine world. Super Horse is supposed to combine the original qualities of the Quarter Horse with all the bells and whistles that current breeders and show types demand—stuff that doesn't seem to belong to an animal whose ancestors trod the same ground as Geronimo, Kit Carson and Sitting Bull. Tails that float and flow like Pegasus sailing through a child's dream, eyes so large, dark and luminous they could belong to an urchin in a black velvet painting, a coat so sleek and flat you have to touch it to make sure it hasn't been varnished. And the feet. Tammy Faye Baker would lust over the high shine on these horses' hooves. Watching them perform in today's show ring, no amount of imagination can place them on the trail during spring round-up, sweat drying in white streaks on their flanks and mud way past their hocks as they corral that last stray.

Still, the legend of the Quarter Horse is enduring, at least for those of us who grew up on mid-century Westerns starring real men like John Wayne and Clint Eastwood. And it was that image that drew us to the breed.

SOMETIME DURING NEARLY twenty years of urban living together, the seed of land lust found its way into our hearts. It lay there untended, surviving as we moved from the north shore of Vancouver to Victoria's inner city Gorge Waterway to a tidy, middle-class neighbourhood on the edge of Toronto's Forest Hill. For three years we lived on a typical 30-by-110 foot Toronto lot, sharing fences with our neighbours, hearing their arguments and parties, waving as they set off for work, admiring their gardens, envying their sport utes, scowling as their dogs yellowed our front lawn—not owning a property so much as being part of a street. Sometime during those three years the seed began to grow.

When we walked into the room where Adam Souter shot himself, the seed took off like a weed after a good rain. The house, in a small town forty-five minutes west of Toronto, had seen better days. Built in 1849 and set on six acres hived off the original hundred-acre dairy farm, its grey stone façade glowered at the head of a long expanse of uncut grass. Souter had built it for his bride, and when she abandoned him for another man before they married, the grief-stricken farmer stood at the tall front windows in a small sitting room just off the kitchen and shot himself in the head. His initials are carved into the stone lintel above the front door—A.S. 1849.

The house was a mess—the old couple who had lived there

143

for fifty years had slid into that dream world of the elderly. She liked to wear three hats at once and couldn't bear to throw anything away, including garbage. Some time in the distant past, things, to put it kindly, had been let slide. The fields had decades worth of uncut grass folding onto itself and hiding a midden of vintage trash; the pond, choked by decades of fallen willow branches, was a fetid horror; the outbuildings were many and ramshackle.

The barn was more holes than boards and how it remained standing in its condition was a mystery of physics. High up on one giant beam Adam had again carved his initials, perhaps hoping that many other generations of Souters would come along to add theirs beneath his. Sofas, chairs, tables, rotting carpets lay in the feed bins, the cattle run-in shed and what might have been stalls for horses. The massive oak floorboards, crusty with accumulated manure, were warped and the cobwebs were so thick you could have stuffed a pillow with them. The hayloft had long ago been claimed by raccoons and the smell, as you ascended the ladder, went far beyond revolting. Around the property skulked twenty-eight cats, actually seven or eight adults and three litters of kittens, all of them wild. Numerous feline corpses in various stages of decay littered the drive shed.

We were thrilled.

The day we moved in, June 25, 1997, was not a high point. The temperature had soared to 34 degrees and it was so humid a fish could breathe the air. The owners had left behind many reminders of their fifty previous years. Garbage was strewn over the property as if it had fallen off the back of an overfull truck. The crowning glory of their leaving sat in the drive shed—a twenty-four-cubic-foot freezer, packed to the tightly closed lid and long ago turned off. It took all day to find someone whose nasal hairs were sufficiently cauterized to get rid of the putrid thing. The smell lingered for days.

Just as we were at the point of exhaustion and despair, the Portuguese Cowboy arrived. We heard him nearly a kilometre away, clop-clopping on the paved road. His mount, Kate, a Belgian, was as tall as a house with feet as big as catchers' mitts. The Portuguese Cowboy had ridden up from his spread, Sun Rise Acres, "down the way a bit," to welcome us to the neighbourhood. And, by the by, "would anyone like to go for a ride?" As quick as you can say "childhood dream," Alison was up and on Kate's back. The massive horse, gentle and willing, trotted us in turn, all over the property, untroubled by the debris and weeds.

Mike deSousa, the Portuguese Cowboy, left the Old Country when he was ten with the notion that one day he'd like to have a ranch and breed horses. Today he has twelve Belgians at varying stages of development and two stallions. Mike's the kind of guy who takes three horses to a horse sale intending to thin his herd and comes back with four. The kind of guy who spends two precious days off fixing his hay wagon and readying his horses in order to give a birthday hay ride to a twelve-year-old and her friends. Mike's magical appearance on his great horse transformed our day.

We had the land, a sort of barn and farming in our souls. We were ready to produce—something. We investigated garlic, cut flowers, sheep and chickens. "Oh, I tried just about everything too," the Portuguese Cowboy told us of his own what-to-farm odyssey. "You name it, I've tried raising it. I had a go at meat rabbits one time. But you've got to have a hell of a lot of rabbits to make any money at six bucks apiece. I had this lady come by once and she asked me how much for the rabbits. I said, 'Six bucks.' Told her it was the going rate, costs me almost that to keep 'em.

"Well, she didn't want to pay six bucks. She wanted to pay five bucks. So I said, 'Okay, five seventy-five.' She didn't want to pay five seventy-five. So we went back and forth and she was complaining like hell over a couple of nickels. Finally I got so mad I said, 'You don't want to pay me what it costs me to raise these rabbits. Fine. Okay. No problem.' I just went running all the way down the cages and I opened every damn door and let 'em all loose. 'There,' I told her. 'Go get your rabbits. They're free.'" The neighbours are still puzzled about what happened to their gardens that year.

Draft horses had a grip on the Portuguese Cowboy's heart, and soon after his rabbits scattered to the four winds Belgians took up residence and haven't left. Our hearts kept coming back to baked beans, dusty trails and tumbleweed. Quarter horses.

The Quarter Horse is a single breed with many branches, each with its own specialty. There are Quarter Horses for barrel racing, reining, flat racing (a quarter of a mile, of course), cattle penning, pole bending, western pleasure and, increasingly, English riding. In Ontario the most popular Quarter Horses (those that command the highest buck) are either western pleasure mounts that bear some resemblance to the big-hipped, sturdy working originators of the breed or English-style hunt seat animals. The latter, though registered Quarter Horses, often have a measure of thoroughbred blood. They're tall, refined creatures who are shown in English tack. Both western pleasure and hunt seat Quarter Horses are bred for the show ring. Round and round they go. Walk, jog, lope for the western ones; walk, trot, canter for the English. These Quarter Horses wouldn't know a steer from a stewing pot. But they can move like a dream. Trained right down to their eyelashes, the best western pleasure and hunt seat Quarter Horses take movement to a fine art with all the precision of an Olympic skater doing intricate figures on the ice.

TO BREED HORSES YOU need brood mares. Our quest for good mothers to nurture our remuda brought us before a greater cross-section of saints and sinners than we'd ever had the pleasure of meeting before. We found one lovely thoroughbred mare, intending to breed her to a quality Quarter Horse stallion. "She's got papers, right?" we asked the dealer.

He peered at us and smirked. "Papers? Of course she's got papers. You think I'd sell a horse without papers?" He turned to his briefcase and whipped out a sheaf of certificates, fanning them in his hand like a riverboat gambler massaging a deck of cards. "I've got lots of papers. Just pick one that looks like the horse and I'll take care of the rest." Another breeder offered us a former hunter-jumper for $1,000. "Hey, she'd be a great cross with a Quarter Horse. You'd get one gorgeous baby. She moves so pretty—a real daisy clipper." We were a little concerned that this one also seemed to lack papers, though the friend of the former owner's third cousin's boss reportedly had them and would offer them up as soon as we asked. Still we were concerned—the going rate for a thoroughbred brood mare was in the $2,500 range, and even indifferent hunter-jumpers who still have a few years in the show ring left don't sell for much under $5,000. "That's meat price," the breeder told us reassuringly. "How can you lose? It's meat price." Meat price is the unlovely, but descriptive, term to express the bottom line worth of a horse—the price it would fetch at the slaughterhouse.

We ended up taking her, and though we tried three times she never produced a foal for us. But she's a lovely, friendly mare and a good riding horse.

Horses are like chocolates. It's almost impossible to stop at one. Nor did we. Barely were the fences up when one mare became five. World championships danced in our heads. We had the basics: two paddocks, one rickety run-in shed to give them shelter from the elements while outside and hay in the now clean and raccoonless loft. Next we needed a stall or two for all those babies when they arrived the following spring.

FIVE MEN PERCH ON A variety of discarded chairs thrown into one end of what was once a hockey arena. Since the last player bloodied these boards in 1989, it's been the Ancaster Stock Exchange, a space devoted to the buying, selling and showing of cattle and horses—the dream of a man who thought he could make money running a high-class facility devoted to livestock, mainly horses. But like many dreams, this one drifted away and the Ancaster Stock Exchange is going out of business as a horse facility. The men have come for the auction of its assets.

The five wait patiently during the early going. Three of them are hefty, needing superior belts to hold their girth. Their large beefy faces exhibit all the expression of a frying pan. Those who play poker with these men lose. The other two are cadaverous with long, deep lines creasing their cheeks, necks like buzzards, and buttocks that have never come close to filling out their jeans. The five have already been waiting nearly three hours for the items they're interested in to hit the block, but the set of their faces indicates they are perfectly willing to sit there for hours yet. These men will wait until Armageddon to save a buck.

The auctioneers have been rattling on since just after breakfast, and hundreds of items have been snapped up by pickers, flea market dealers and a cross-section of the Ontario horse industry from one-horse hopefuls to a smattering of the elite. The five have hardly moved a muscle, except for the steady roll of their jaws as they chew gum.

"Heard a lawyer owns this place," says one.

"Fool," snorts another.

"Damn fool!" barks a third.

"Horse type," hoots a fourth.

"That makes two damn fools!" drawls the fifth.

The final sally is greeted by a series of barking laughs more like coughs. It has the air of a set piece that the five have run through before. The contingent from the Cattlemen's Association have spoken. There is no one, at least in the opinion of "sensible" farmers, more foolish than those who make horses their livelihood.

"It's like trying to run a race with your shoelaces tied together," offers Randy, another cattleman who's sidled over to stand beside the five. He's casing the auction for a cheap tractor. "Someone might do it *by mistake*. But who'd do it *on purpose*? Who'd walk to the start line, bend down, tie their laces up and then say, 'Okay, let's run this here race.' You wanna *know* who'd do it? Well, I'll tell you—a *horse* person, that's who. Ever notice how they never call 'emselves *farmers*. There's a reason. They'd be *laughed* at. Yes, *laughed* at by real farmers."

"Fools!" choruses the Cattlemen's Association. They're really enjoying this. Alison, eavesdropping beside them, somehow feels no urge to volunteer the information that she's a "horse type" here to buy a stall.

Everything goes. One bidder tries to pry up the rubber matting lining the hallways and entrance to the show ring.

"Wanna put this on the block?" he hollers during a lull in the action.

"Dunno," the auctioneer hollers back. "Let's have a look."

The two men squat down amid the crowd to contemplate the matting and are joined by the owner, the auctioneer's second in command and a smattering of bidders who claim expertise in such matters.

"Expensive stuff," comments the owner as he has at most items auctioned so far. "Those stall mats this big"—he stretches his arms, indicating about half the width of the rubber on the floor—"would cost you sixty-five bucks just for one," he proclaims enthusiastically. Everyone nods agreeably; they don't believe a word of it. But even the owner is forced to admit that prying up the nailed and screwed down matting will surely rip it to shreds. "They really save horses' feet and legs," he adds lamely, as if to convince the crowd that he's not a complete idiot for laying something down in a walkway that cost more than wool broadloom. The people drift away and the owner looks down at the floor. "Maybe I'll try and get this stuff up later." No one but the cattlemen heard. They wink at each other and continue chewing placidly.

Next comes the dirt. Not just any dirt. Specially made, triple-A quality, hoof-pampering, hock-loving dirt. A reining horse could slide a mile in it, a western pleasure mount could glide like a cloud across it and a barrel racer could explode out of the start in it. This is where the owner of the Ancaster Stock Exchange really shines. Though his beloved facility is about to be turned over to antique shows and truck pulls, he's eager to demonstrate the care he took in selecting just the right footing material for some of Ontario's finest horses. He launches into a not-so-brief history of the dirt. The auctioneer humours him for a few minutes then shoulders him aside with "Got a bid? Got a bid? Who's got a bid?"

The auctioneer is off and running, and in no time at all three successful bidders have split the dirt. They are pleased with themselves. The five chew on.

Finally the auction arrives at the most anticipated lots. Stalls. Yards of them, rows and columns and columns of them. Virtually everyone has been waiting for this moment. They have suffered through dishes printed with cowboy hats, deep fryers, oddments of furniture, garden hoses, fire extinguishers and the dirt. Everyone is waiting for the stalls—especially Alison, who imagines their sleek, clean lines dressing up her ancient, near-death barn.

At the first lot, down in the belly of the arena, one of the helpers explains that this unique group of folding stalls was recently used by a circus to hold elephants. No one seems to have any elephants but they certainly should do for horses.

The owner breaks down the original costs of these splendid items—$600 each for the fibreglass panels (no chewed wood to worry about), $250 for the steel supports (no stallion could take these out), $300 for the grill work and $800 for a single door. Even the five cattlemen, who wandered down with the crowd, are impressed.

Horse people will go to great lengths to tell you what a bargain they got on their stalls. In truth, everyone pays too much. It is a relatively small industry with a select clientele and the most basic new stall with a bottom-of-the-line door can cost $750. Add in the extras like feed chutes, opening grills, collapsible hay racks and rubber seats under the bolts to reduce noise on the grill work and the price doubles or triples easily. The Ancaster Stock Exchange stalls are Cadillacs, no question about it.

Shyness overcomes the crowd. No one utters a word when the auctioneer bellies up and lets loose his chant. Finally, Tina Gaul, who runs a summer horse camp near Peterborough, Ontario, makes a tentative offer, $325 each for a row of eight. The owner looks a little panicky. The cattlemen smile. By dint of humorous bullying, the auctioneer pushes the final bid up to $475. Tina Gaul takes it. "I don't know how I'm going to get them out of here," she says cheerfully, eyeing the purchases that will do her trail horses proud.

"Wait till the last lot goes," sneers a standardbred trainer. "She'll be sorry. I say $300 each, tops."

What he doesn't know is that Tina Gaul is married to Chris Gaul, an equine vet with a legendary reputation for thrift. There is no way they're ever going to pay too much for anything. "We run an organic farm because Chris is too cheap to buy chemicals," Tina explains in illustration about her husband, who always knows three ways to do something more cheaply. "Have fun and spend no money" is his mantra.

One of Chris's favourite jokes concerns a Saskatchewan farmer who placed an emergency call early one morning to his vet. Hastily bolting his breakfast, the vet flung himself into his car and sped twenty-four kilometres out of town to the man's ranch. "What's up, Bob?" he asked, grabbing his bag out of the trunk.

"Oh, nothing much," replied Bob.

"Everything's pretty much okay around here."

"Okay! What do you mean—okay? I thought it was an emergency!"

"Nah, I just wanted a ride into town to get my truck. Your call fee's cheaper'n the taxi."

Chris roars with laughter each time he tells it. He can tell good jokes standing in a manure-filled stall up to his armpit in a horse's rectum at two o'clock in the morning.

Six hours after the auction began, the tiring crowd puts to bed the last bid on the steel-supported, fibreglass panelled stalls—$825 each for a row of twelve. Even a few odd doors end up going for almost as much as Tina paid for an entire stall. Those familiar with the stock market will recognize the dynamics of a buying frenzy.

Randy the cattleman shakes his head as he walks toward the tractors he's come for. "Why?"

The five get up with much grunting and stretching. None has put in even a single bid on anything. "Goddamn horse people!" spits one as they head out the door.

Alison, priced out of the stalls, buys five swinging cattle gates for $50 a piece—a real steal. They'll work quite nicely as stall doors. There is one small hitch—each gate is a different size, with different hinges, and all are made to be welded to a steel post, not bolted onto a wooden one such as we have in our barn of ages. Each stall will have to be custom-made to fit the cheap gates. We did a little pricing, two-by-fours for the dividing walls, three-quarter-inch plywood for the back, angle brackets, extra long bolts, some welding work and two-by-sixes to tie the stalls together overhead. Tina Gaul got a bargain.

Then there's the chewing issue. Three-quarter-inch plywood and two-by-fours, though plenty expensive, are no match for a horse's teeth. We've seen horses chew through the side of a stall leaving a horse-shaped silhouette right out of a kiddie cartoon. So that meant more money to buy special metal caps to run along all the exposed edges to thwart the chewers. We were stymied.

Brick skids came to the rescue. We spotted them advertised as pallets in the local paper and promoted as good material for stalls. They were perfect—nearly a metre wide by a metre and a half deep and nearly five centimetres thick. Each pallet consists of strips of unidentified incredibly hard, incredibly heavy wood tongue and grooved together then bolted through the entire length. If that isn't enough, a heavy-gauge steel cap runs along both ends. Rough looking, a bit like the beat-up wood used for concrete forms, a single skid weighs more than forty-five kilograms. A few stalls of this stuff might bring down our entire barn, we worried.

Fireman Dave, who placed the ad, was using the skids on the floor of his barn where he stored vintage tractors. A very earnest guy, he told us these "pallets" had been brought up from South America and he could "let us have some" at $22 apiece, cheaper than plywood and a lot stronger. "I'd like to see the horse that could kick or bite through that!" We estimated we'd need about thirty and bought four on the spot to try them out for size in our barn. The Portuguese Cowboy dropped by and immediately saw the potential for the unusual pallets, especially for his stallions, who move the walls of his barn around like a bellows. Within twenty-four hours of our getting them home, various trucking and farming neighbours put in orders for 150 if there were any extras.

Then Chris, the vet, dropped by. He immediately spotted what we were still calling pallets. "Brick skids," he said with comfortable authority, "you've found out about brick skids. Great! How much did you pay for them?" he asks, getting right to the point.

"Twenty-two dollars," we said proudly. "They come from South America, some kind of exotic hardwood."

"South America? Twenty-two bucks? For all four, right?" We shook our heads.

Chris swallowed a snort. "They're brick skids, and this area is full of brick yards. South America! Twenty-two bucks! I paid three bucks . . . each. The guy must have seen you coming." It wasn't the first or the last time someone saw us coming in the horse business.

We found an entire brick skid culture in our part of the world. It is a secret little group that husbands its source of skids zealously. Chris used them to build his stalls and also cottages at Tina's horse camp. "There's nothing cheaper and they certainly aren't going to blow away," he said with fervour. It is the measure of the man that he offered up his own source; we broke speed records driving there and buying up as many as we could lay our hands on. We built three indestructible stalls and then an immense patio on the side of our house with plans for a giant compost bin, run-in shed and even a dock for our pond—should we ever find more.

Horses, stalls, barn still standing—we were set to begin our breeding operation. In the interests of research, we decided to spend some time at southern Ontario's Quarter Horse shows to learn about the gorgeous specimens we intended to produce on our own small farm.

ELEVEN YEARS OLD, Annabelle's little body glows with sequins. They swoosh down from her shoulder blades, dance coquettishly across her chest, wrap themselves around her waist and disappear up her back like the tail of a dying comet. Her legs are tightly encased in soft suede chaps with an elaborate fringe that waves and flirts when she walks. Struts is more accurate. This little girl moves with a saucy confidence that bounces her from one step to the other. The same fringe, dyed turquoise to match the chaps, adorns her amber shirt. Swirls of black and turquoise stand out on her honey-coloured boots, and on her head sits a black hat. What a hat. Its felt is so lustrous you want to stroke it, but the silver is what really catches the eye. A thick band of medallions interspersed with turquoise beads circles the base of the hat, ending in a complicated corsage of braided horsehair and feathers.

"You got him dirty!" she shrieks. The red suffusing her cheeks battles with the cerise lipstick enlarging her lips. "He's dirty!"

"Oh, shut up," mutters the teenaged trainer's assistant, carefully pitching her voice so Annabelle doesn't hear. It isn't immediately apparent to Alison exactly what is wrong with the animal, an obviously well-bred, deep bay, Quarter Horse gelding.

"I'm telling Daddy," persists the child. "Look at that!" She points to the horse's white hind sock. Sure enough, a faint greenish stain. Manure. The teenager was chatting with a friend when nature erupted from her charge, and instead of descending neatly between the animal's legs the poop had cascaded down one side. Annabelle is jumping—Tinkerbell in full fury. Her event is next.

The assistant dives for the bucket, producing an array of bottles, combs, cloths and sponges. After diligent squirting and scrubbing, the stain melts away. Meanwhile the Daddy, the trainer and the Mom, hairspray and lipstick in hand, appear. Not even a show veteran like Annabelle can resist chewing her lips—not when she's eleven. Dad, pot-bellied and fortyish, wears penny loafers, a golf shirt, Bermuda shorts and a Rolex. Hanging about the periphery, he asks first his wife, then the trainer and finally the assistant when the event will end. His tee-off time is two hours away. They all ignore him. The Mom is an aerobic masterpiece in hand-tooled cowboy boots, black Roper jeans, butterscotch bomber jacket with acrylic nails dyed to match and about two kilograms of gold spread over fingers, chest and earlobes. Her heavily streaked cap of hair is artfully windswept. She's having the time of her life, commenting knowledgeably to her glazed-eyed husband about one horse's hocks and another's tail set.

The trainer is Ms.-in-between. Assertive without being pushy. Knowledgeable but consultative. Supportive though not personally involved. Being a horse trainer is as much about salesmanship as it is about teaching.

Annabelle's class is called Youth 13 and Under AQHA Western Pleasure. The initials stand for the Texas-based American Quarter Horse Association, which is sponsoring the event. The AQHA is an international organization but the Americans, being American, call it American. In truth, they have a point. There is something undeniably Yank about the Quarter Horse. A Swedish or even Australian Quarter Horse doesn't quite seem to fit, though Germans, who love anything even vaguely cowboyish, have been getting into Quarter Horses in a big way in recent years.

It is March and the first show of the season—Quarterama. The parking lot in the Canadian National Exhibition grounds on the lakeshore in Toronto is jammed with trailers ranging from shoddy one-horse step-ups dripping rust stains and slathered with primer to mammoth rigs big enough to accommodate the population of a small country and outfitted with sufficient gadgets to keep James Bond occupied for hours.

The elite of Ontario Quarter Horses fills the stalls on several levels in the Horse Palace, joined by a good measure from Quebec and the United States. In the area between show rings and stables, several acres of tables are piled with horse stuff of every description—magic grooming potions, secret formula leather cleaners, hundreds of kilograms of silver baubles and sufficient saddles and bridles to outfit Napoleon's cavalry. Every now and then a ripe rounded drawl perks up the chatter of flat, unaccented conversation. Montana, Oklahoma, Georgia. Competitions range from the slow-moving western pleasure classes and elegant hunt seat events to heart-stopping barrel racing, reining and the entertaining cutting and penning where horse, rider and cattle face off.

But underneath all the flash, pomp and glitter, this is a stone-cold business. Everything is for sale and everyone is on the look-out for a better horse. Even Annabelle, who adores her big bay, is campaigning for an upgrade. She's bored with the trunkload of ribbons from Ontario and Quebec shows. The bay isn't World Youth Championship material. Mom is eager, Dad resigned.

Horse people are wizards at arithmetic. They can reel off, right down to the last farrier visit and cup of oats, how much they pour into each animal. A favourite phrase when a buyer eyes a prospective purchase is "Well, you know, I've got a lot into him." Which invariably means the price is double what the creature is worth. Any hesitation by the buyer prompts recitation of The List, which generally includes the fancy stud fee, vet bills, training expenses, showing costs—all laid out as if to say to the buyer, "See what I've done for you with this horse."

Then there are the savvy sellers who have taken lessons from Germaine Greer—offer no excuses, make no apologies. They slap on a price tag high enough to purchase the average new car, step back defiantly with a look in their eye that says, "I dare you to question it," and leave the buyer in terrible turmoil. Without The List, a person feels unbalanced; without the recitation of justifiable expenses buyers have nothing to fall back on—except their own judgement, a commodity sometimes in short supply in the horse business. Nonexistent, if one is to believe the Cattlemen's Association. It makes a person almost believe the horse might, just might, be worth the price being asked.

The announcer urges the twenty-five entrants for Annabelle's class to enter the arena. The next few minutes are all tactics, worthy of a military campaign. Horses and riders wait their turn in the holding area at the arena's entrance, some circling slowly, others just standing. Mom and the trainer consult closely. Who to follow? Who to avoid? Which horse and rider will make Annabelle and her gelding look better than they are in comparison? Which will make them look worse? The bay has a lovely slow jog, but his lope lacks the necessary fluidity and pace.

Oddly, for a breed designed to cover a quarter of a mile like a jackrabbit eluding a coyote and trained almost solely for the explosive job of cutting cattle out from a herd, once in the ring—on the rail, it's called—all of that is supposed to disappear. The pleasure in western pleasure is as slow as the air on a muggy August afternoon. The horses seem to jog in place as if they are on treadmills, and the best of them at the lope rock infinitesimally forward, covering as little ground as possible.

"DEAD HORSE WALKING, if you ask me!" sniffs Mary Jo Walsh in the sprawly, y'ahlly accent of South Carolina, adding several syllables to each word. "Day-ed how-arse." She's sitting in the stands, and her inflection and volume make her clearly audible ten rows in either direction. "Look at that! Damn thing looks like it's got a goddamn poker up its goddamn bum. Look at that! Ain't no goddamn lope. Dead horse walking. What in hell's that goddamn hitchy, jumpy gait. Like the goddamn thing's getting goosed each time it moves."

Hank pokes her with the toe of his $400 Ariat boots. "Settle down, Mary Jo," he soothes. "Have some popcorn."

Scowling, Mary Jo plunges her hand, as tanned and shiny as a piece of well-oiled leather, into the double buttered tub her husband offers. "Sheeeeeit! Gives me a goddamn bellyache seein' what they do to Quarter Horses."

Hank and Mary Jo are "usin' horse" people, waiting for the Absorbine Junior Barrel Racing Sweepstakes. They've purchased a barrel racing mare from some "good folk" in Ohio who are showing her here one last time. They intend to retrain the spunky, athletic mare for cutting cattle. "I seen her work some cows just once," explains Hank. "Jes playin' around. And man that baby's jes all ate up with cow!" Hank and Mary Jo have been cutting and penning cattle since they were "barely off the tit." They've faced down recalcitrant heifers in thirty-two states and as far away as Quebec.

"Those froggies sure can ride. Kinda surprised 'bout that," Hank ruminates. "First time I went to a rodeo in this place, Rivers Doo Loop, or somethin'—back in 1988 or somethin'—and they rode the silver right offa my belt buckle. Kinda funny hearin' 'em talk though, sorta like baby babble. Laugh too. Gosh damn, laugh. I never heard a buncha people laugh so much. They laugh at everything. But those froggies sure can ride."

Mary Jo is frowning at the horses jockeying for position in Annabelle's Youth Western Pleasure. "My kid showed up in all that paint I'd whale her right to Sunday!"

"Settle down, Mary Jo." Hank proffers the popcorn tub. They've had this interchange before. "Lemme watch this one an' we'll go git some donuts."

Mary Jo scowls some more. "Dirty old man, you ain't lookin' at the horses."

A flashy palomino piloted by an older girl crowds against Annabelle's mount, and the two girls shoot each other black looks. "Don't let her push you," coaches the trainer. "Make her go first. She likes to get behind you and force you to move faster." A striking brown-faced roan mare with an anxious child on board fidgets at the entrance. Roan is a marvellous colour, a bit of nature at its playful best. Neither bay nor grey, chestnut nor black, the speckly shades mix and melt into each other. Match this! the improbable blend of hues seems to say. The girl onboard clearly wants Annabelle to enter ahead of her. Annabelle nearly obliges. "Hang on, not yet," the trainer hisses. "Stay away from that one! She kicked someone yesterday, and the stupid judge only noticed the other horse shy. The roan just sailed on past—and placed, if you can believe it!" Both parents cluck and shake their heads. Imagine.

Suddenly, unexpectedly, Annabelle becomes a kid. "Hey, there's Janey! Janey! Come in with me."

"No!" the trainer shrills. "You'll pass her on the lope. Wait." A rangy chestnut with long white socks, a swishy tail and a generally happy disposition sidesteps into the arena to join the throng walking along the rail. "Ugh. Quick! Go!" urges the trainer.

"She looks like Wal-Mart," observes the mother.

"Exactly," the trainer nods. She's right. Everything about the chestnut is wrong. The tall stockings make him look as if his forelegs are driving up and down like pistons at the jog instead of the desirable, almost straight-legged gait, and the girl's orange and white outfit clashes horribly with her horse's coppery coat. Annabelle and her mount look as polished as the Queen on parade in comparison.

Round and round they go. Walk, jog, lope, turn and do it again. The horses respond to invisible cues from the legs and hands of the well-schooled children. The judges line them up and walk along the row, watching as each horse is backed up one by one. Parents and spectators applaud every performance. They all look so devastatingly cute. The horses are almost flawless to the untrained eye—even Chestnut White Sox and his orange-clad rider look pretty good.

Annabelle's turn. The bay scoots gracefully backward, appearing to bow slightly with each step. Annabelle's parents and the trainer clap enthusiastically.

Who knows what happens next? A bird darting across the arena. A sudden hunger pang in the cavernous gut. The whiff of cougar a few thousand kilometres away. Up shoots the bay's head. The ideal Quarter Horse carries its head and neck no higher than the line of its back, a vestige of its working-class roots when it had to look where it was going and keep its eyes on the job at hand. Some are so extreme it seems their noses will surely drag in the dirt—Mary Jo's Dead Horse Walking.

As if a Quarter Horse head and neck popping up like a startled llama wasn't bad enough, the bay takes it upon himself to jump forward, *unbidden,* then crab-walk into the nearest horse like a barge tossed sideways by a swell.

"Ahhhhh!" the trainer growls.

"Ohhhhh," the parents moan. For Annabelle and the bay, it is over. There will be no win today, nor even a placing. Scenting the rank odour of recrimination the trainer, without actually seeming to move, drifts over to another customer preparing for the next class. She'll hear all the complaints later anyway, but she'd just as soon not get her ears filled in close proximity to other trainers and riders. It will be her fault. She expects it. Annabelle's parents have spent $18,000 on a six-year-old Quarter Horse (on her recommendation, for which she pocketed a ten per cent finder's fee), ten months of training for the horse at $550 a month, two lessons a week for Annabelle at $30 a shot plus at least another $200 monthly in sundry extras ranging from shoeing and worming to clipping, braiding and bathing. And that doesn't even include show fees, trailering, etc., etc. The etceteras are important to trainers. They are the bits and pieces that add up to new paint on the fence, siding on the barn and a smart-looking horse trailer and mega-truck that shout "Winner!"

*   *   *

LINDSAY GRICE IS ONE of the finest Quarter Horse riders and trainers ever born and raised in Ontario. Other fine riders and trainers will no doubt quibble—or object strongly—but even equine dolts can recognize she has something special. Lindsay is tiny, compact and neat—like a gymnast—with a smile that seems way too big for her body. Back in pre-lib days she would have been described as pert. Even swathed in layers to stave off the mid-winter winds that find their way into her indoor arena and turn it into a tomb, she always manages to look colour coordinated in an outfit that would do for a luncheon date downtown.

Inexplicably, twenty years of training, showing and coaching haven't stamped their brand on her small, manicured hands, which seem more appropriate for a Bay Street office than the physical rigours of working with horses.

The horse world is famous for lousy hands. Manicures and horses are as compatible as umbrellas and windstorms. Even if you manage to avoid the grunt work of heaving twenty-kilogram hay bales, wrestling overladen manure carts and schlepping feed buckets back and forth, it is on the verge of impossible not to create havoc with cuticles, knuckles and palms. Hand-pulling manes to create a thinned, shortened fringe that shows off a horse's neck to advantage, and is easier to braid or band, is hell on the finger's delicate skin. Endlessly lunging steeds in big circles to ratchet their energy down a notch, and training them in the thousand different ways one can from the ground before bum hits leather and the riding begins, turns palms into something resembling a toad's back.

Then there's the riding itself. Taking a Quarter Horse from early in its second year, just before it's broken to saddle and bridle, to the premiere Ontario event, the Breeder's Futurity, later in its second year, entails about 175 hours in the saddle, upwards of

300 annually for more mature three- and four-year-olds. And the hands never rest. When you watch the finished product in the show ring, nothing seems to move, except the horse. But training is a world of endless motion and adjustment. Hands slide constantly up and down the reins—a rough calculation puts the distance travelled by hand in the training of one horse in one season at sixteen kilometres, and all over a leather road. In an average season Lindsay has fifteen horses in training, in a busy one as many as twenty. But the hands never tell. Nor the face or body. At thirty-five she still could pass for a first-year college student.

You could easily assume the blond horsewoman is a soft, easy-going person who charms her way through life. And you'd be wrong. Lindsay Grice is legendary for her toughness. It's too much for some. "She's so, so . . . how can I put it? Hard," observes one former client who is showing at Quarterama with another trainer. "I wuv my wittle Charlie," she coos at her steed, who has bumped her with his nose, then she turns to Alison. "But Lindsay always made me feel guilty whenever I gave him a treat or a pat. I just can't help it!" she adds breathily. "We wuv each other, don't we, Charlie." The horse, knowing what's coming, waits patiently, head hanging over the stall door for the inevitable treat, grabs it out of her hand, then pointedly turns his haunches to her.

"Keep them out of your space," advises Lindsay. "No treats. Never. Not ever. There are other ways to reward a horse. You'll have nothing but problems if you're always giving them treats."

We fell into the "wuv" trap the first summer with our small band of broodmares. Somewhere during the second week, after daily trips into the field with pocketfuls of treats, we learned what Lindsay was talking about. No sooner had we gone through the gate one fine summer morning than the previously docile herd turned into a thundering mob, sweeping down on us, bucking, kicking, shoving each other—and us—in their eagerness to get into our pockets. We gave the carrots to the rabbits from then on.

Lindsay is also showing at Quarterama in one of the prestige events—Hunter Under Saddle Junior AQHA. Junior refers to horses under four. Twenty-six young animals float into the arena, tails undulating and heads held low like shy debutantes—a sea of gleaming horseflesh, mostly bay, piloted by black-coated riders with iron thighs all clad in cream-coloured breeches. Lindsay has her show face on. Steely yet soft, rigid yet flexible—the way she rides. Her eyes are fixed at a point between the ears of Generally Charming, an Ontario-bred horse, just turned three and only one month into intense training that owner Joanne Black prays will pay off at the end of the summer with a win at the Ontario Breeder's Futurity.

Quarter Horses are still within reach of the average middle-income person—barely. Quality dressage mounts and jumpers can easily cost six figures. You're not going to win either of the two biggest events in the Quarter Horse world, the Congress in Ohio or the World Championships in Oklahoma, on a shoestring, but you can own and show Quarter Horses without being filthy rich. Joanne, mother of four children under thirteen and the wife of an electrician, is far from rich.

Joanne had a nice Quarter Horse for several years. When horse people say an animal is nice, it's akin to teenagers referring to a classmate as having a good personality—damning with the faintest of praise. There was nothing wrong with Joanne's previous horse, but it would never take her to the finals at Quarterama, let alone make the cut at the Breeder's Futurity. She has always dreamed of a horse that would take her all the way. The job of a trainer like Lindsay isn't limited to teaching the horse and rider, it also often includes finding the horse—sometimes at any price, this time only at the right price. Joanne almost didn't get the young mare. Lindsay had spotted her months earlier but passed on her because the $15,000 price tag was far too high for Joanne. But with a bit of haggling the breeder, eager for one of her horses to be trained and ridden by Lindsay Grice, agreed to take Joanne's four-year-old horse as part payment.

Quarterama is the first show ever for Generally Charming. It's a tough event for Canadians. With the country still imprisoned by winter, horses do what they're supposed to do in the cold—grow hair, plenty of it. Big, fuzzy coats are as big an *ugh* on the show circuit as fat is on a runway model. Mostly kept inside their stalls, save a few hours' medicinal turnout each day, they're mummied by hoods, neck protectors, blankets, leg wraps. In the end, if nature has her way, there are always clippers but the look is never as "slick" as a horse that is naturally shed out. Trainers like Lindsay and owners like Joanne spend almost as much time getting their horses "slick" in the dying weeks of winter as they do in training the animals.

Every horse at Quarterama has a gorgeous, billowing tail. They ripple, flow and cascade down the animals' hocks. Impossibly long, impossibly thick, impossibly shiny, not unlike the Breck girls' burnished locks, which any normal female would swear were fake—as are the tails. Fake. Generally Charming has a perfectly good, self-respecting tail of her own. But without augmentation it would appear thin and insignificant next to the great amplified clouds emanating from the well-muscled rear ends of the animals parading into the Horse Palace main ring.

During the early Mary Quant era, women wore falls, synthetic pony tails to give that extra boost no amount of teasing could duplicate. A pound or two of bobby pins later, the artifice was incorporated. As long as the winds stayed away and no rain descended, it kept pride of place atop a woman's head. Women with falls laughed differently than those without. You couldn't throw your head back for a good old guffaw without threatening to dislodge it. And guffaws just don't work with the head immobile. Titters, on the other hand, were quite manageable.

Doctoring the tresses of a horse isn't unlike adding a fall to a woman's hair. But you can't tell a horse not to poop or swish its tail. Generally Charming wafts into the ring in what seems to be perfect form. But Joanne, watching anxiously, says she's tight, tense like an athlete with pre-race jitters. Mark Grice, another trainer and Lindsay's ex-husband, studies Generally Charming as she make the first circuit. The mare's problem is much more elemental than nerves, in his opinion. "She has to pee."

It is as hard for a horse to move easily and gracefully with a full bladder as it is for a human being. It can even be dangerous, especially for a horse that has been worked hard. Some trainers believe horses that come back from a race or exercise session with a full bladder are more prone to "tying up"—severe, and sometimes fatal, muscle cramping. One standardbred trainer we know has taught her horses to pee when she whistles. It's a great party trick.

Mark and Lindsay Grice were once the perfect Quarter Horse couple. A handsome pair, they had known each other since Lindsay was eleven and Mark not much older. Quarter Horses came to be their lives. On the show circuit if Lindsay didn't win, Mark often did. They built up Kilmanagh Valley Farms in the low hills of Caledon, just north of Toronto, into one of the best-known Quarter Horse facilities in Canada. They also had at stud Tresrullah, a gorgeous hunt seat horse that Lindsay rode to claim the Ontario high point Junior Hunter Under Saddle title in 1990.

Mark, mustachioed and always immaculate, looks like he

167

stepped right out of a Marlboro commercial. He has a rare eye for very young horses and also broodmares. He found a $1,000 thoroughbred mare in the United States, bred her to Tresrullah and the result was Rock N Rullah, which went on to win a World Championship title in 1998. Another offspring, Trulah Rula, took a second at the World's and two more Tresrullahs won Ontario Breeder's Futurity and Quarterama titles—a strong record for a young stallion. Lindsay and Mark, and the stallion Tresrullah, have gone their separate ways but Quarter Horses are still their lives.

Mark points to an almost invisible hunch in Generally Charming's back as evidence of her need to urinate. It isn't the only clue. She's infinitesimally agitated and her tail wiggles a fraction. "She's cranking her tail," Mark observes of the faint movement, as if the young horse were waving it around like a flag on Canada Day. "She has to pee."

Lindsay is a veteran of the show ring. There's no hint anything is wrong except for a small tightening of her eyes as she focuses harder on the animal between her legs that isn't quite doing what she wants.

Just at that point, a minor scene erupts at the gate where a few competitors are still waiting to make their entrance. In sweeps a woman on a horse, that much is knowable. What kind of horse is a different question. Short, bouncy and white-socked, the flaming red chestnut bears little resemblance to the tall, mostly bay steeds levitating around the ring.

It is an open event, meaning both professional riders and amateurs are eligible to compete. But most of the horses are being ridden by pros like Lindsay, whose livelihood depends on their performance. No weekend fun or hobbyist passion for them, it's all business—also politics. "I'll give you first through fourth," offers Mark before all the horses are even in the ring. "It's politics. The judges wouldn't dare not place them highly." He reels the finishes off, listing as one through three the current "hot" pro trainers on the circuit, one American, two Canadian. "The only way they won't place is if their horses lie down in the middle of the class."

The new entrant has amateur stamped all over her from her horse's long unbraided mane to the thick chin strap holding her hat on. She is a glorious contrast. If the other riders were miked, a collective groan would be audible even at the back of the stands.

As everyone else moves sedately at trot on the rail, The Amateur sails past as if late for her own wedding. Faces twitch. A man from Michigan riding an exquisite black loses control of his show face for a moment. Horror writes itself across his features as the woman nearly sideswipes him in her hurry to set a record for the most circuits of the ring in a single class.

She does everything she isn't supposed to do. The other horses' heads bob low and loose. Her gelding, neck erect and straining, looks like a kid standing at the back of a parade trying to see over everyone's head. His legs drive up and down. The others swing their front legs from the shoulder in the ideal hunt seat flat-kneed cadence. In Quarter Horse competition, high knee action is considered ugly—the less you see of the knees the better.

"I don't know what kind of a trot that is," sneers the Portuguese Cowboy, comparing the horses to his beloved Belgians. "Looks like they've got pins in their legs or something. I like to see a horse trot up nice and proud." Belgian breeders love lots of knee action and heads held high, precisely the stuff the Quarter Horse world loathes. With horses, anathema in one breed is perfection in another. Thick and stumpy is as desirable to owners of the five-gaited Icelandic ponies as it is undesirable at Quarterama.

"Oh god," shudders Mark as The Amateur charges up the back end of Generally Charming. "Stay away," he half-whispers, fearful that the animal will distract Lindsay's horse, "stay away."

Two- and three-year-olds are teenagers with minds still floating somewhere between foal and horse. The mind of a horse is a curious thing. And these days it is also fortune fodder. What goes on between the ears of an equine has turned into a billion-dollar industry. Whisperers, touchers, nostril blowers, healers and reasoners are all hell bent (for a nice fee) on providing some insight into the hows and whys of horse behaviour. And we eat it up. It's hard to imagine anyone without a dog shelling out $50 to listen to someone lecture on the subject of canines. Not so with horses.

HALF AN HOUR WEST of Hamilton, Ontario, the crowds flocking into the indoor arena at Black's Equine Centre are testament to the notion that everything to do with horses can, with a bit of a stretch, find a connection to the nature of human beings. And Monty Roberts is the grand champion of making that connection. Roberts wrote *The Man Who Talks to Horses* (several decades on the *New York Times* best-seller list). Part evangelist, part carnie, part therapist, Roberts is the kind of natural-born horseman who could probably train horses by serenading them with a violin.

As it is, his shtick is to go mano a horso, taking a young, unbroken horse and, after thirty minutes of communing with it in a ten-metre diameter round pen, convince it, through what he calls "join up," to accept saddle, bridle and rider. Many people in the audience will never have anything to do with horses, unbroken or otherwise, beyond the odd nose-to-tail trail ride. But they're prepared to sit in a drafty building, crammed thigh to thigh on uncomfortable bleachers, because they want to believe that the problems of humankind can be faced and repaired in some similar fashion—with determined and unbending, though humane, methods.

Roberts' first challenge is a pushover: a Quarter Horse gelding which, true to his breed, is more accepting and trusting than fearful and suspicious. As he works the horse, Roberts is constantly talking and working the crowd. With one breath it's a comment on how he's doing with the horse. With another it's a life-affirming story of how he rose above harrowing abuse at his father's hand when he was a kid. Peppered throughout are barely veiled, sarcastic references to "my competitors," none of whom is the least bit shy about mocking him in return. There's a rumour around that one of Roberts' competitors, if not all of them, is raising money to erect a statue of Roberts' father in their hometown.

Roberts spends the full thirty minutes with the horse but it's clear to onlookers that the animal is ready for a saddle after five. "That horse's broke all to hell," growls a paint and Quarter Horse breeder. "Maybe it had a shot or something to calm it down," he suggests to Dee Dee, his companion, who has recently moved from western pleasure horses to barrel racers. She squints at the animal walking quietly and carrying a rider around the pen. "Bet it's been lunged to death," she states firmly.

Lunging is a critical training tool for a young horse. The animal circles a trainer, connected by a long line, moving from gait to gait, developing athleticism, conditioning and good manners. Lunging is used also by many riders to work the oats out of their mounts prior to riding. Many a high-spirited, jumpy horse has been lunged into tranquillity before prospective purchasers come to call.

Even those who have come to Roberts' demonstration for a dose of equine spiritualism are visibly disappointed.

Roberts smiles as the Quarter Horse calmly leaves the pen. He's more than a consummate showman, he feels through every pore in his body how the crowd is reacting. His intuition is eerie. Just as the man finishes suggesting to Dee Dee that the horse might have been drugged, Roberts raises the issue himself, chiding those who might think that of him. The man reacts as if his pocket has just been picked.

Roberts knows what his crowd wants to see and understands that by not giving it to them with the first horse, he'll hook them even harder with the magic he weaves on the second. A gentle tease.

The next horse, a gorgeous two-year-old part Hanoverian, prances in. When the audience collectively sucks in a breath of admiration, the animal freezes in terror. His body quivers from nose to tail. Then he suddenly remembers he's a horse. Flee! Flee! He snorts around the pen, dashing back and forth, desperately looking for a way out. Roberts smiles again. There is no talk of doping or horses worked into a state of acquiescence behind the scenes with this one. For twenty-five minutes Roberts works, driving the horse around and around the pen with flicks of the long lead line in his hands. Never letting him get close, he keeps him moving, all the while discoursing about the animal and life. The jammed arena is hushed and rapt.

The audience begins to identify with the animal. They have all been there: frightened, disenfranchised, cut off from the herd, seeking warmth and belonging. The horse begins to show signs of wanting to come in from the cold—submissive lip smacking and chewing, head dropping, shoulder turning in. When Roberts finally, gently, relents and allows the horse, now desperate for contact, to come in to the centre of the pen and "join up" with him, the audience cannot withhold a sigh of relief. Suddenly everyone feels embraced and loved.

A shudder of pleasure ripples through the arena as Roberts pauses for the first time in his performance and whispers, "He's ready." He slowly raises his hand and gives the animal a scratch on his head. Minutes later, on goes the saddle and bridle and, after a couple of false starts, a rider follows. A few can't resist leaping to their feet and cheering. One woman dabs her eyes. A middle-aged man is unabashedly weeping. "God love you!" shouts out a man from the stands. "You're a good man," another tearfully testifies. This has nothing to do with horses.

Even the Quarter Horse trainer who has been bragging that he broke his last three horses on the walk from field to barn ("Ya gotta let 'em know who's boss, make 'em respect your space and you'll never have any trouble with 'em. There's no *voodoo* shit about it.") is guardedly impressed.

At the end of the demonstration, the audience, fulfilled and smitten, files past tables of Monty Roberts trinkets, books, videos, T-shirts, sweatshirts and some pricy statuary. The items are going fast. Roberts takes a chair nearby and begins a solid hour of answering questions and autographing purchases.

AT QUARTERAMA, LINDSAY Grice isn't thinking about Monty Roberts, his abusive father or his trademark "join up" technique with horses, she is focusing on the mind and movement of Generally Charming. The magic words "you are now being judged" have not yet been uttered, and without seeming to shift a muscle she is trying to stretch out her horse, relax her, take her from a trot to that state of motion more akin to clouds scudding across the sky than a horse making contact with the ground.

Mark watches, his body twitching and leaning, vicariously trying to control her horse. The tail! That impossibly long, flowing, fulsome tail. Partway down the appendage something is sticking out. Another tail—the false one. Only a few years ago augmenting a Quarter Horse's tail was a hangin' offence or at least cause for embarrassment if you got caught.

But, like so many things in life, something is a terrible thing in the horse world until it isn't, until the next terrible thing comes along to replace it. The issue of false tails has all but disappeared, replaced by the controversy of "cutting" or "numbing." In a show the Quarter Horse tail is supposed to lie flat or "packed" against its hindquarters. It gives the horse the appearance of being all business, of focus on the job, not happy-go-lucky swish and crank and I'm-just-galloping-around-the-meadow. It is the rare horse with a tail that naturally stays tucked against its back end at all times. To achieve the look, breeders, trainers and riders used to cut the tail's nerve. Of course it meant the horse could no longer protect itself effectively from flies or lift its tail completely to poop.

Today most Quarter Horse people use an alcohol block—alcohol injected into the tail's nerve, which numbs it for about six months unless the operation is botched by an amateur who can't find a vet willing to do the job. Many use small-animal vets to do the numbing. After you've docked the tails and sliced the ears of a schnauzer or doberman, an alcohol block on a horse's tail seems very minor indeed. Once you know what to look for, the "dead" tails are easy to spot, but most judges ignore them, preferring the illegally achieved packed look to the natural swish and crank.

Most in the Quarter Horse industry hate the practice, but refusing to do it is a little like trying to compete in Olympic weightlifting clean. You'll feel virtuous but you'll never win. Dave Lewis, who trucks horses for a living and is passionate about reining horses, steadfastly refused to mess with his horse's tail. He had a beautiful mare who could spin on a dime and slide a mile, creating a rooster tail of sand behind her. Competition after competition, he placed fourth or fifth behind inferior horses whose lifeless tails clung to their hindquarters. Finally Dave gave in and suddenly the red ribbons were his.

After one circuit of the ring, Generally Charming's tresses are so much askew the bound end attached to the real tail sticks out like a rude organ. Mark is out of his seat so fast the woman in front of him spills her French fries and gravy. He catches Lindsay as she rounds a corner and speaks to her urgently over the boards.

An amateur in such a situation would do the human thing— the head would rotate to look at the offending protuberance, eyes would roll, a frown would form and the rider would scuttle back to the entranceway for a frenzied fix-up, then fling herself, clammy with panic, back on her horse. Lindsay doesn't even blink but glides back to the entranceway where owner Joanne, who loathes the false tails, does a fast stitching job. Just as she finishes the announcer intones, "You are being judged." The competition is on.

Lindsay hopes for a top three finish but ends up a disappointing fourth under one judge and seventh under another. Mark shakes his head. As the class waits for the results, Generally Charming spreads her legs, lifts her tail, humps her back and lets loose a hot stream of urine. "She had to pee," mutters Mark. He nails the top three finishes and the horse he picked for fourth ends up fifth. "There's no magic about it," he smiles at an impressed Alison. "You just have to know who's riding. The horse almost doesn't matter."

It has been a long winter of working hard with Generally Charming, who came to Lindsay as a very green three-year-old.

Quarterama, coming in March, is still very early in the program for the young mare but both Lindsay and Joanne had hoped for better. As is often perversely the case, slaps and strokes come together. The reward doesn't come in the form of ribbons but an offer—US$30,000 for the horse Joanne had anxiously shelled out $10,000 plus a trade-in-horse to buy just eight months earlier.

What to do? It's a particularly hard question for Joanne, who is neither rich nor perpetually at leisure, the stereotype of those who show horses for fun. Generally Charming is her first great horse and $30,000 is a lot of money by anyone's account. But if she sells, it's unlikely she'll be able to buy a similar or better horse for the same amount of money. "Where," she asks, "am I going to get the chance again? People like me don't just go out and buy a quality horse like this. I've got one right here."

She decides not to sell. Once the blah performance of Quarterama is behind her, Joanne, an ebullient though modest amateur in heart and mind, is hard pressed to contain her glee as she and Generally Charming proceed to motor through the competition at show after show. Loaded down with ribbons by the early summer Ontario event—another -ama, Summerama—she cheerfully talks about her dream, showing at the Quarter Horse Congress in Ohio. For her it would be like going directly from little league baseball to the World Series.

Sport, from minor hockey to Grand Prix jumping, is a groin-kicking universe where parents eat their own, where psychological sabotage is entertainment and where friends embrace with daggers barely concealed. There is no such thing as gentle sport, though there are gentle moments. They shine like a soft halo over everyone involved with such endearing power that athletes, parents and onlookers come to believe that sport is a friendly, character-building place to be. One of those blessed moments comes at Summerama with Lindsay aboard Joanne's horse, riding once more against fellow pros in Junior Hunter Under Saddle. That day it is the perfect pairing. Horse and rider speak without effort, listen without straining, the horse seeming to obey even before the cues are given.

Two judges make their decision. One ranks Generally Charming first and the other places her second. The crowd cheers its approval. Out of the ring, Lindsay is almost gasping with pleasure. She has a hard time bending words around her grin. "Sometimes . . . sometimes . . . it's just so . . . so . . . perfect. Sometimes everything just works. All the buttons you install in a horse, they just work." Well wishers gather, her rivals among them, eager for her assessment of the ride; they all nod happily, basking as if the moment had been theirs.

Across the field but a world away, Quarter Horses of an entirely different sort are earning their oats. Dave Hickey, his wife, Judy, and a happily smiling group sweat and chat under the early summer sun as they wait their turn for a victory picture. If you hadn't read the program, you would never believe the three horses at the centre of the group come from the same breed as the animal Lindsay Grice just rode to top honours.

Hickey's group is showing halter horses, the Arnold Schwarzeneggers of the equine world, bred for conformation and looks. Halter is all about muscle—big, bulging, hang-out-over-your-shoes, ready-to-come-ripping-out-of-the-skin muscle. Depending on the beholder, halter horses are either gorgeous specimens or hideous mutants.

Lindsay, sipping a cold drink at Summerama's café, ponders halter horses after her triumphant ride. "They're crazy," she states flatly. "I just don't get the appeal. Look at that one." She points out a massive three-year-old black stallion dancing at the end of a lead shank as if it were being attacked by an entire hive of bees. His handler takes two steps forward then circles, two steps then another circle, eventually crossing the short stretch of grass. "I guess the classes are entertaining to watch when they flip out," she observes as the black, as if on cue, goes straight up in the air. "If I ever do anything terrible—like getting a speeding ticket or something—don't send me to jail. Just make me haul around one of those halter stallions for a year. That will be punishment enough!"

"I *like* a little muscle on a horse," says a beaming Dave Hickey while casting his eye over the three generations of beefy halter horses sired by his stud, An Awesome Mister, all waiting to have their picture taken as winners in their respective classes. "And I like a pretty horse with good conformation. But I do like a horse that can do something," he adds.

Rare is the animal that crosses over from halter into the "do something" category. Halter horses are bred so specifically for muscle, conformation and looks that turning them into performance horses would be like taking Arnold Schwarzenegger, years ago when he was the world body-building champion, and trying to turn him into a gymnast.

"Ride them! Oh god no, you don't want to ride them," dismisses a shocked owner when Alison, watching a Summerama halter class, asks if she's ever swung a leg over any of her animals. "They'll lose all that bulk. You work really hard to put the weight on them and it would all be wasted. Besides," she adds, "their legs really can't support their weight at anything but a walk. You don't want to add a rider to it."

"So," Alison inquires, "what do you do with them when they're finished showing?"

"Welllll . . ." the owner pauses for a moment. "They're not much use, to be honest. You try to get rid of them as quick as you can."

More than a few think it is folly to take halter horses and embarrass the poor animals by trying to make them into performance horses. "I love people like that," one of Ontario's top trainers says cheerfully. "Horse owners with way more money than sense. That's how people like me earn a living."

When Dave and four other minority owners bought An Awesome Mister in 1992, the stallion was already on the road to becoming a rare two-way horse. After winning a world championship at halter in 1989, he'd been ridden to second place at the Quarter Horse Congress in Ohio, the biggest horse show in the world (promoters boast it offers seven acres of shopping if horses aren't your thing). Dave sent An Awesome Mister back to the Congress in 1992 and the horse came away with two wins in western pleasure.

Until An Awesome Mister came to Ontario, there had never been a Congress *and* World champion in the province. Hickey swept in, stallion in tow, not with the idea of just breeding horses but with a program. He tackled his plan as he did projects taken on by his construction company: one step follows another, the walls after the foundation, and so on.

The first year, Dave bought a slew of mares of all types, good and indifferent, to breed to An Awesome Mister and tried to sell the best foals to people who intended to show them. A stunner of an offspring does a stud's reputation no good if it is hanging out in someone's backyard. Once he discovered the "best crosses" for his stud, he got more selective about the mares that were treated to Mister's semen. Then came An Awesome Mister–emblazoned baseball caps, T-shirts and deck chairs.

Within three years Awesome thises and Awesome thats were filling up classes from Thunder Bay to Niagara, and every second person seemed to be wearing a Mister cap or T-shirt. "He certainly goes all out," sniffs another breeder at the 1998 Ontario Breeders' Futurity as she peers at the special corner devoted to An Awesome Mister that Dave has set up, complete with chairs and a constantly running video extolling the stallion. "I think he's getting a little overexposed, don't you?" whispers her companion as two men, sporting caps with the horse's name, stroll past.

"He's a nice horse," drawls another owner with a lesser horse at stud. "If you like a horse that's drugged half the time, wears orthopaedic shoes, is really short and is HYPP single positive."

Dave rolls his eyes at the mention of such criticisms. "I really don't like to think it's jealousy," he says earnestly, "but some people . . ." He lets it ride. Some in the industry are scandalized that Dave is freely breeding a horse carrying the gene for HYPP, a disease akin to epilepsy. An Awesome Mister is single positive, which means he may or may not come down with the disease and he may or may not pass that gene to his offspring. Though far fewer horses die of HYPP than colic and the mortality rate of single positive horses is about the same as the general population, there is much fear of the disease. Many believe deliberately increasing the risk of spreading the disease in a breed already too narrowly defined genetically is irresponsible. On the other hand, many don't care—quite the contrary.

Halter people often seek out horses that are single positive. Through some quirk that no one has yet fathomed, the HYPP gene makes horses muscle up more quickly. Even around western pleasure and English show circles, the topic is likely to raise as many yawns as eyebrows. Looks and movement matter, looks and movement are ribbons on the wall and money in the bank. The infinitesimal chance that a stunner will turn into a shivering wreck or drop dead in a fit are no worse than a thousand other things that can happen to show horses.

Inside the immaculately clean, concrete-floored breeding facility at Dave and Judy Hickey's Heritage Farm in the rolling hills near Peterborough, the subject of all the envy, admiration and condemnation couldn't care less. A stallion's life comes as close to heaven as it's likely to get on earth. Like a person who has won the lottery and retired from work, a stallion need only eat, sleep and fornicate. There are pressures—quality and quantity of sperm, quality and quantity of offspring—but those are owner worries; the stud, of course, is blissfully unaware.

For all that, An Awesome Mister is feeling a little tired. It is late May, near the end of the Quarter Horse breeding season. Ejaculation every second day during the week and some weekends since the first of February has begun to pall. Virtually all that is left for Mister's attention are problems: mares that have absorbed or aborted their fetuses or inexplicably refused to follow the rhythms of nature and allow sperm to meet egg.

Dave and Judy Hickey are weary too. "I gotta tell you, I'm getting sick and tired of doing it every second day. Mister is too," says Dave as he gears up for another session of what he calls a "chess game." With douches of this, shots of that, lights to bring mares into heat early, charts and tests, Dave plays with nature. Like all serious breeders he is trying to beat the odds of producing foals out of every mare. The odds are lousy—just sixty-six per cent of all bred mares will drop a healthy, live foal.

Chris Gaul, the vet, has his own medicine chest of potions and a battery of strategies to take on nature's stubborn statistic. In spite of that, he admits the near futility of trying to do an end run around that powerful force.

"You meet a breeder who says he's got an eighty per cent record and you're talking to a liar," he roars. "It's incredible! You get these people together and they're all talking about breeding and they'll tell you they haven't had a mare miss in three years. And then everyone suddenly has the same results. Every goddamn one of them! Oh sure, you'll get a hundred per cent one year and then twenty-five per cent the next. Eventually nature gets you."

Chris confesses he's not sorry when breeding season is over. "I'd hate to be a reproductive vet. These fellows, they're depressed all the time. It's awful. You don't want to talk to them, they're so gloomy."

Fifty years ago, a stallion owner loaded his stud into a wagon and cruised the countryside during breeding season—a little like the milkmaid in the musical *Oliver!* who wanders the streets at dawn singing, "Any milk today, mistress, any milk?" Any mares today, mistress, any mares? If your mare's fertility cycle happened to coincide with the stallion's appearance, you invited the owner in, gave him a meal and a glass of something bracing, perhaps offered a bed for the night and let the stud loose in the field. It was called "live cover."

"Live cover!" shudders Diane Howe of Pinedale Quarter Horses, which specializes in breeding hunt seat Quarter Horses. "Live cover," she repeats disbelievingly. "I didn't think anybody did that anymore."

Live cover means biting, kicking, thrashing . . . violence. Equine sex is not pretty. Stallions who routinely breed in the field are often sorry specimens loaded with battle scars. The hind end of a horse is a dangerous place to be. There are no wounds of war on An Awesome Mister. It has been a long time since his organ has been anywhere near a flesh-and-blood equine vagina.

Mister's hooves echo on the concrete floor as he nears the breeding area. "He's what I would call a sensitive stud," observes

Dave. Some stallions will breed a fence post in the middle of winter but An Awesome Mister is fussy. The mood has to be right. Hickey has developed a set routine to help him along. First he is taken out the back door of his stall. Then he is lunged for ten to fifteen minutes. The handler puts the chain from the lead shank through his mouth like a bit. "When that chain goes in his mouth, he knows what's going to happen," says Dave. "When he comes out here, he can holler and he can talk to you. That chain's a signal. It gets him going."

Dave is like a baseball pitcher with a rabbit's foot in his back pocket, special socks on his feet, a four-leaf clover tucked inside his hat and his underwear on inside out. He pours some water into the drain and it splashes into the catch basin. "We always do that," he explains. "It's part of the routine." An Awesome Mister, hearing the water, snorts and stamps on the other side of the door.

Dave Hickey, who walks, talks and looks as if he's spent every second of his life in the saddle, has a way of fixing you with his eyes and explaining something with the seriousness of a person unveiling the mysteries of quantum physics. He is an intense man for whom planning, a program and a regimen are essential elements in the successful progress of life for both horse and humankind. Then an abashed smile takes over. "Sounds a little silly, I guess. But you don't want to leave anything to chance."

While Dave is warming up Mister, Judy is warming water for the "sleeve," the inner part of the artificial vagina. A little like an old-fashioned, hard-sided hot water bottle, the vagina has a cap on top where the water is poured to warm the long, rubbery tube inside. "You gotta be careful with this," Dave emphasizes. "Too cold and it puts 'im off, too warm same thing." And the pressure must be exactly right. Too much water makes the sleeve tight and the stallion can't, or won't. Too much give and he'd just as soon wander off and eat grass as do his duty for the gene pool.

Two mares, Boston Impress and Barpasser's Sweet Image, are standing quietly inside the bars of narrow breeding stalls. These are the tease mares, there to help arouse Mister. Any old mare in heat will do but in this case they are also there to be bred. One of the mares has a foal, thirty days old skittering anxiously around, desperately trying to reach her udder through the bars of the pen. There isn't enough room inside the pen for the foal. Rick, the Hickeys' vet, is bustling back and forth. "Did you give her a bump?" he asks Dave. "Yes, we did." The bump is HCG, a hormone, a way of trying to fool Mother Nature. The trick is to inseminate the mare just as she is about to ovulate, sending a ripe egg scooting down the fallopian tube and into the uterus where the sperm can do their fertilizing job. Given at the time of breeding, the shot will ensure ovulation occurs. If it doesn't, the sperm just hang around inside the mare, waiting for the egg. The sperm usually die within forty-eight hours and the unovulated egg simply shrivels up.

Judy slides the artificial vagina into the "dummy." A cross between a torpedo and the mechanical rodeo bulls still found in some western bars, the dummy is padded for easy and comfortable mounting, and well wrapped with bright yellow electrical tape. There aren't too many yellow mares around, but since horses can't distinguish colour that aspect of the business doesn't bother An Awesome Mister.

The door to the breeding area slides open. In he comes. He is staggeringly beautiful. Though a world champion halter horse, he now has none of that blow-it-out-your-skin muscle. Just a dark, almost midnight, coat that ripples and tenses when he moves. An Awesome Mister is surprisingly small—something his detractors love to point out and something visitors are surprised by. A favourite story about the stud involves a German horse buyer squired around by Dave Hickey. As he likes to do, Dave brought out An Awesome Mister for show and tell. "Hmmm! That's a nice looking pony," noted the visitor. "Now where's the stud?"

There's nothing a stallion owner hates more than someone denigrating the height of his animal. And there's an entire art form in the industry devoted to prevaricating about size. The code word for a horse that is actually the height claimed is "honest," as in "he's an honest sixteen hands," which generally means "I've really measured him and I don't mind if you bring your own stick along and check for yourself."

Dave smiled, "You don't have to be big to be good." He gently reminded the visitor, who was wrestling to haul his foot out of his mouth, that An Awesome Mister was a rare double champion at halter and in performance.

Dave turns the water off in the drain. "Some people thought I was crazy but I was sure this was a horse that could perform. Some people told me I was just wasting my money. Fooled them, didn't I?"

An Awesome Mister dances into the room, hooves ringing against concrete. Everyone falls silent. "He likes it quiet, no distractions," Dave says in a low tone, shooing non-essential personnel to the edge of the large room. As one of the barn workers leaves, she clumsily knocks over a pail. "Ssssh," hisses Dave.

Mister, unperturbed, eases into his routine, heading straight to the two securely penned mares. They look about as glad to see him as the average patient does the dentist. The mares' pens are securely fortified, allowing Mister to caress them but offering no opportunity to return the favour with a kick. He sniffs, snorts, licks and bites. There's a heavy bone-breaking clang as Boston Impress's hoof lets him know how she feels about the business.

Mister works the mares. He rubs his gorgeous dark head against Boston's hindquarters, inhales deeply, then moves nibbling and sniffing toward her neck, making an odd throaty sound as he goes. He chews at her withers and she squeals. His penis descends and grows hard. The six people in the room breathe shallowly and watch intently. It is, after all, near the end of the season, and Mister's enthusiasm is waning. The worst thing that can happen to a stud owner is to come up short on semen. Nature doesn't wait. Mares not bred today may ovulate and the egg will be wasted. It will be another twenty-one days before they are ready to ovulate again.

Though the breeding season is winding down, six mares, three on site and three in the United States, are waiting for semen. Their owners have paid a US$1,500 stud fee for Mister's precious fluid. It isn't the highest stud fee in the Quarter Horse world. Some of the most famous horses, like Zips Chocolate Chip of Texas, command $4,000 or more. But Mister is still young, with only six generations of offspring. All it takes is one or two foals landing top honours in a big American futurity, the Congress or the World Championships, to add a grand or more to a stud fee.

An Awesome Mister's dance drags on, and for a few minutes it looks like that is all he is prepared to do. Suddenly Hickey barks softly at the handler, "He's ready! Take 'im over." With his giant organ bouncing beneath his belly, the stud crabsteps over to the dummy. With a great grunt and heave, he's up and pumping. Seconds later a flood of precious semen erupts into the artificial vagina. Mister, still clutching the dummy with his front legs, drops his head and rubs it, to an anthropomorphic human eye, lovingly against the yellow tape.

Now the work begins. Judy and Dave hurry into the small lab attached to the breeding area. "We've got to have a good collection today," says Dave, peering at the baby bottle liner full of semen they've pulled out of the vagina. He reaches his finger in and draws out what looks like soft, clear Jello. "This time of year stallions have gel. I don't like it. It's useless," Dave growls.

Judy prepares to mix the semen with an extender that lengthens the life of the sperm in shipment. Dave pulls out a semen counter. Quantity of sperm and motility are critical. "Goddamn it!" he fusses. "I don't like what I got. Too much gel here." He sucks up a bit of semen into a thin glass straw and tries to place a drop in the counter. "Son of a bitch!" he mutters. "Got a bubble!" Impatiently Hickey blows out through the semen and tries again.

Judy is already pouring the semen into the extender. "Dave, what're you doing? Just leave it. Leave it."

Hickey persists. "Got it! One hundred ninety-five! Put it down as 195." The reading is well above the acceptable 100 sperm per millilitre, meaning live, progressively motile microscopic tadpoles madly swimming upstream. Hickey breathes deeply. "I've got enough semen to breed twelve and a half mares and we've got six to do so, we're okay."

The doctored sperm goes into syringes, the syringes are packed into three special Styrofoam containers and a man, hovering nearby, jumps into his car and drives the containers to Buffalo, where he'll put them on their respective flights to Texas, Idaho and Ohio.

Then they prepare to inseminate the three mares on the property. Boston Impress is one big problem. "What a hell of a mess," Hickey says, eyeing her meticulously prepared chart. "Look at this! First a yeast infection. We treat her with iodine. Then she wouldn't go into heat. We hit her here." He stabs his finger at a date in April. "Hit her again here."

"Sometimes I wonder why we do it. Nothing but problems."

His wife pokes him. "Oh, come on. You know why." She turns to Alison. "He knows why. He loves it."

Dave groans. "Yeah, I do but I'd sure like to get this mare in foal." He turns to study the chart again.

After breeding, the waiting game begins. At fifteen to eighteen days an ultrasound provides the happy or depressing news. Up the rectum—brood mares spend more time with objects up their bum than a gay prostitute. The vet inserts the head of the ultrasound, and its sound waves penetrate the intestinal walls, bounce across the thick protective layers surrounding the womb to search out a round black blob that looks a little like a giant insect's eye. Foal.

In the small window of the monitor attached to the ultrasound, the blob undulates innocently. This is a critical time for detection; in a few days the embryo will detach and float freely inside the womb, making it much harder to detect. Some vets can, or claim they can, detect the fetus by rectal palpation. No need to resort to the ultrasound and an extra $35 or $50 in expense for the client. But if you are panting for news of an impending foal, you pay the money. Only "backyard breeders" would even think of going with the flow and letting a vet, up to his or her armpit, opine "I'm pretty sure she's pregnant." You pay the money.

ABOUT THE ONLY THING that turned out as planned with our own breeding efforts were the brick skid stalls, which have proved to be utterly indestructible. We certainly haven't come close to Chris Gaul's sixty-six per cent success rate. The fruit of our first year's breeding program was one foal out of four mares bred. Our lovely, meat-price thoroughbred mysteriously aborted or absorbed what she was carrying. Another, also a thoroughbred, was a beautifully put together mare but she was owly-tempered and a little too quick with her hind feet for our liking, so we sold her "in foal," as they say. She did carry her baby to term, but the poor thing was born with twisted back legs and had to be put down. We felt terrible for the gentle young woman who had bought her to start her own breeding operation.

Then came Cameo, a giant chestnut with a face like a camel and withers so high and sharp she'd castrate any man fool enough to ride her bareback. She too carried her foal to term. Early one morning, after taking turns waking up to check the video monitor we set out in the stall, we saw the process under way. Cameo was down and straining, head stretched out with the effort of popping out her baby. Horses foal incredibly quickly— you never know what predator is lurking, waiting to pounce. Sometimes less than a few minutes pass between the water breaking and the whole baby being delivered. We read more books about horses giving birth than we did manuals on human babies when our two girls were born. We knew we had to hurry if we wanted to catch any part of the birth. Hearts pounding, we broke speed records dashing to the barn. When we arrived, Cameo was back on her feet with the limp, half-born foal hanging out of her. David grabbed the distraught mare, howling in her agony, while Alison tried mouth-to-mouth on the baby. Round and round the stall Cameo paced—ten men couldn't have held her still. Whenever she could, Alison breathed into the foal's nostrils. Finally, the exhausted mare dropped to her knees and lay down, grunting and heaving, trying to rid herself of the thing.

It was a filly. Black with two white hind socks and no hint of Cameo the camel in her delicately shaped head. We buried her beside the barn.

Easter saved us. Mr. Twenty-Five Per Cent came snorting into the world at six on Easter morning. We doted on him. Saucy, confident and dreadfully spoiled, he was a fine sorrel Quarter Horse colt with a big blaze like his momma's and enough white on his feet to make him flashy. Everyone loved him and everyone cried when we sold him, surprisingly to the first people who came to look. Our youngest daughter wouldn't leave her room for the entire day.

In 1999 we hit Chris Gaul's magic sixty-six per cent average, two for three, with one fetus absorbed again. "Sixty-six per cent, huh?" queries Chris. "Lemme see, twenty-five per cent last year, sixty-six per cent this year—that'd make your record about forty-five per cent, wouldn't it?"

"Forget last year," we mutter. "We're sticking with sixty-six per cent."

"Oh good," encourages Chris, "you're getting the hang of things. That's the way breeders do it unless, of course, their last year was a great year. Then they remember it." He sighs and shakes his head. "They're all liars." Chris is a kind man, as kind as they come, but we notice that he carefully hasn't excluded us from his generalization. We are, after all, horse breeders.

CHAPTER FOUR

NORTH AGAIN

SEATED NEXT TO DAVID on the flight from Vancouver to Whitehorse is a couple in their mid-thirties. They're returning from a holiday in "Vegas" and the slight yellow pallor of their skin speaks of days spent in the casino, not pool side. He's a small, rumpled, talkative man who looks so much like Woody Allen that David almost calls him Woody by mistake several times. He's a surveyor "in between" jobs. As David listens, he suspects that the between has been a lot more frequent than the in. "Things aren't great up here right now," the man explains mournfully. "Commodity prices are awful and a lot of mines are shutting down."

The wife, a dour bulky matron much larger than her husband, stares resolutely ahead, taking no part in the conversation. In the next few minutes David learns much more than he ever wanted to know about their trip to Nevada—they are "in betweeen" winning streaks—interspersed with more gloomy prognostications about Yukon's economy.

"So, what do you do anyway?" Woody demands after a long blackjack play-by-play. David explains that he's a writer doing some research on trapping.

"Oh ho! Is that right? Well, I can tell you a lot about that. I've been around trappers all my life. Ada's father was a trapper." He leans over to his wife. "Isn't that so, Ada?" There isn't a flicker of response from the woman. "He was one of the best around, been at it from the beginning"—which would make his father-in-law more than a century old. Woody glances at Ada again hopefully, but she isn't breaking her silence. A put-upon air wafts up from her like drugstore cologne. As the conversation idles on, Ada loosens up to drop the occasional word into the men's discussion, instructing her husband to "tell him" this or "tell him" that but never turning her head to look at him. Encouraged, David tries to speak directly to the woman, thinking to organize an interview with her father, but when he does, her lips snap shut like an oyster that's been prodded.

After pointing out other people on the plane who are trappers or come from trapping families, the man segues unexpectedly into a harangue about "conservationists" and their interminable war against trapping and, by inference, the northern way of life. "Those bastards don't have a clue. If they ever ran a trapline . . ." is the gist of it. Though David hasn't expressed an opinion about anything, even the weather, the man lumps him in with the bastards. The blander David's replies, the more heated he becomes, as if David is provocatively arguing against something he holds dear. Soon "they" and "them" is replaced by "you" and "your kind."

The man is now talking as if he's spent his life on the trapline. "When did you start trapping yourself?" David ask neutrally during a brief lull. The man lapses into a sullen silence for the remainder of the flight.

IT'S HARD TO CHARACTERIZE Whitehorse as this kind of town or that sort of place. Its personality isn't writ large upon it. Yukon's image is unrelentingly romantic—the gold rush, sourdough fortune seekers, saloons, bawdy houses and a host of iconoclastic individuals so extraordinary they make the denizens of Cannery Row seem ordinary in comparison. Unfortunately, none of that verve and eccentricity is reflected in Whitehorse, Yukon's capital. The nondescript buildings hunker down, looking bored to death. The stock of old buildings is small and undistinguished. Most of the new "old" structures have that faux frontier character found in Yosemite, Banff or any other western tourist town. The rest of the construction is standard fast food/strip mall interspersed by bureaucratic dullness. No call of the wild here.

The lack of snow isn't helping Whitehorse. It's an abnormally warm and snowless November. Just a thin greyish dusting covers the landscape, mere centimetres where there should be half a metre or more. In the dingy, colour-starved early winter light, the land depends on the snow to beautify, covering a wood slash on one side of the road and an unidentifiable rusting hulk on the other. The north glows in summer, when life erupts so strenuously you can almost hear things grow. The winter coat softens and energizes in its own way. The ecstasy of animals and children after snowfall is testament. A white landscape is also easier on the soul when the niggardly winter light reflects weakly off ice crystals. But this grey half-world, an uneasy transition between the two seasons, leaves everything flat and lifeless—waiting.

We'd been praying for snow. No snow means no trapping. Even though the animals have already acquired their thick, lustrous winter coats by November, without snow the terrain is far too rough for traversing the trap lines. Travelling to the Yukon from Ontario is staggeringly expensive, nearly $2,000 for the flight alone. A family of four could spend a weekend in Disneyland for the cost of crossing the 60th parallel. So we thought snowy thoughts from the moment we booked David's flight, but as the date drew closer, each call to the north elicited the same doleful "not much yet" from the trappers. Finally, when we couldn't wait any longer, David left, hoping that the weather would make up for lost time as he flew toward Whitehorse.

Amid the grey sameness of the town, Hawkins House, a multi-hued, two-storey Victorian house, stands out in glorious technicolor. Built in 1992, the bed and breakfast features the best in old world charm and hospitality with pick-up-your-spirits breakfasts of sourdough pancakes spiced with wild berries, salmon paté, whipped cream, citrus butter and moose meat pie.

The first night, after a wretched dinner of alleged Greek food eaten on the premise that it's hard to ruin it, David stumbles onto his second Yukon surprise, the world's greatest bookstore, Mac's Fireweed Books. It's open on a Monday night and jammed with people. The staff is knowledgeable even about obscure topics and the selection of books about the north is vast. David browses for hours.

The next morning an hour's flight at 9:00 a.m. will take David to Dawson, where Poncho Rudniski is waiting to take him out into the bush for a trapping primer. Nine o'clock comes and goes. For twenty minutes David stands in the airport waiting room with thirty other puzzled passengers. Finally, a serious young female clerk appears to announce there will be a "few minutes' delay"—no further explanation.

There's no sign of a plane on the runway or a flight crew in the airport. Sometime after ten the clerk reappears to announce that the plane is delayed because of a bad snowstorm in Dawson. At least that's good news for trapping, David thinks. Complaining desultorily about the vagaries of air travel in the north, the group drifts away toward the coffee shop. David telephones Poncho to tell him about the snowstorm delay.

"News to me," drawls Poncho. "I was outside ten minutes ago, must have missed it."

"How far away is the airport?" David asks.

" 'Bout twenty miles," Poncho responds. "But it's not snowing there either. Called them about twenty minutes ago to check on your flight. Didn't say a thing about snow. Maybe they missed it too."

David rings off and hustles over to have a word with the clerk, who calls to the pilots cooling their heels in the hangar. The story is quickly adjusted. It seems the real problem is a snowstorm in Old Crow.

"What's that got to do with getting to Dawson?" David demands.

"Wellll, it's the next stop," the girl responds evasively.

"It's the damn pilots!" explains a burly man sitting nearby and eavesdropping. There is a distinct edge to his voice. "They don't want to get stuck in Dawson overnight, so they won't leave Whitehorse till they're sure they can get all the way through." The man goes on to explain that he has important business in Inuvik, the plane's final stop. "I've been here three days, waiting for the plane to go," he snorts in disgust. "Each day it's the same thing. I end up spending all day at the airport, before they finally decide that the flight's not going. And I'm not the only one."

The clerk stands looking at David with as bland an expression as she can muster. David glares back. "So what's the bottom line here?" he asks quietly.

"I have no idea when we're going to go, but I'm not supposed to say that," she admits in a voice barely above a whisper. "But I think you'll get to Dawson today. I'm pretty sure."

"This is the north," Poncho explains when David calls with an update. "Things don't always turn out the way you expect. Especially on planes. Relax. I'm not going anywhere. I'll see you when you get here."

It takes an hour and numerous fruitless enquiries about charter flights and car rentals before David realizes that he has no other choice but to take Poncho's advice. He breathes deeply, buys a cup of coffee and gets acquainted with his fellow waitees. The burly eavesdropper turns out to be a travelling salesman peddling medical supplies on commission. Another older man, so grizzled and worn he has to be a prospector or trapper, turns out to be a schoolteacher in Old Crow. He urges David to visit. "The friendliest place in the world," he claims.

There is a Native family returning from taking their mother to a Vancouver hospital. They don't say what's wrong, but it's clear the news wasn't good. The mother, a wee shrivelled woman of at least ninety, is dwarfed by her wheelchair. She doesn't speak a word of English, but her smile is luminous, and despite the wait she's clearly enjoying, as best she can, what seems likely to be her last adventure. In Vancouver, her son and daughter-in-law bought gifts for their children, several goldfish, which they've transported in two large clear plastic bags. They've spent most of the last three days shuttling back and forth to the bathroom adding fresh water to keep them alive.

"Least they've got something to do," grumps a French-Canadian, built like a stump. Dark-haired, sad-eyed and sporting a week-old five o'clock shadow, "Just Call Me Frenchy" is the most upset by the delay. He lives in a cabin far in the bush with no running water or electricity. He's vague about exactly where he lives and precisely what he does for a living. "A little of this and a little of that" is all he'll say in his heavy accent. The Yukon is one of the few places in the country where you can survive, often quite nicely, without a job. Though the climate is as harsh as any in Canada, there are dense forests, rivers and lakes of fish and plenty of game. Unlike the Northwest Territories, where the barren terrain makes most gravitate to the towns, in the Yukon people can spread out and, with a little of this and a little of that, make do with what nature has provided.

Frenchy was counting on at least a few hours of daylight to get his supplies in, chip some ice for water and start his fire. "Messing around in the dark chopping wood. That's how a guy gets hurt. Like to see those bastards try it."

Eventually David relaxes enough to delve into the small library he's purchased from Fireweed Books. You don't dip into Yukon lore; it grabs you by the heart and the funny bone.

"Buzz Saw" Jimmy, for instance, was twenty-six when he worked his way to the Yukon as a fireman on a steamer in 1899, or thereabouts. Riches eluded him but his real bent was tinkering and inventing. He fashioned his namesake soon after the big rush petered out by crossing an old tractor with a Model-T Ford and a metre-high saw blade. The result was a mobile wood cutter with metal wheels and a lot of unidentifiable bits of metal sticking out here and there. It looked like something Dudley Whipsnide, the villain of movie serials, would use to dismember the damsel in distress. But the oddball contraption cut ten cords an hour, which pretty much gave Buzz Saw a corner on the Dawson firewood market, until he fell into his machine sometime between 1915 and 1917 and sheared off a leg.

After a peg leg took the place of the original, Buzz Saw went back to work, only to fall into his machine again a few years later. Onlookers were aghast to see him lying on the ground with his severed limb beside him. "I fooled you that time, you son of a bitch!" Jimmy sneered at his contraption, which had cut off his wooden leg.

During the Depression, Buzz Saw Jimmy placed a series of ads in the local paper, showing his sense of style if not his encyclopedic knowledge of the great poets.

PROSPERITY FOR A NEW YEAR
Now the year is over,
"Night is drawing nigh,"
Shadows of the Woodpiles
"Steal across the sky;"
Try and Knock Out Depression
With a Truck, a Saw and I.

SEE Jimmy Buzz SAW

That's That!

A mon's a mon for a' a that,
Business is business so that

He can make some money
Get himself a honey
Go where it's sunny
Is that so terrible funny.
—Longfeller

SEE Jimmy Buzz SAW

The construction of the Alaska Highway in 1942 brought another wave of characters north. One of them was Wigwam Harry Fieck, born in 1900 in Stratford, Ontario. He drove a truck for the U.S. army until the road was completed, then began digging basements, cesspools and any other large holes that were needed, by hand. He dug at a furious machine-like pace until the job was finished. Once he dug a basement for a man who was too slow to pay for Harry's liking, so he filled the hole back in, all in one night.

In later years, Harry earned a few coins performing sleight-of-hand tricks in bars and entertaining customers with his trademark Wigwam Harry jig. Observers described it as "half highland fling and half Indian war dance. . . . Whatever it was, he could really dance, there was artistic sense to it." Wigwam Harry's income was small but his needs were even smaller—a drink now and again and accommodation in a series of cardboard and scrap lumber shacks. He even lived for a time in a discarded piano box.

Of course, not all the characters were imports; many had been there all along. Johnnie Johns, born into the Tagish Nation, was one of the best big game hunting guides in the world. Trophy hunters from all over North America and Europe sought him out at his base in the Carcross area just south of Whitehorse.

"In the thirties I took out as many as seventeen hunters at a time.

199

I was making $100 per day, per hunter. It wasn't all gravy. I hired one guide for each hunter and I had to feed the horses. My ponies were bred for the Yukon; they could dig through snow to the grass and come out fat in the spring. I treated my hunters on the rough side, and they liked it. I didn't wait on them. In fact sometimes they waited on me. My hunters were big shots from Europe and the States. But I took them out and made men of them."

"We do not furnish women or liquor!" warned Johnnie's promotional brochures. "Bring your own."

BY THE TIME DAVID FINALLY boards the Dawson plane at 2:00 p.m. he's completely and determinedly relaxed. "It's the north," he keeps repeating to himself, even when the plane remains in the air for an additional hour circling Dawson "because an air ambulance is on the runway." He says it again when he notices that the port side wing doesn't appear to be more than five metres from the trees as the plane lands. Once on the ground, he can't resist asking the baggage attendant about the air ambulance. "Air ambulance? What air ambulance?" the man queries. "Hasn't been anyone take off or land here all day."

"It's the north," David says with conviction.

The road from Dawson's tiny utilitarian airport into town is one of the least attractive entrees to a community he's ever seen. It's downright stark. The road is surrounded by giant, turd-like curlicues of tailings left behind after a century of various mining operations that have come and gone since the Klondike gold rush, and there's little else to recommend it.

But the town itself is everything a southerner envisions. Pretty and compact, Dawson is nestled in a tight little valley against a crook of the Yukon River. With plenty of older character buildings and ultra-wide boulevards, the town seems to have grown naturally and pleasingly outwards from its central core. It's a people town made for promenading and socializing. And there isn't a fast-food outlet in sight.

Like any tourist town, Dawson has a summer and a winter face. But here the two faces don't seem to come from the same family. At the height of summer, it's a hot, throbbing place bursting with six thousand people swarming the hotels and bars, happily living out for a week or ten days the wild freedom legendary in the north. Officially, two thousand people reside here full time, but fewer than half of them actually winter in Dawson.

In summer the hills, covered with growth, frame the town like a picture, but in January they're more like an open fist gripping Dawson by the throat, strangling it as 50 below Celsius settles in, each day duplicating the previous one and guaranteeing a replica the next.

By 9:00 p.m. in November it's hard to buy a meal in town. All but three hotels are closed for the season, and though the few year-round bars will work up a sandwich on request, nothing resembling a restaurant is open. The sounds of night echo along Dawson's wide, empty streets. David walks briskly past boarded-up hotels and stores that remind him of ghost towns in British Columbia's interior and the western United States, except there is ice underfoot instead of earth.

With winter barely begun, daylight sneaks in at 9:24 a.m. and lasts, after a fashion, until 4:36 p.m.. The dimness of the light feels gentle, almost soothing, as if you're wearing a weak pair of sunglasses all the time. It seems quite dark to David the day he arrives, but the driver of the hotel shuttle, a young man wearing only a T-shirt and shorts, though it's 20 below, assures him that November is nothing.

"Hell, in December you can't hardly see your hand in front of your face. Not that you want to go outside and look." With an average of seven and a half hours of daylight, and –16 degrees, November is positively summery compared to December, which can only manage four and a half hours combined with an average temperature of –25. And in January the temperature averages –30 and can sink below –40 for prolonged stretches. Light and temperature are critical matters in Dawson. The official rise and set of the sun is front-paged in the paper alongside the temperature and comments on the character of the cold.

In the early 1880s, Jack McQuesten, a local store owner, invented the sourdough thermometer, which consisted of bottles each containing a different solution—quicksilver, coal oil, extract of ginger and Perry Davis painkiller—placed outside on the window sill. When the mercury froze, it was 40 below; when the coal oil froze, it was –45 and the ginger –50. If the painkiller froze, northerners didn't move away from the fire. Gradations of Perry Davis painkiller were used to gauge really severe cold; it became whitish at –50, crystallized at –56 and froze solid at –60.

"Where Perry Davis painkiller has remained frozen for a period of seven weeks at a time, ice worms have been known to attain a growth of 27 inches," noted the *Dawson Weekly News* on October 15, 1909. "These are much sought after by the Indians who eat them raw with Snyder's Ketchup."

Dawson's men and women are heavy; not exactly fat, but sturdy, with a sense of force and endurance—perhaps an extra kilogram or so for the cold. David fits right in. Older folks seem worn down, ground down, eroded to an essence, but what's left is a bright and sprightly vitality, rare in the southern elderly.

The Eldorado Hotel, where David checks in, is like all the others in town, not shabby, just well-used. It's clean and comfortable and the staff are friendly. The Bonanza Dining Room is solidly built for determined scarfing. The two-storey hotel reserves its entire second floor for non-smokers, but the dining room resolutely belongs to tobacco—each and every table sports a no-nonsense ashtray that could survive an impact with a stone wall. The customers look like they just stopped by on their way to, or back from, the gold rush. You half expect someone to snork a wad into a spittoon.

PONCHO RUDNISKI HAS BEEN waiting, first at home and then at the Eldorado, for hours. He and David have been talking all day, from Whitehorse and from the airport in Dawson. They lapse into the easy familiarity of old friends.

Without much probing, David learns that Poncho is forty-two years old and a Yukoner born and bred. He has lived in the north all his life—never considered going anywhere else. His father nicknamed his older brother Cisco and he got Poncho, both taken from a 1950s television western. Poncho has never seen the show, so David doesn't mention that Poncho was the very overweight, not too bright, butt-of-jokes sidekick to the Cisco Kid.

Poncho's first nine years were spent in Keno, a tiny mining town about two hundred kilometres south and east of Dawson where his father worked in the lead and zinc mine. Poncho, his brother, two sisters and two half sisters attended school at Mayo, a slightly larger community fifty kilometres west on a gravel road. The majority of the children in that school were native and the rest a polyglot of miners' offspring, some transients and some the kids of longtime Yukoners. The relationship with the natives was an uneasy one. "You learned to run or you learned to find a way to get along with them," says Poncho bluntly.

When Poncho was nine, his family moved to Dawson, and

shortly after that he met Black Mike Winnage. Black Mike had drifted to Dawson from Fairbanks in 1917 doing a little of this and a little of that, wood cutting, trapping, mining—whatever earned a dollar. For a time he ran high-class poker games at the Westminster and Occidental hotels in Dawson and dressed the part of a millionaire gambler with spit-polished shoes in the latest style, dazzling white shirts, bow ties and an impressive black moustache.

After the Depression struck and the stream of gamblers slowed to a trickle, Winnage turned to carpentry, specializing in fixing buildings that had been tilted by permafrost, a perpetual problem in Dawson. By the time Poncho met him, Black Mike had concentrated on trapping, and he had his own way about it. He specialized in catching beaver, an art in itself. In winter the beaver is trapped through a hole chopped in the ice. Black Mike baited the trap with a fresh sapling. When the beaver swam to it, a snare closed around its body. A rock, attached to the snare by a tripwire that was fastened to another rock on the bottom, pulled the animal down and quickly drowned it. To make the trap work, you needed rocks the size and roughly the shape of a big loaf of Italian bread with sufficient girth for fastening the wire. Round ones wouldn't work.

It was Poncho's job to haul the rocks from Black Mike's cabin to the beaver dam, several hundred metres away. "It was backbreaking work," Poncho recalls. "And they had to be the rocks beside the cabin, even though the ones by the water were exactly the same. I still don't get it."

Poncho left school when he was fourteen, mined in the warm months and went trapping in the winter. He married Tammy at twenty-four, and his two strapping sons came along in the next five years.

Poncho is an easy guy to get along with. His wide-open face is readily creased by a smile, and you sense that what you see is what you get, nothing hidden in dark corners of his personality. He's about 5'10" and packing around 215, mostly hard, pounds. It's not a threatening bigness. Poncho has that combination of hardness and softness peculiar to retired boxers, men who have nothing to prove to themselves or anyone else—their manliness isn't in question.

Turns out Poncho was a decent, knock-around, light heavy-weight who tried out for the Canadian Olympic Team in 1980. Unfortunately, that happened to be one of the best years ever for Canadian amateur boxing with a talent pool that included Lennox Lewis and Sean O'Sullivan. Poncho didn't make the team. He's also a decent hockey player and stood between the pipes for the 1997 re-enactment of a historic game between Yukon and Ottawa's Silver Seven. He's passed that skill on to his sons. The elder boy is the size of Eric Lindros and plenty tough. There wasn't enough competition for him in the north, so Poncho and Tammy decided to let him go to school in Penticton—but not alone. For the last three years, Poncho and Tammy have split the school year between them. She goes south with him from Octo-ber until December and Poncho takes over in January. The younger boy, not as big, but with considerable hockey skill, isn't really interested. He's more like his father, preferring the trap line and his skidoo.

About the first thing Poncho tells David is that he's picked the wrong guy. "I went out for the first time this week and got two weasels and a squirrel. Maybe twenty bucks' worth." He peers at David as if giving him time to change his mind and head back to the airport. David searches for something encouraging to say but ends up with a weary, "Oh well."

In truth, after two days of flying, endless delays and three time zone changes, he fleetingly hopes Poncho will say that at four o'clock with darkness fast closing in it's too late to head out. A leisurely dinner, a glass or two of wine and a wide-ranging discussion of trapping would suit him fine. Tomorrow would be soon enough to get down to the real thing. The thought had never occurred to Poncho. "Let's saddle up!" he orders.

At Poncho's house, five streets over from the Eldorado, David puts on his long johns (newly purchased for the trip), toque, scarf, Jean-Claude Killy "Sur la Piste" jacket and ski gloves. He senses Poncho's disapproval of his attire, but nothing is said. Armed with the all-important pocket notebook, David jumps into Poncho's mint condition 1961 dark green Dodge truck. "Tomorrow, we'll spend the day at the Tombstone Mountains. Tonight'll be just a taste."

The line they head to is the closest one to Poncho's house. He's been thinking of abandoning it but laid out traps specially so David could see the historic Ridge Road that was the main route into the mines during the Klondike gold rush. "It might be interesting for you and maybe I'll catch something at the same time. Though I didn't do so good here last time." By the time they reach the road, all David can see is a purple bruise of trees and hills and the occasional mouldering roadhouse, illuminated by the headlights, along the famous route.

"Trouble with this line is it's too damn close to town." For the life of him David can't figure out what Poncho is talking about. Eight kilometres away from a town of a thousand in winter?

"It's a posted trapline," he explains at David's quizzical look. "But people still insist on walking their dogs along here. Like there's no other place! I hate when I find a dog in my trap, but what can you do?"

Encroaching civilization is a problem faced by many trappers and Poncho isn't the only one to find the odd dog in one of his traps. Most quietly dispose of the animal rather than face an irate and sometimes irrational owner. "Don't forget that basically everyone is armed to the teeth up here," one trapper told David to put the matter into context. "People also poke sticks into the traps to set them off."

"Animal rights?" David asks.

"Nah, just assholes amusing themselves."

The asshole problem forces Poncho to conceal the traps so that they're not visible from the trail. "If it's right there, the assholes will bugger it up, but they won't go looking for it." He sets the traps fifteen or twenty metres off the road but then they're hard for him to find too.

"What about the animal rights' groups?" David prods.

"Once you only had to worry about Greenpeace in Vancouver. Then they set up in Whitehorse. Now it's your next-door neighbour who's looking funny at you when you load up your truck with traps. Most of the people who've lived here for a while are fine about it, but the transients are bad and the civil servants are the worst. A lot of them don't seem to understand that this is a way of life and a living."

When they reach the trapline, the struggle between man and nature begins banishing the annoyances of civilization. David had always considered trapping to be a relatively simple, if violent, procedure. His experience consisted of trapping mice and the occasional rat, and using live animal traps to relocate troublesome raccoons who take up residence in our ancient barn. You bait the trap, catch the animal and, if dead, gross out the children, then dispose of it. How hard can this be?

The first trap is full. A nice plump frozen marten lies in it. It's a beautiful ferrety creature, about sixty centimetres long nose to end of tail, with a lush dark brown coat and a black fringed neck. Its unglazed eyes stare into the gloom and it appears to be asleep. There is no sign of a struggle.

"Damn it!" explodes Poncho. "Look at the goddamn tail!" The marten's body is thickly furred but the tail is hilariously bare. It looks more like a bony earthworm than a tail. "That marten's a beauty," he moans, "Fifty, sixty dollars. But with the tail like that it's worth maybe five dollars. Maybe."

"What happened?" David asks. Poncho gestures toward the trap and a jumble of overlapping animal tracks. "See, there's the marten over there." He indicates a delicate solo trail emerging from the west, more like a brushing of the snow than an actual print. "Those marten tracks are about three days old. He just ran along and jumped right into the trap.

"Over there, that's wolverine." Poncho points to much larger, more authoritative prints leading toward the trap then skirting around it and heading back to the trail. "The bugger stood there, had a good look at the trap and then went on his way."

"Why wouldn't it eat the marten?" David asks.

Poncho shrugs. "Don't know. We haven't seen the last of him, though."

"Is that wolverine over there too?" David walks over to a line of tracks about three metres away that appear identical to the others.

"Rabbit," Poncho snorts, swallowing a laugh of disbelief that anyone could mistake one for the other. "And you saw the lynx track on the trail, right?" Deciding honesty is the best policy, David admits he hadn't seen any tracks on the trail, much less lynx tracks.

Poncho crouches over the trap and picks up a single black feather. "This is the bastard that did it." A raven had patiently stood there, pulling every scrap of fur off the marten's tail but not touching anything else.

"I must have done something bad to an Indian in a previous life." Poncho grimaces. "Guess it's payback, huh? There's ravens all over the damn place now that they've closed the dump," he shouts over his shoulder on his way back to the truck. "Let's go!" He backs the truck up a good fifty metres so David can see lynx tracks running along one side.

On this line Poncho has set his traps out at a rate of about one every 1.5 kilometres or so. Sometimes, depending on the terrain, he might set them closer together, but on average they are almost exactly one per 1.5 kilometres. Part of it is a conservation ethic. "You've got to let some get through. If you over-trap, you'll be wasting your time for years afterwards." Poncho shows David one area where a trapper has laid out a Maginot Line of traps, more than a hundred in sixteen kilometres, catching everything on four legs.

Even if he didn't care about the results of over-trapping, Poncho couldn't afford to do it. Each of the small Conibear traps intended for marten costs eight to ten dollars. Usually the animal freezes so tightly into the trap it can't be released without damaging the fur, so trappers simply take the whole thing back with them, animal and all, for thawing later. Without spares you'd have a lot of blank spots in the line.

David quickly discovers that there is much more to trapping than simply baiting a trap and setting it out. Leg-hold traps, once the trappers' staple, were banned except for certain circumstances three years ago. They were replaced by Conibears, the dominant brand name. They are all-metal traps and come in a variety of sizes, depending on the intended prey.

The Conibear 120, primarily used for marten, consists of two ten-centimetre metal squares, the wire about the diameter of a coat hanger but heavier gauge. The squares are held apart by a spring mechanism and the tripping device sits in the centre. The animal has to stick its head right into the middle of the trap to get at the bait. When it is triggered, the trap snaps shut, with a motion like a butterfly closing its wings, only faster, usually hitting the animal in the neck or shoulder, making a quick, humane kill. Trappers, initially angry about losing the leg-hold trap, have come to appreciate the Conibear because it doesn't mess up the fur and it's safer to handle.

Because of the Conibear's design, it can't lie flat on the ground like the old leg-hold but must be propped up inside something else. Trappers often set the marten traps inside a small rectangular wooden box, about fifteen centimetres square and forty-five centimetres long and open at one end. The trap is set just inside the open end with the bait behind it. The marten tries to get at the bait through the trap. Sometimes the marten boxes are attached to a tree sixty or ninety centimetres off the ground to keep mice out. And the trap itself is always fastened with a chain or wire to a tree or an anchor pole. If the trap gets sabotaged by a larger animal and dragged away, the pole will usually catch between two trees where the trapper can retrieve it.

For lynx and wolverine, there are identical but bigger Conibears that are set on edge and situated so that the animal has to walk through it to get at the bait. The trapper builds an elaborate backdrop of branches and boughs, called a cubby, to disguise the trap and prevent animals from getting the bait from the back. Ideally, traps are set in high traffic areas and where there are natural cubbies in place.

Driving along the trail is a chiropractor's special—if Disney could recreate it, they'd really have something special in the way of an amusement ride. The slower you go, the longer it takes, but if you speed up, the jolt factor increases logarithmically. David tries to write as Poncho drives but when he checks the notebook in the headlights all he can see are seismographic squiggles, five centimetres tall and completely indecipherable.

"You're not supposed to drive along here," Poncho admits after a stomach-compressing thud that ends with their skulls brushing the roof. "But what can you do? There isn't enough snow here for a skidoo. And I have to check my traps."

If Poncho is still annoyed about the marten tail, he doesn't show it. His good cheer is legendary, and even people who have never met him know Poncho as a cheerful guy. But as trap after trap turns up nothing or bits of mutilated fur, David senses that his good cheer is requiring an effort. At eleven o'clock, after six straight hours of work in pitch black, Poncho calls it a day. Heading back to Dawson, David asks him point-blank how he's feeling about his meagre take of two marten and one chewed-up lynx, not even enough to pay for the gas. But Poncho won't go so far as to concede he's disappointed. "I'm hoping when we go over the hill tomorrow, we'll have a good trip. I need a good trip. I want to call the wife with good news tomorrow night."

As a precautionary measure, David starts the next day by wolfing down the Eldorado Hotel's special Greenhorn-Heading-Out-for-a-Trapping-Adventure breakfast—three plate-sized pancakes, a side of bacon, a three-egg omelette, home fries and toast. Poncho, who arrives with a trapper friend, Bruce, just as David is finishing, limits himself to coffee, explaining that he doesn't eat breakfast. How, David wonders, can a 200-pound-plus man hit the trail with only coffee in his belly?

Bruce's main purpose this morning seems to be to tell them that he's been up to Poncho's Tombstone line the week before in his all-terrain vehicle.

"Went all over," he says solemnly. "Didn't see a thing, not a mouse track up there."

Poncho only grunts and changes the topic. For a time they fence back and forth, Bruce adding details to the game survey he's done on Poncho's trapline and Poncho changing the topic. Eventually, Bruce stretches in his chair and lets out a sigh that gives the waitress a start.

"Guess you'd better get going," he says. "Daylight's wasting." David looks outside. It's 7:00 a.m., still pitch dark and will be until at least 9:30. Poncho and Bruce chuckle comfortably. It's a northern joke.

Back at his house, Poncho again looks over David's garb. He doesn't say anything, but it's clear from his expression that Jean-Claude Killy's "Sur la Piste" will have to go. He hauls out shredded snowmobile pants, a tattered but bulkily warm ski jacket and a pair of snowmobile boots with heavily insulated soles. The pièce de résistance of David's outfit is a handsome pair of handmade beaver fur gloves, giving David a close kinship with Sergeant Preston of the Yukon. Topped off with a red toque and tartan scarf, he sets new standards for wilderness fashion. He feels very "fashiony," as our daughter used to say, and more than equal to whatever the Yukon can throw at him.

Earlier, Poncho arranged to rent an extra machine from Ivan, another trapper. After much negotiation, he gets it for the bargain-basement price of $100 because Ivan has read one of our books.

Ivan is a stolid fellow who throws around words like they were manhole covers. "Ever driven one of these?" he asks David, meaning the specific model. He looks surprised when David says he's never driven a skidoo period. Ivan shoots Poncho an are-you-crazy? look.

"I'll give him a good once-over," Poncho assures Ivan. "Nothing to it."

Ivan looks dubious, something he's rather good at. He then tells David that the 'doo has been recently serviced.

David starts hauling out his wallet.

Ivan holds his palm up. "When you get back is soon enough." "If you get back" remains unsaid but hangs in the air.

As David and Poncho are settling into the truck, Ivan casually adds, "I think it might be leaking some gas."

"Let's saddle up," Poncho instructs, ignoring him. They stomp out to the truck—adrenalin is starting to flow. By 8:00 they're loaded. Poncho has packed a teflon sled he built using hockey sticks for ribs with his traps and bait—a frozen-solid, skinned beaver, his secret animal attractor recipe (more about that later) and their lunch. "Tea and gumwiches," Poncho says with a wicked smile. David doesn't ask. David supplies six giant chocolate bars for dessert. Remembering Ivan's warning, they sniff and poke around the skidoo for signs of a leak.

"How about we bring some extra gas?" David asks, looking at a jerrycan beside the house.

"Nah," Poncho responds expansively. "Don't need any, we have two skidoos."

Just as they start backing out, Bruce arrives in his truck. His main purpose in coming by seems to be to remind them, as he had at breakfast, that he'd been up on Poncho's trapline recently and hadn't seen any tracks, not a rabbit, nothing. Poncho again only grunts at the information and changes the topic, giving a detailed description of where the truck will be parked, where they're heading and when they expect to return.

"If you're not back by midnight, I'll come looking," Bruce vows.

At the parking area, about eight kilometres from town, Poncho's "good once over" on the skidoo consists of a brusque, "Right hand controls the throttle, left hand the brake, steer with both hands, it's easy. Let's boogie!"

By the time David looks up from the control panel, Poncho is nearly out of sight down the road. David boogies. The first thing he discovers is that forty kilometres per hour on a skidoo is as fast as he's ever moved before.

Wind whistles by his face, scenery shoots past. What a blast. Flashback to his first two-wheeler bike, a used Schwinn that seemed rocket-powered when going downhill. And then to an MGA sports car he owned in his early twenties. It was the last of the true sports cars, with wooden floorboards, paltry shocks and almost no clearance from the road. A hundred and sixty kilometres an hour seemed like flying. But this is faster, much faster.

After ten or fifteen minutes, David begins to gain on Poncho, who is a blur of snow kicked up from his machine. But every time he gets close, Poncho, assuming that David is getting the hang of it, speeds up more. It's a compliment of sorts, but pretty soon David is clinging by his fingernails, the throttle completely depressed and flying, absolutely flying. It's fun. Gloriously, scarifyingly fun.

Once he sneered at snowmobiles as noisy, wilderness-destroying machines. But they're damn exhilarating, no denying it.

They travel by road for half an hour before turning off on a survey cut line, which they follow deep into the bush. The road is easy going, the cut line less so with plenty of dips, undulations and debris on the surface. It's also narrower, barely 1.5 metres wide. Does Poncho slow for this new terrain? Not on your life. Every once in a while, he turns around and flashes David a big, contented grin, or gives him a thumbs-up and speeds up some more.

From the cut line, they turn off again onto a trappers' trail barely as wide as the skidoo. The only hint that anyone else in the world has ever been here is a faint track left by Poncho five days earlier when he set out his traps.

Poncho's Tombstone Mountains trapline is a 135 kilometre loop. It climbs gradually to a plateau with the reward of a grand view of the range. For fifty years trappers have been working this line, first by snowshoe or dog and sled and then with machine. Poncho and David will cover the 135 kilometres in a day and be back by evening, but a few decades back the trapper had to live in a cabin or tent on the line and take four or five days to service it, living off the land because everything had to be hauled in. Pelts and fresh meat would be cached along the line in small secure rooms often built on stilts.

The trail takes the path of least resistance, with switchbacks and unexpected dips the norm. Flat doesn't exist. In places the trail shoots up so suddenly it seems impossible to walk up, let alone drive a skidoo up. Going down is a bowel-liquefying experience. Poncho has already sailed to the crest and charged down the other side. Fallen trees lie across the trail at odd angles, and in a few places branches stick up like punji stakes.

Occasionally, just to mix things up, the trail disappears entirely into a sink hole. Here and there rocks are dangerously visible through the snow and occasionally the trail is so rocky it looks like a creek bed. Along some stretches a thirty-metre chasm threatens, centimetres away from the edge of the track. Poncho attacks each obstacle at maximum speed. David, bumping far in his wake, buttocks clenched, hands welded to the handles, concentrates hard on keeping his balance and his tongue in his mouth so he doesn't bite it off.

Poncho rides with a knee up on the seat, giving him more visibility and the leverage to lean into corners like a motorcycle racer. It also looks cool. David tries it and discovers too late that the trail is banked the wrong way on a turn; over the machine goes. With each tip the skidoo stalls, and it sometimes takes a dozen heaves on the starter to get it going again. After a few such exercises, he gives up and sits firmly on the seat, both feet planted and pointing forward.

David had wondered why Poncho chose the smaller skidoo over Ivan's. The answer is clear when he sees Poncho start his machine with a turn of the key. Northern courtesy, David realizes, stretches only so far.

Speed is David's best friend and worst enemy. The bumps are less jarring when he throttles back, but the machine is also less stable and the tips more frequent. When David speeds up, the machine keeps to the track better but goes alarmingly airborne when he hits the many logs spread across the trail.

About a kilometre and a half before the start of the trapline David rounds a curve to find Poncho waiting with a grave expression on his face. What could be so serious? Have they been magically transported to a Jack London novel and are surrounded by ravenous wolves? If so, David knows what to do. He's read his Farley Mowat. He would immediately establish an impenetrable perimeter around them by peeing on all four corners of the compass. Doubtless Poncho could contribute to the cause. But Poncho sadly shakes his head and points to a set of tracks strutting down the middle of the trail. "Wolverine," he growls, then he's gone.

The day of trapping doesn't begin auspiciously. At the first site they find the marten box smashed to kindling and the ground trampled as if a parade had come through. There's a beautiful marten head—but that's it. Every speck of its body has been eaten, with the head tossed aside insolently. The trap is nowhere to be seen. After fifteen minutes of searching, they find it frozen into creek ice about thirty metres from where it had been set up, still attached to the branch that acts as an anchor for just these situations. It takes another fifteen minutes to chip it free.

"Wolverines like their little jokes," Poncho says with a philosophical air.

A big Conibear trap, set in case a wolverine came along, has also been tripped and the cubby scattered. Despite Poncho's long experience with the trapper's nemesis, he isn't sure how the wolverine has managed to demolish it without getting caught. He speculates that a marten had actually been caught in the big Conibear, making it safe for the wolverine to yank the carcass out.

"Just the luck of the draw," shrugs Poncho. "You watch. This bugger's going to do the entire trapline. And I don't have another big trap set for quite a while."

The second and third traps are both tripped. This time the wolverine delicately slipped its paw under the box and flipped it, trap and all, into the air, freeing the bait, which he scarfed down. Otherwise the sites are almost pristine, with no excess footprints. The animal walked directly up to the trap and tripped it, no fuss, no muss—all in a day's work. The wolverine took the most direct route from trap to trap, staying on the skidoo trail if that was the shortest distance between points or cutting cross country if it wasn't. As the day wears on, David becomes schooled in deciphering tracks, easily identifying the martens' trails and, all too often, the wolverine's.

The fourth trap looks as if a fury has been at it. Again, the box is kindling and the ground trampled but this time the snow is packed down as if a marching band on speed has been practicing there. Violence is everywhere, spots of blood here and there, tufts of marten fur and spots where the raging wolverine has scraped the snow right off the ground. What there isn't, is any sign of the trap or the anchor pole attached to it.

Anchor poles are usually between two and two and a half metres long and five to seven and a half centimetres in diameter. They should look as natural as possible, a branch blown there by the wind, so the animals don't sense the hand of man. They don't weigh much; a wolverine could sneeze them away. They're merely intended to drag behind if the trap is dislodged and get hung up in the dense underbrush. As an experiment, David tries to pull one of the poles through the bush and within seconds it is stuck and he can't begin to budge it. "I can't move them either," Poncho admits. The wolverine has no such problem.

They spend half an hour looking for the trap, and though there's plenty of wolverine sign, there's no trace of the animal or the pole: no branches, no bark, nothing. "I once got so mad when a wolverine took off with a trap I kept looking for hours," Poncho says as they search. "I wasn't going to give up and let that wolverine get the better of me." Today he gives up quickly because he has no idea where to look. The animal and the trap have disappeared. "Maybe he ate the damn thing," Poncho wonders.

The previous night's poor take, coupled with the shambles he's found at the first four sets, puts a dent in Poncho's optimism. Each grin fades a little quicker than the one before and what started out as "oh well" degenerates into "oh shit" and then a glum nothing. David envisions a parade of ruined fur and destroyed traps—a very long day.

But the fifth trap is a surprise. As David pulls up, Poncho is cradling something in his arm, looking hard at it—a beautiful frozen marten, completely unscathed. The wolverine has been all over the site, striding around, examining everything as if to say, "I know all there is to know about this set and I choose not to touch it."

"They're strange creatures," sighs Poncho. "It's like he's saying, 'If I don't leave a few, Poncho will get discouraged and stop playing.'"

Wolverines are the Don Rickleses of the animal world, nasty little tricksters with a vile sense of humour—their biggest punch line is that they can back up their pranks against all comers. Pound for pound, they are by far the toughest and fiercest animals going—they won't back down from anything. Ranging in weight from twenty-five to forty-five pounds, they look rather like small bears. Cumbersome looking when standing still, they're actually fast and versatile, their small, sinewy bodies possessing power out of all proportion to their size. When it comes to the things that animals do, wolverines are near the top in everything: digging, running and climbing. Nor do they lack for personality, and what's between their ears comes close to human intelligence.

Marten all behave more or less the same: they scent the bait, run toward it and jump right in. Wham! Sometimes you can follow their tracks and see that they've targeted the trap as far as fifteen metres away, sprinted directly to it, no pausing, no caution—strides lengthening as they near their mark. Then the fatal dive.

Wolves are devilishly clever, but it's hard to know where pack

219

intelligence ends and individuality begins. Lynx aren't particularly smart, but they're so shy they're hard to catch. Trappers say that if they're only caught by the leg, lynx will fight briefly, then give up and stand still until someone comes and incites them into a frenzy of fear. Like marten, they never seem to get trap-wise.

Not so the wolverine. The dumb ones get trapped quickly, the others wise up fast after getting clipped in a trap, but not fatally injured. And they're the utterly elusive ones. It occurs to David that trappers are inadvertently but selectively removing the least intelligent wolverines, creating an ever brainier super race, bent on outwitting trappers. First trappers, then the world.

Poncho's solution is a snare, a simple device but difficult to set up well. A heavyweight braided wire is fashioned into a noose. The animal's first rush of movement through the noose tightens the wire; the more the creature struggles, the tighter the choke. Unpleasant to witness, but snares are fast—usually doing the job in seconds. Of course, the art of the thing is to get the animal to place its neck into the noose in the first place. Wolverines don't exactly stand still while you distract them with one hand—card tricks, perhaps—and quickly slip it over their heads with the other.

The snare separates the canniest trappers from the rest. They search for signs of the animals' favoured routes, preferably a wolverine superhighway with obstructions on either side to keep them from straying, and string up the snare at head height, secured to both sides of the trail. It's important to make the area surrounding the snare look as natural as possible, so they decorate it with twigs and line the approach with branches to encourage the wolverine to keep to the centre. Most animals, even wolverines, prefer not to walk on twigs, particularly if the points are upright.

Wolverines have an excellent sense of smell but here it works against them. If they catch a whiff of man, normally they'll be gone in seconds, but a seasoned trap raider expects man scent near a set, so he'll be pretty confident that humankind offers no particular threat. Occasionally, a wolverine charges through a snare and gets caught over its shoulder or around its stomach, giving him time to fight.

"I've seen them chew down every tree around trying to get the one the trap's attached to," Poncho says with a combination of rue and respect. "If they can't chew the trees down they'll chew off their legs. I've caught plenty of them with three legs. The stub grows over as if it never was. They seem to get along fine. One old boy was blind in one eye when I caught him. The other eye didn't look too good either. But he was plump as could be. Didn't look like he'd ever missed a meal."

The sixth and seventh traps have been tripped by the wolverine using its patented flipping technique. "It's too bad, if he hadn't flipped the traps we would have had two marten. There's marten track all over the place."

The two men develop a routine. Poncho zooms ahead. David catches up at the set. He gives David a little synopsis of what he saw and an interpretation of what has happened. David jots in his notebook. Poncho zooms away.

After a while, the aura of the bush works its magic on David. It is like those winter moments in a deserted city park, Sunday morning in a school yard, or early in the day when you're the first one up the ski lift. We make a lot of noise just being. Even thinking can set up a rattle inside. But every now and then, in those times of perfect solitude, the brain quits churning its wheels. With two children, dogs, horses, rats, rabbits, cats, phones, faxes, TVs, computers and radios, David has forgotten what quiet really is. Here it's so silent he can hear the air moving—not wind, just air slipping around delicately caressing his ear.

At traps eight and nine, plump martens lie captured and untouched. At each one, the wolverine has stood about thirty centimetres away for a considerable length of time, as the indents of his paws show, and studied the trap with the marten in it, then moved on. Poncho is pleased but cautious in his optimism, certain that this wolverine still has surprises in store.

"Maybe this one would rather have a little sauce on his marten," Poncho speculates. "Make a note. I'll be sure and bring some along next time."

At the tenth trap, a weasel has stolen the bait, but at the eleventh he or a kin got his come-uppance. The slender creature is exquisite, all white, densely furred and about thirty centimetres long. Despite its beauty, the weasel is worth only about $6. The watching wolverine has been here too, looking but not touching.

Bonanza at the next three traps. All contain excellent unscathed marten. "I really didn't expect anything in this stretch," Poncho laughs delightedly. "And certainly not with this damn wolverine hanging about." The wolverine studied the first two traps but moved on. At the third, he ate the bait by insolently tilting the box over, taking the bait out, then letting it fall back into place, but he didn't disturb the marten. Some trappers fasten wire mesh on the bottom of the box to keep the wolverine away from the bait but Poncho feels that this just irritates them.

"Make a note," directs Poncho, "that wolverine is sure fooling that Poncho."

Weasels are in the next two traps, both of which have been studied by the wolverine. Poncho stares at the tracks, shaking his head. "I'll be interested to see what he does with the big trap."

Poncho has a large Conibear trap at the next set, but David

gets the feeling he doesn't really want to catch this wolverine any-more. Poncho doesn't begrudge the wolverine taking his bait or even his pranks along the line, but he hates the wanton destruc-tion. Bush vandalism.

"I've had the same wolverine wreck an entire trapline, a hun-dred traps! I came upon him when he was just finishing pissing on my last trap. He just stood there looking at me." Infuriated, Poncho tried to run the wolverine over with his skidoo, hitting it twice in the process. "I was so mad I couldn't help myself. You never saw a more surprised wolverine when I hit him the first time. He just didn't believe that I would do it. But you know I hit him at thirty miles an hour and he didn't even feel it. I ended up catching him in a trap a week later and he wasn't hurt in the least."

This wolverine is different. He has a sense of proportion—it's as if he were in a game with Poncho, one Poncho now doesn't want to end.

Poncho needn't have worried. David pulls up to find him frowning at the big Conibear. Somehow the wolverine tripped it and ate the bait. It's far too big to flip over, so how did he get at the bait without getting caught? David imagines him springing the trap by poking at it with a long stick held between his two front paws. Poncho grunts in such a way as to acknowledge he wouldn't be half surprised if the animal had done just that.

After tripping the trap, the wolverine coated its trigger—a for-midable feat of marksmanship—with a long stream of pungent blue-green urine. For good measure he trashed the nearby marten trap, ate all but the marten's head, then pissed on it as well before sauntering off.

Poncho's sense of affinity, of oneness with the wolverine, van-ishes as he feverishly goes to work building a larger and more formidable cubby. This is the only way Poncho can figure out that the wolverine might have managed to trip it. By the time he's finished there are enough poles driven into the ground to build a fair-sized stockade.

"Let's see the bugger get through that!" Poncho exclaims. But the construction project is really just a little backwoods therapy. He knows full well that the wolverine can get through it if he really wants to—they can get through just about anything. His face tells the story. It's been a good day so far but he thinks it has ended right now.

But then three traps hold perfect martens, fur intact. Untouched except for a long squirt of urine on each. This bothers Poncho not at all, as it doesn't damage the fur. David wonders if the wolverine is annoyed because Poncho had unsportingly set a trap aimed specifically at him. Perhaps the wolverine feels insulted that Poncho thought he'd be caught so easily. Anthropomorphizing perhaps, but it's easy to ascribe human emotions to these animals.

At the next set, Poncho unwraps a wire securing the trap to a tree. It's gnarled and twisted back on itself like fouled fishing line and was here long before Poncho came along. The wire has been broken several times and been twisted back together again as it held trap after trap against the tree. Where it circles the tree, it has bitten deeply into the bark as the tree slowly grew. "This looks like it's caught twenty or thirty marten over the years. The cheap old trapper who used to work this line kept using the same wire over and over again as if it were gold." David reminds Poncho that a cheap old trapper is still using the wire.

Unexpectedly, the wolverine strikes again. The next two marten boxes are tidily flipped over and the bait gone. There are tracks everywhere, so if the traps hadn't been sprung there would almost certainly be marten in them. From three metres away, the next marten looks untouched but its carcass is riddled with tooth punctures ruining the fur. Poncho only shakes his head. The punctured marten turns out to be this wolverine's going-away present.

The next trap is the twenty-fifth, about a quarter of the way around the line. In it is a particularly fine dark marten with dense, silky fur almost uniform in colour. A beauty. For the first time today there is no sign of the wolverine. Nothing, no mess, no tracks, nothing. He's gone.

David estimates that it's about noon. Neither he nor Poncho is carrying a watch, which somehow seems right for this day in the bush. They've been slowly climbing all morning. The sky gradually clears as the day advances with wan patches of light blue visible between the high clouds. Occasionally the sun struggles through but it is unlike the sun of the 49th parallel. It seems to come from a different solar system—bigger than in the south but as faint and powerless as a dying flashlight. The sickly rays do little to lift the pervasive early winter gloom. All the same there's a gentleness to the illumination, a weak caress.

In the southern United States, they call the half hour before dusk "dark thirty," when the fading light softens objects and gives colours a muddy dimension as it casts eerie half shadows that tease and fool the eye. It is considered the most dangerous time to drive and also appears to trigger the appetites of those with murder or rape in their personality. But here dark thirty lasts all day, draining colour from the landscape and distorting the already stunted trees. It feels other-worldly.

Though it is near lunchtime and they've been pushing hard for hours, David is curiously not hungry, despite the fresh air, which is usually a great appetite enhancer. From experience, he knows that it's best to eat periodically in the bush to keep up strength and maintain body heat, but if Poncho has read the standard backwoods guides he pays them no heed. There's no way he's stopping and there's no way David's going to suggest it.

Poncho has reverted to his ebullient self. Everything is going better than expected. The night before, Poncho had said he'd be satisfied with a dozen marten, and they already have that many piled on the sled, though some are mauled.

"Let's boogie," he yells after resetting trap twenty-five.

At trap twenty-six they're met by a different wolverine. It's a World Wolverine Wrestling Federation tag team. From his tracks, big as fists, he's about twice the size of the first, a granddaddy. "As big as I've ever seen," observes Poncho, who doesn't speculate on what this means for the rest of his line. That trap and the next three are casually flipped over and the bait eaten. Wolverine number one quartered the whole area even when he'd left the trap untouched. This one simply sauntered over to the trap, gobbled the bait, ignored the marten, then headed off to the next.

He did it again farther down the line, leaving a particularly beautiful dark marten alone but eating the bait. There's an abandoned Conibear cubby nearby made from an old oil barrel. Here the wolverine varied his routine, carefully examining every part of the cubby, but not damaging it in any way.

The big wolverine flipped the next nine traps in a row before the marten got to them and ate the bait. "We would have had marten in those traps, because there's tracks everywhere," sighs Poncho. The wolverine then gave Poncho a break, leaving two martens but eating the bait and sauntering insolently off.

A five kilometre gap separates them from the next trap. This section of the trail could have been designed by the producers of the James Bond films, with inclines so steep you need full speed to get up them and downhills so precipitous they seem like luge courses. Large logs every few metres or so add a bit of excitement, along with hairpin turns and stretches so rock-strewn they resemble creek bottoms. David slows before he hits the first log parked at the bottom of a hill, waiting to catch him in his full-tilt descent. He brakes frantically but still hits it with a tremendous smack. The skidoo doesn't make it over the log but he does.

David can see Poncho's tracks from his vantage point in the snow. He's blithely sailed over the log, landing several metres beyond. There's no alternative. David can't get around the log and it's firmly frozen to the ground. He must do an Evel Knievel. By dint of considerable effort, David pushes the skidoo, which has no reverse, back about twenty metres before the hill stops him. Throttle cranked down, he runs at the log, hits it full force . . . and is airborne. It's glorious! And he lands, still upright. Suddenly the logs are no longer obstacles. David looks forward to the next one.

The trail widens somewhat, making conditions right for poplar to take root. They're thin things, about two centimetres or less in diameter, two to three metres long and thicker at the base than at the tip, making them springy and resilient, like whips.

The saplings grow 45 degrees toward the middle of the trail, seeking the light and creating a criss-crossing gauntlet of whips running ninety metres or longer. They come at David suddenly, furiously whacking his face as he hits the thicket going forty kilometres an hour. With his eyes focused ahead, trying to keep Poncho in sight, there's no time to protect himself. He tries ducking behind the windshield, which is only about forty-five centimetres high. That limits the lashing somewhat but cuts his vision to almost nothing. When he slows, the snowmobile threatens to tip as the trail banks hard.

He can't use his right hand for protection because it's on the throttle. He tries a left forearm shield, but then he can't see well, and as the course changes or obstacles appear he loses control of the machine with only one hand guiding it. There's really nothing for it but to take the whacking. At 20 below with the wind chill lending extra crispness to already half-frozen skin, the poplar lashes feels as if they're cutting to the bone. David is certain blood is coursing down his face, but when he pulls off a glove to check is surprised to find nothing, not even welts. But the stinging remains.

At the end of the five-kilometre trapless stretch, the trail veers west and climbs steadily. The dim sun is at their backs, lighting the trees in front with a gauzy glow like the phony snow-covered plastic Christmas ornaments of the 1950s.

Now Poncho and David meet wolverine number three, an entirely different critter. The first trap in this section was sprung by a whiskey jack, an overly friendly member of the jay family that seasoned campers curse and have dubbed the "camp robber." It's still stuck inside. This wolverine ignored the whiskey jack but used the bait as a centrepiece of his calling card. "Bugger pissed all over it so no one else will eat it," grumps Poncho.

At the next set Poncho had located the trap about a metre off the ground, nailed to a tree. Apparently affronted by the change, which meant he couldn't flip the trap, the wolverine smashed it. At the next set, he pulled the marten out of the trap and ate every scrap, then went on to destroy two more traps and eat the bait. Poncho says little, repairing what he can with a "here we go again" slump to his posture.

Just to keep them off balance, the wolverine suddenly changed his gambit, leaving a nice, perfectly intact marten in the trap. "He licked every inch and pissed all over it but there's no chew marks," says Poncho, marvelling at the turn of events. The bait was eaten. At the next trap exactly the same thing.

"Pissed on, licked all over but not chewed. Make a note. Poncho is really confused."

As they reflect on the perversity of the wolverine, the pallid sun starts to drop below the horizon, painting everything with a washed-out reddish tint like a faded bloodstain. "We'd better hurry up if we want to have our gumwiches and look at the Tombstone Mountains. You want to see that," advises Poncho. "It's a pretty sight. Let's boogie."

At the next trap, the wolverine turned the tables again, biting a single chunk out of the marten's neck, ruining the fur. The bait is eaten but nothing else is touched. The next three traps are marten-less, flipped, but not damaged and the bait eaten. Then comes a slightly chewed marten, just enough to ruin the fur, but nothing is eaten, including the bait. Three more flipped traps. And another about-face—three lovely martens in a row untouched, with only the bait eaten and no calling card. The wolverine's fury apparently abated and his belly full, he wandered away from Poncho's line.

With just enough light to see by, Poncho pulls over to a large clearing and announces that it's time for lunch. The vista is very fine; the Tombstone Mountains and surrounding peaks are not as jagged and threatening as they are in places like the Selkirk Range of the Rockies, where foreboding overcomes you just looking at the hard, black faces and deep crevasses. Surprisingly, trees grow nearly to the top of these mountains. Below, a valley snakes around the skirt of the range and disappears into the distance.

David estimates from the almost non-existent light that it is about 4:00 p.m. He hasn't eaten for at least eight hours, and although he still doesn't feel really hungry, he's starting to feel the cold; it's time to stoke up the furnace. Poncho hasn't eaten since the night before, but David doesn't sense that he's particularly hungry either. Poncho hauls the sandwiches out of the bag, handing a packet over with the flourish of a waiter in a five-star restaurant. He watches David intently, saying nothing.

David hefts the offering. Solid as a rock—frozen too hard to pry open—but he can see a piece of spam, prem, spork—call it what you will—poking out between the slices of bread. Poncho's gumwiches are basically processed pork. Everyone of early middle age or older knows the plain, squarish tins with their own attached key and can recall the odd metallic taste of the meat in school lunches or fried as a bacon substitute with eggs on a camping trip. Poor man's paté. Not David's favourite but guaranteed to establish a presence in the stomach. He sets to work with far more gusto than the sandwich warrants. It's frozen so there's little taste.

"How do you like your gumwich?" Poncho asks with an over-innocent look. He laughs at the sound of David's teeth crunching through the layers.

"Fine," David responds, "but I prefer them cold. Couldn't you have brought some ice?"

"Tammy was angry when I told her I was making you gumwiches. She said I should make you something edible. But I told her if you want to learn about trapping, you had to eat like a trapper."

The tea is lukewarm, the sandwiches barely edible and the chocolate bars like Popsicles. Still, a grand meal in a gorgeous setting with good company.

"That's Bruce's line down there," says Poncho, nodding toward the valley below. "He's got one of the best lines around. You can get everything there—lynx, marten, wolverine, wolf, the works.

He doesn't even have to work for it!" The last statement is said with an I-don't-really-mean-that laugh.

After savouring the landscape for a long moment, Poncho continues. "You remember Bruce telling us that he'd been all over here in his quad?" David, mouth glued shut, nods. "He told us he didn't see any animal tracks at all, didn't he? I haven't seen any tire tracks, have you?" he asks, knowing that if he didn't David surely hadn't. "Trappers never like to tell the truth to each other."

They're less than two-thirds of the way through the trapline with the light fast disappearing. "We're really going to have to go now," Poncho announces. David's not sure what he means other than moving faster, which he doubts is possible. Though he doesn't say so lest Poncho take it as a challenge.

As darkness settles in, the wind picks up and the temperature starts dropping. David's still comfortable in his trapper gear, especially the Sergeant Preston gloves, but each time he takes the gloves off to take notes, his fingers stiffen up in seconds. Soon it doesn't matter. It's all he can do to keep up with Poncho, who's taken boogieing to a new level. They exchange a few words at each set before he roars off.

A new wolverine checks in after lunch, and this one turns out to be a pleasure to work with. In a stretch of twelve sets, there are eight martens untouched—the bait is eaten but no pissing, chewing or damage to the trap. The wolverine has casually looked things over, eaten the bait, then moved on to the next trap, apparently content with the offering.

Poncho grows more exuberant at each stop. With twenty-plus furs, he's well beyond his hoped-for goal of a dozen. The only thing spoiling his fun is a miscalculation when he laid out the traps in the first place. "I didn't see any tracks through here so I put the traps wide apart," he laments. "But I saw plenty of tracks in the next stretch—that's where all the traps are."

As fate would have it, Poncho is skunked on his next twelve sets. There's only one marten in the lot and all that's left is the head. "I could have sworn this would be the place we'd definitely get marten." He shakes his head. "Experience helps. But you never really know what animals are going to do or where they're going to be."

Then the tide turns again, eight straight untouched marten, all inspected by wolverine number four and, for some unfathomable reason, ignored. Poncho is so thrilled he no longer cares to ponder the reasons for the unexpected benevolence.

"Make a note. Poncho's happy. Poncho's very happy. You can trap with Poncho anytime."

It's now dark. Light doesn't so much retreat as get sucked out of the day. For a while David enjoys watching the fairy glow of snow crystals flicker in the headlights. The night black of the north is like a blanket dropped over your head and pulled tight. The air is perceptibly cooler on the face and each puff of breeze stabs at the skin. Inside the beaver gloves, David rubs his fingers together constantly to keep the circulation going and the chill at bay. Each time he gets off the skidoo the cold starts moving up his legs. There is no thought of taking notes now.

Skidoos have headlights, of sorts, but their illumination ineffectively bounces off the darkness of the wood-enclosed trail. Curves now come without warning, and logs seem to spring up out of the shadows. The whip gauntlet changes from a painful irritant into a horror. After the first face-smack nearly knocks off David's glasses, he tucks them in his pocket and sallies forth more slowly.

David assumes Poncho is also slowed by the obstacles and the night. Hardly. If anything, he's moving faster. Each time he arrives at a new trap, Poncho is pulling out. Poncho is on the good side of the wolverine and he's still netting one marten in every second or third trap.

The munificence comes to a halt four traps from the end of the line. The benevolent wolverine has given way to the first wolverine, who ransacked the initial two dozen sets. Every single one of the last four traps is trashed, the bait eaten and, in two cases, the marten ripped to shreds but not eaten.

Though it's starting to be seriously cold, Poncho sets to work building a snare for number one wolverine. "Make a note. Poncho's tired of this wolverine."

Poncho stands on his skidoo looking back happily at the huge mound of furs on the sled. The pile is so big that David can't see him from behind when he's hunched down over the skidoo—the only thing visible is the red tail light and then only when Poncho goes around a corner.

"Let's boogie," he hollers, and roars off. The trapline is a loop, and they're now back close to where Pancho set the first trap. Because they are slowed down by the full sled, it will be a couple of hours yet before they reach the truck.

The going is easier once they leave the trapline and move on to the survey cut that will take them back to the road. There are fewer whip gauntlets as the bush opens out enough to offer a clear view of the sky, which is alive with shooting stars. The thought of the truck's heater at the end of the trip keeps David in a positive frame of mind. Every once in a while he sees Poncho's red light dancing reassuringly in the distance.

Despite the speed of the skidoo, the wind chill and the dark, David is still enjoying his new-found skills of log jumping, pell-mell bobsled runs downhill and grinding trips up. Part-way up one of those inclines, the skidoo stops—no dramatic coughing, wheezing or shuddering—no warning. It just stops. In the same instant the headlights shut down. There's no battery in Ivan's snowmobile.

No black has ever been darker. David takes all this in as he fruitlessly pulls the starter rope, cranking until his arm is numb. Nothing. He has no way of checking for sure but he knows in his heart that he's run out of gas.

As his concentration shifts from starting the skidoo to his circumstances, David realizes how truly alone he is. He hasn't seen Poncho's red tail light for at least fifteen minutes, and even though he strains he can't hear anything. He flirts with panic for a brief moment, teasing himself with the sensation. He was ten when he got lost in the woods—decades ago, but the terror floods back as if it were yesterday.

The memory rattles around for a few seconds before David sternly reminds himself that he's a grown-up now with many years of camping and hiking under his belt. Still, night is the source of our most ancient fears and this is a very black night. He refuses to dwell on the fresh wolf tracks they saw along this stretch on the way in. As his ears shed the skidoo's roar, the bush starts to come alive with the little murders of the animal kingdom. "At least I have my pocket knife," David says to himself as he checks his pocket.

David knows there's nothing to worry about, really. Poncho is boogieing as fast as he can, probably rehearsing his midnight conversation with his wife. Eventually, he will realize David is no longer with him, likely when the trail hits the road. Then he'll stop and wait for him to catch up. At worst he'll get all the way to the truck, which is an hour and twenty minutes away, leaving David with a nearly three-hour wait until he returns. Most likely Poncho will notice sooner.

One thing he knows for sure is that Poncho will be back. If for no other reason than that the other trappers will never let him live down losing David. And in the background there's Bruce, who has taken on the solidity and reliability of the Rock of Gibraltar in David's mind. Bruce knows where they are and he'll be along if something happens.

If he had to, if something happened to Poncho, David could walk out. But that kind of decision would wait for the morning. The only way he can get into real trouble is to leave the skidoo and get himself lost.

All these thoughts flash through his mind in seconds as he hunkers down to wait. Oddly, the time passes quickly. Once you decide not to be scared there is much to listen to and watch. During a meteor shower, David feels his body easing into a languid state, calm, relaxed, like the first stages of sleep.

Hypothermia, he thinks with a start, propelling himself to his feet to try to shake it off. But when he stands up, his thoughts don't seem any more muddled than normal. Cautiously he recites the alphabet, his address and the names of his children and their birth dates. Not hypothermia at all but pure and total relaxation, a state so foreign he didn't even recognize it. It's a nice feeling. As it turns out, Poncho is almost back to the truck before he turns around. Almost two hours pass before David hears a faint putt-putt far in the distance.

As Poncho comes roaring up beside David, it's obvious, from his worried expression, he's been red-lining the skidoo in his haste to get back. He's also dropped the sled.

"Out of gas?" he asks.

Poncho feigns complete lack of concern that David has been alone in the wilderness for two hours in the dark. It's a façade. Later Poncho tells David about a police officer he took with him on his line. In broad daylight the man's skidoo got stuck. And Poncho, zooming ahead as is his wont, didn't notice. The officer leapt off the skidoo and ran screaming and weeping after Poncho, almost unhinged at the prospect of being left behind. "It was pathetic," recalls Poncho.

"I think it's the gas," David confirms, hoping that the skidoo will now start, but not after one pull. He needn't have worried—there isn't a drop left in the tank, and the 'doo won't be going anywhere. They haul the machine off the trail and squeeze on to Poncho's. David is so pleased to be on his way again he doesn't immediately notice how god-awful uncomfortable it is. Poncho's skidoo is none too big for Poncho, let alone for a pair of 200-plus-pounders. They look like adults on a kiddie fair ride.

Perched behind Poncho, David can sit down on the very back edge of the seat. Staying there is a different matter. There's no back rest so he has to cling on tightly to Poncho's waist. He can't see a thing through Poncho's back but the discomfort comes with a bonus—he's nicely shielded from the wind. Poncho, on the other hand, gets the blast of freezing air full force because there's now no room for him to scrunch down behind the steering wheel. It's all incredibly cramped and precarious. At least, David thinks with some consolation, I'm safe from the whip gauntlet. At that moment a branch the size of a baseball bat catches him on the side of the head.

They manage about two kilometres before Poncho stops. David falls off the left side of the skidoo, lands in a snow bank and waits numbly for some feeling to creep back into his legs. Eventually, he stands up and hobbles around in a crooked C shape. He assumes Poncho has stopped out of courtesy, but there he is on the other side of the skidoo twisted up like an octogenarian.

"We'll stop every couple of kilometres," Poncho assures David as they reluctantly wedge themselves back on the skidoo.

"How far do we have to go?" David queries.

"Don't ask," Poncho responds, too sore to offer up a token "let's boogie."

Just as David reaches the point of almost complete paralysis, Poncho stops again. This time they fall off on the same side, almost on top of each other. Lying there, flat on their backs, the two men groan piteously as they stare at the stars. Poncho starts it. A weak chuckle. David catches it. They bellow and guffaw and snort until they can't laugh any more.

"We're almost back to the truck," Poncho says with the dying sigh of a laugh.

"What bullshit!" David shouts, and they're off and laughing again. This time when they moan to a halt, frozen tear tracks crease their faces.

After several more laughing breaks, they make it back to the truck. No sight ever looked sweeter, but there's a moment of anxiety when the truck won't start. Poncho coaxes it patiently and eventually it rumbles to life. Now this is a prime-time ad for truck sales, David thinks idly. Sitting at more than 20 below for fourteen hours in the middle of the northern bush and not plugged in. He thinks about offering the idea to Dodge in between winces as his feet, hands and face thaw and prickle. When they're both warmed up enough to stretch and savour the comfort of the truck, Poncho becomes more and more exuberant about his catch, asking David several times to consult his notebook for a total. As best as David can figure it, he has at least forty but toward the end, the quantity and quality of his note-taking deteriorated. They drive back to Dawson in a warm daze.

Poncho seems relieved when David refuses his offer of tea. A hot bath is a lot more tempting, and in truth David is afraid that he'll offer up the last of the gumwiches. They arrange to meet at nine the next morning. Poncho vaguely tells David to call when he wakes up. It's 10:45 and only the bar is open at the Eldorado. He heads to his room, eats a pack of airline peanuts, drinks four glasses of water and falls into bed, the bath forgotten.

"Christ, who's this?" demands a groggy voice. "Dave! Is that you? What in hell are you doing up?" Poncho's incredulity at 8:30 the next morning is worth a lot. David's been up since 6:30. Not that he isn't tired—he's far beyond that. Seven hours of sleep was about as effective in quenching his weariness as the peanuts were in satisfying his appetite. Jet lag popped him out of bed and no amount of trying could bring sleep back. It never occurred to David that Poncho might be still sleeping. He expected he would have been up for hours cleaning furs, cutting bait, doing something vigorous and northern, all on a single cup of coffee.

David learns later that Poncho had a long midnight phone call with his wife, Tammy, then was roused in the wee hours of the morning to rescue Ivan's girlfriend and some of her friends from a party where everyone who had transportation was too far gone to find their keys, let alone drive anywhere. The details are hazy but David gets the feeling that Poncho is not unused to saddling up and riding to the rescue.

They meet around ten in the Eldorado's coffee shop and again Poncho passes on breakfast, leaving David to wonder why he isn't rail thin. Before bed the night before, Poncho had carefully counted his take: thirty-six marten and two weasels, worth about $1,800. By far the best he'd ever done in one day considering the low price of fur these days.

"The golden years were 1980, '81, '82," Poncho recalls fondly. "I made $85,000 each of those years in two months. The prices were really high, as much as $800 for a lynx. Those were the days. After that everybody jumped on the bandwagon. Before that no one was interested. We haven't had a decent year since."

After coffee (David's furnace was well stoked with everything vaguely breakfast on the menu), they headed over to Henry's Garage, which is as close to a clubhouse as exists for the fifty or so trappers who work around Dawson—they call themselves the 8th Avenue Trappers Association. Despite their congeniality, trappers are generally solitary people—have to be in order to survive long stretches in the bush. Poncho's Tombstone Mountains line can be done in a long day, but many lines still require at least one night on the trail. Ivan's trapline, for instance, is 145 kilometres north of Dawson and he usually spends more than a month at a stretch on the line.

Poncho and Henry had one of the few trapping partnerships. They met when Poncho was thawing highway culverts with jets of steam before spring thaw to avoid flooding. Henry, a smallish, wizened fellow of around seventy who looks a little like a two-legged marten, was the foreman of that outfit and already known as a trapper's trapper.

Sixty years ago, Henry and his father earned a living cutting firewood by the cord to feed the voracious appetites of the steamboats plying the Yukon River. Together, working dawn to dusk, Henry and his father could make $20 a day. Decent money at the time, but the work was back-breaking.

"One day I put out a bunch of traps around where we were cutting," Henry recalls. "I didn't really know what I was doing. I can't even remember where I got the traps, but I got four lynx; twenty bucks a piece. That's the day I became a trapper."

Poncho was already an experienced trapper when they met but compared to Henry he was a neophyte. "I knew how to catch mink and beaver and I'd read the books about marten and the rest, but Henry showed me that most of what I'd learned was wrong." One of the textbook techniques Poncho used was covering the trigger of a leg-hold trap with tissue paper to keep snow from interfering with the mechanism. He followed the procedure religiously, often wondering why he rarely caught anything. "Henry told me that the paper made the snow on top melt, then it would freeze into ice, forming a crust." The animal simply walked safely over the trap on the bridge Poncho had obligingly provided.

For years, Poncho and Henry worked a trapline running from Dawson to the airport. "That was the best line," sighs Poncho. He had to give it up as the town expanded, driving away the animals and attracting an increasing number of dogs.

A few years back Henry had a stroke. He still goes out on a line with his son, but he's not up to the kind of work that was routine for over half a century. Mostly he spends his time tending to the fire in his garage and giving advice to whoever happens by. Before they leave the coffee shop, Poncho cautions David not to mention the four wolverines they'd encountered yesterday.

"If you tell Henry, he'll get all upset and want to go out and see their tracks. He'll analyze it and analyze it, talk about them endlessly. Drive us all crazy. He'll bug me until I take him for a look. Then I'll blow a whole day with him poking around."

A dozen or so trappers rent space in Henry's Garage at any given time, and half a dozen or so more drop in for coffee. It's a large comfortable space, heated toasty warm by a wood stove, with plenty of space to store traps, and clean and hang furs.

Poncho is absolutely exuberant this morning but he spends the drive over prepping David for the reception at Henry's.

"They're not going to be happy," he says a dozen times in a

dozen different ways. "We've got too much fur. A few days ago a couple of guys came in but they just had four or five marten. Everybody was happy. Made a big fuss about them. It was easy to be happy, they only had four or five marten. We've got more than thirty. They're not going to be happy. Not with what we've got. And they haven't been getting any."

Poncho looks over at David. "I left the lynx and marten we got on the Ridge Road back in the freezer. Don't tell anyone we've got more in the freezer. They're going to be pissed enough as it is."

Poncho's right, the other trappers are none too pleased. Poncho and David haul his take into the garage and pile it ostentatiously in the middle of the floor. Henry scuttles out from his adjacent house with a welcoming smile on his face, which vanishes when he sees the immense pile of marten, most still frozen into their traps.

"Oh, you got some marten, eh?" he mutters, his eyes gone flat and hard. Then he disappears back to his house without another word.

"What'd I tell you?" says Poncho. "There's no getting away from it, we trappers are really jealous of each other."

At his moment of triumph, Poncho finds himself bereft of an audience. For a time he concentrates on showing David the intricacies of skinning the marten, which are just beginning to thaw. Hardly a word is spoken as they work. Marten are small, requiring concentration to peel back the fur from the carcass, taking care not to puncture or tear it. When the pelt is free, it is turned inside out, then stretched and tacked in place on a small board resembling a paddle, where it's left to dry. It takes David a good hour to do one properly. Poncho, though much faster, will still be occupied for the better part of a day doing the rest.

Bruce shows up about eleven; Ivan arrives shortly afterward.

Their reaction is studiously muted as they steer the conversation to their own traplines and previous great catches, both real and imagined. Henry returns and scuttles about the periphery, feeding the fire and aimlessly puttering at nothing in particular but with a sense of great purpose.

During the any-topic-but-Poncho's-furs part of the conversation, Bruce mentions that he dozed off while watching TV the previous night. "Must have been tired. I was dead for twelve hours straight." Poncho and David exchange glances—so much for Bruce's Rock of Gibraltar assurances that he'd be there to rescue them if they ran into trouble.

They laugh about the gas episode. Bruce and Ivan chastise Poncho for his negligence. "Any experienced trapper would have brought extra gas," Ivan states sagely with Bruce's vehement agreement in the background. Poncho is too pleased with his pile of furs to rise to the bait.

David is now familiar with the Trapper Body Type. There are actually two distinct categories: the heavy-set powerhouse and the compact dynamo. Both Bruce and Ivan fall into the heavy-set/well-fed group. Bruce, dark-haired and mustachioed, is part native, with a boyish look and manner that belies a sharp tongue that can sneak up on you and shave a piece of your hide before you know it.

Ivan has a bulky dourness about him that goes well with the set of his body. He always seems slumped and semi-relaxed when he's sitting or walking, but he too can verbally cut to the bone when he unlimbers his tongue. Poncho later tells David that he's more than earned his disposition. A few years earlier his wife, then manager of the Eldorado Hotel, suddenly took ill and died, leaving him alone with two young children.

"I think he's still mourning," observes Poncho. "But he's a great father. Drives his kids down to Whitehorse for skating and that sort of thing." It was Ivan who rented David the skidoo and then steadfastly refused to take a dime for it because it ran out of gas.

Neither of them, in fact nobody David met or heard of in the Yukon, makes a living from trapping alone, but to hear them talk it's the only thing in their lives. Poncho works during the warm months for a gold-dredging operation that has a small tourist operation on the side. Bruce drives heavy equipment, and Alex owns two huge bulldozers, which have been largely idle the past two years because of the recession in the Yukon caused by low mineral prices.

Everybody has coffee, and they've pulled up a stump into the middle of the room. Poncho, removing the marten from their traps, is the only one standing. The 8th Avenue Trappers Association is now in session.

"Pleased you're finally making something of yourself," says Bruce, nodding toward Poncho's pile with the air of someone who could do the same in an afternoon should he decide to exert himself.

"I'll take you out later in the week and show you how to bait a trap," Poncho volunteers kindly. "Actually, Dave here could teach you a thing or two if he had the time."

"I've forgotten more about trapping than you'll ever know," Bruce retorts.

"You're a trapper?" Ivan asks Bruce querulously. "I didn't know that. Have you ever caught anything?" He turns to Poncho. "Did you know that he was a trapper?"

"News to me," shrugs Poncho. "All I've ever seen him do is his moose call and that's none too good."

"If I did my real moose call," counters Bruce, "you'd get so excited I'd have to shoot you."

The genial abuse continues for an hour. Inevitably, talk turns to the wolverine, its foibles, fancies and destructiveness, each tale topping the other.

The final story is about a line cabin that had been ripped apart by the mother of all wolverines, which coated everything with urine, leaving the mess uninhabitable, then, before leaving, penned a note dissecting the trapper's psychological frailties. The little group lapses into the comfortable silence of people who have had a pleasurable give and take. Even Henry, still fiddling around on the periphery, seems happy.

After a vast, disc-cracking stretch, Bruce announces that he's heading home to "lie around a while."

"Gee! I thought you were going to do something different today," says Ivan with mock surprise, then he too is gone.

Before Poncho and David leave, they retrieve the furs that Bruce and Henry had surreptitiously transferred from Poncho's pile to their respective benches.

"Bruce is just having his joke. He knew I'd notice. Henry used to be the best," Poncho says a little sadly. "He's having a hard time since his stroke."

While they pack up, Poncho slips over to Henry's house. Being nosy, David follows and overhears him organizing a trip to take Henry up to the trapline to see the wolverine tracks. Poncho makes no mention of it when he gets in the car.

That evening David treats Poncho to dinner at the Westminster Hotel, one of the three still open in Dawson. It's a slightly upscale version of the Eldorado with some highly polished wood, less threadbare carpets and a menu a step above the scarfing safari of the Bonanza Room. As an appetizer, Poncho orders the large-size main course of poutine, which has enough chips, grease and gravy to satisfy a pro football team. It's gone in a heartbeat.

"Make a note," Poncho says with a contented sigh. "Don't tell my wife what Poncho's eating for dinner." Sorry, Poncho. Then he tucks into the main course, a roast chicken, and he still has room for dessert, apple pie à la mode.

Poncho leaves David at the Westminster to wait for the Dawson City Taxi, which will take him to Stewart Crossing, two and a half hours south.

GETTING AROUND IN THE Yukon, particularly for a visitor in winter, is something of a conundrum. Car rentals are expensive, much more so than down south. And when you add up the rental, mileage and gas, the cost is precisely the same as what you pay to fly from Whitehorse to Dawson. While David was sitting fuming in Whitehorse waiting for the plane, he called a few rental places and discovered that not only is the car rate the same as flying but each of the firms' rates are identical. Curious, David called all six agencies listed in the Yellow Pages. Down to the last cent per kilometre, dot of i and cross of t, everything is the same.

At the last one he asks a particularly friendly voice on the phone, "What gives?"

"This is the north," the voice responds with a chuckle, as if that phrase explains everything. After a time, when David doesn't reply, he adds, "We all know each other. If one of the other guys drops his rates, we'll hear and drop ours. By the end of the day everybody'll be the same—only lower. Who needs it? So we don't bother with that stuff. Makes life easier."

There are only two real alternatives to renting a car—hitch-hiking or taking the Dawson City Taxi. Hitchhiking in winter is technically feasible, but it involves a lot of hanging around in gas stations and coffee shops, situated roughly eighty kilometres apart, and cadging rides—certainly possible but hardly conducive to keeping a schedule. The Dawson taxis, actually GMC Suburbans, do the six-hour run between Whitehorse and Dawson nearly every day. They leave each place in the early evening and arrive at the other about 1:00 a.m, stopping a few times along the way.

The taxi from Dawson is driven by a dapperly uniformed young man who fills in David's paperwork efficiently, issues him with a ticket, loads his suitcase, then submerges himself into his Pink Floyd and obscure British comedy tapes for the entire trip. He answers David's questions with the brusque manner of one who has something better to do.

In the back sit three young women in their late twenties—obviously veterans of the trip, they come armed with pillows for the haul to Whitehorse. For a few moments, David tries to listen in on their conversation, something about boyfriends and husbands who won't go away or did go away. But their chatter soon blends in with, then gives way to, the roaring of the road.

The taxi pulls into Stewart Crossing right on time at 8:30 p.m. The gas station has been specially opened by a friendly, blond woman just in case any of the passengers has to go to the bathroom or needs a quick dinner of a chocolate bar and pop.

"It's a couple of hours to the next stop, so you could get pretty stuck," she explains.

David tells the woman he's waiting for Danny—she finishes his name, McDiarmid, then picks up the phone. "I'll run you over if he's not in," she offers, but Danny's there in five minutes. About the first thing he says is that he doesn't know why David wants to talk to him anyhow. "I do everything the same as Poncho," he maintains, but David is welcome nonetheless.

The driveway to the McDiarmid place begins almost at the

edge of the gas station and continues about four hundred metres into dense woods, before opening into a clearing several hundred metres across. The truck's headlights catch ghostly apparitions, supernaturally tall, clanking, howling and barking to raise the devil. They're sled dogs, all standing on top of their houses and rattling their chains with the frenzy of their greeting to Danny. Around the houses the ground is worn into deep ruts. There is no way anyone could sneak up on this home.

After introductions, David and Danny settle down over coffee to chat. Danny wants to know every detail of David's time with Poncho. He too has a good chuckle about running out of gas, before again wondering why David is bothering with him.

Despite Danny's protestations, he and his wife, Dorothy, are different. For one thing, they weren't born in the north. Danny and Dorothy were high school sweethearts from Vancouver who visited Yukon shortly after graduation in 1974 and quickly decided that it was the only place for them. Danny had known about trapping since he was a boy from family stories about his great uncle, who was a Yukon trapper in the twenties, and two of his father's brothers, who also had lived in the north.

When Danny and Dorothy moved to Yukon, they immediately went deep into the bush and set about learning how to manage without all the amenities of life. It was true back-to-the-land survivalism, something many of us dreamed about in the seventies but few attempted, at least for long. They made their own fish nets, cut and peeled logs for fences, learned how to hunt and developed all the make-do, jerry-rigging skills essential for life in the bush. Cash came from their trapline.

When their three children were born, Danny and Dorothy educated them for several years in the cabin before finally deciding to move to the big city—the metropolis of Stewart Crossing, population not listed anywhere but no more than sixty. The gas station is pretty much it, other than a small grouping of houses hunched around the junction in the road. Just behind the gas station is a summer lodge that is a historic site, but it's being closed down because the owners can't afford the cost of bringing it up to code.

There's no motel, bed and breakfast or anything of the sort, so David has a reservation on the McDiarmid's over-sprung living-room sofa, to be shared with a drooling, pushy, overweight yellow Labrador retriever. In the Yukon brochure under tourist highlights for Stewart Crossing, the sole entry is an interpretive sign overlooking the Stewart River. Mayo, about fifty kilometres east, boasts 400 people. The McDiarmid children go to school there with a half-white, half-native group of kids.

On a couple of acres in a deep stand of spruce, the McDiarmids hand-built a beautiful three-bedroom log cabin including a loft.

Like most trappers, Danny has another job. "I worked for years doing building maintenance for the highways department. But there was lots of pressure. You took the job home with you. A furnace breaks down at midnight and you'd have to go out. A lot of pressure. And a big part of the reason you're out here is to have no pressure."

Danny now feels that he's got the perfect job, working as a carpenter at one of the two hotels in Mayo. "He's a trapper too," he says of his boss, as if that explains everything. "So I go out for a few days. Then he goes out."

Danny thinks of himself as a trapper, but in recent years low fur prices have pushed trapping farther and farther into sideline status. Dorothy also works as a mail sorter and campground worker. During the summer, they run Crooked Creek

Wilderness Tours, seven- to ten-day horse packing trips, with everything but personal gear provided, into the Wind River and Bonnet Plume areas north of Mayo. It's as close to an unspoiled place as there is on the planet. David and Danny spend a pleasant hour standing and chatting by the corral. The mountain horses, hairy brutes, are shorter than Quarter Horses but with the same stocky, four-square build.

The wilderness trips have gone well, but business builds slowly and the horses eat up money. The mountain horses fend for themselves wonderfully, but they still need supplements. Hay is as much as $13 a square bale in the north, $100 for the bigger round bales, two or three times what we pay on our farm in Milton, Ontario, an area considered pricey by most horse standards. There's no complaint, Danny's just letting David know how things are.

Dorothy is an attractive, matter-of-fact woman of medium height and build with short, blond, swept-back hair and the polished skin of women who spend most of their life outside. In frontier situations, it is often the women who get the short end of the stick, doing the lion's share of the domestic work, and a good deal else as well, in primitive conditions. But there's no hint of that with the McDiarmids; theirs is a true partnership. Dorothy, puffing away on her cigarettes, presides over a calm, comfortable and close family life that would be the envy of most.

Danny, heavy-bearded and balding, is also of medium height and build. He doesn't exude power like Poncho, rather persistence and stick-to-it-ive-ness, the human version of drops of water eroding a rock. He's a meticulous organizer. Every tool, every item has a place—labelled if its use isn't obvious. Discarded equipment sits clean and neatly placed in the corner of his drive shed in case he should find a need for it one day. Before they set off, Danny creates a lengthy to-do list, ticking off items as they go into the truck.

A city type might consider Danny's ways compulsive but here, with few people and fewer services to rely on, being organized can literally mean the difference between life and death and certainly the difference between a miserable experience and a small setback. The law requires that traplines be checked at least once every five days; penalty for failure: fine at best, loss of trapline at worst. When the weather is especially brutal, it's often not possible to wait for a better day. In rough terrain, it would be pretty easy to fall and break a leg or topple down a cliff and end up concussed. Danny knows that if he gets into trouble, his wife will sound the alarm and one of his pals will come looking for him, but the window of survival can be very narrow at –25 degrees, not to mention –60, which often settles in for days. Hypothermia can kill in a matter of hours.

Even Poncho's trapping expedition, seemingly a model of amiable confusion, was well ordered in its way. There was the gas incident, but then Poncho did have a second skidoo so he wasn't worried. And he was right. The ride back was uncomfortable but hardly life-threatening. Being organized is a trait Danny shares with all the trappers David met, despite casual, come-what-may appearances. Danny's just a lot more obvious about it. And it's a surprise. The buttoned-down, systematic mind doesn't exactly jibe with one's image of the backwoodsman.

Danny is disappointed that he can't take David out with his dogs because there isn't enough snow. He is one of the few trappers still working with a dog team. "I don't use my dogs on every trapline. But I use them where it's rough. They can go pretty near anywhere. It's slow but it doesn't matter how steep. And," he says with one eyebrow pointedly arched, "they don't run out of gas."

After a pause he adds, in case David hasn't fully grasped the point, "The reason I like my dogs is that I know I'll always get home. With a skidoo it's another story."

The chief drawback to dogs is their speed. Despite television appearances in which a dog team seems to be flying at half the speed of light, they cover only about twenty-five kilometres a day. "They're like people, they're out of shape at the start of the season. After a while, they're capable of more." The dogs' slower progress makes a standard eighty- or ninety-kilometre trapline a four-or five-day trip instead of a full-day skidoo boogie.

"Lots of people don't use line cabins anymore. I really like getting out there and using them. It really gets me in the frame of mind. I like being out in the bush. There's nothing to worry about. Nobody looking at you." Danny doesn't say it, but taking the dogs gives him an excuse to stay out longer.

Line cabins, set at strategic points on the trapline, are small log shelters, usually windowless, with a cheap stove and a rough bed. If possible, traplines are laid out in intersecting loops so that the same cabin can be used more than once. The cabins usually have an above-ground cache to store bait and furs. Danny once preferred tents for overnight trips but now concedes the cabins are quite a bit more comfortable. "As you get older, you get less enthusiastic about tents. They're a lot colder than the wood cabins. And it takes a lot longer for the fire to warm them up and a lot more wood to keep them warm."

Danny transfers the last item on his checklist to the truck as if it's a canister of nuclear waste. "Castor," he announces in the manner of one who's said all that needs to be said. Ground beaver castor is the animal lure most commonly used by trappers. Some buy it ready-made from the Trappers Association in Whitehorse at $5.95 for 60 millilitres. Others, especially those who've been at it a few years, make it from scratch. The basic ingredient is beaver glands, which are fermented along with one or more secret additives. One trapper confessed that his special ingredient was strawberry jam; he was a little embarrassed it was so mundane.

Poncho, after a pause for consideration or perhaps to build suspense, revealed that he puts salmon eggs as well as beaver glands, moose brains and other odds and ends into the concoction and allows it to simmer. Normally the most open of men, he would go that far but no farther. "Trapper's secret," he said with a decided smirk when David asked about proportions and method of preparation. He did disclose, albeit reluctantly, that it needed to be "cooked" for at least a year and he has to keep it hidden because the other trappers would take it if they could lay their hands on the stuff.

Poncho's lure smelled, not unpleasantly, like ripe turpentine. Danny's is more pungent, with an undertone of rancid eggs. Like Poncho, he won't tell David anything specific about it except that it does contain beaver glands. He's even a little reluctant to let David sniff it, as if he might detect the ingredients from a single whiff. Danny ages it in a large Mason jar behind the wood stove. "One time it cracked," he recalls ruefully. "Did I ever catch hell!" On another occasion, he carried a jar of it in his coat pocket to keep it warm on the trapline. Somehow it broke when he first set out but at 20 degrees below and riding a skidoo he didn't notice until he got to his trapline a couple of hours later. "By then it had soaked through the whole coat and mixed up with my sweat. I had to leave my clothes outside. I'm lucky Dorothy let me inside.

"One year everyone was talking about skunk oil. I guess I didn't pay close enough attention because I put it on my bait and nothing would come near. Turns out you were supposed to put only a little bit in the castor. I had to move all my traps—wash 'em and steam 'em to get the stink out."

It took some persuading but David managed to winkle out a few secrets from other trappers. Skunk essence is favoured in certain quarters but it's pricy, running around $9.25 for 30 millilitres, though a bit does go a long way. Wolf gland is also popular—when you can get it.

"It costs a lot," says an old-timer, who swears by it, "but then again it's hard to get the wolf to hold still long enough to milk it!" By the time David left Yukon, he had quite a list of additives—anise oil, asafetida, bergamot oil, catnip and cumin oil, fermented egg, fennel, fish and tonquin oil.

THERE'S NOT ENOUGH SNOW for the dogs or even the skidoo, so Danny and David will cover as much as possible of the line by truck, going up the Stewart River toward Mayo about thirty-two kilometres, then cutting northeast and heading as deeply into the bush as the track will allow.

As they move along the river, they can see the leavings of wood-cutters who once plied their trade along the banks. Trees grow slowly here, and the spindly first growth along the river looks barely more than a decade old, though it's closer to fifty years. Every now and then a small solitary stand of mature trees appears. How did the woodcutters miss them? There's no obvious reason and Danny has none to offer. Things grow slowly and rot even more slowly here. In one place, stacks of decomposing logs moulder, in another a pair of crumbling shacks is surrounded by the chaos a colony of pack rats would create. There are mounds of indiscriminate garbage and machinery, the white man's unlovely version of an Indian midden.

Here and there rusting metal objects lie as if their owners had been using them one minute then dropped them the next, walking away, never to return. As Danny and David move northeast, away from the river where the woodcutters' reach ended, spindly growth gives way to stands of spruce fifteen to twenty centimetres in diameter. A section of pine is mysteriously clear-cut. "Pine seeds for genetic stock in Sweden," explains Danny. "Easier to cut the whole tree down to get the seeds. They gave the wood away. It was very big for a time. Now the big thing is morel mushrooms after a forest fire."

After creating a set, Danny stands back absorbing the scene, often returning three or four times to make adjustments—adding a brush stroke here, a layering there, making every one its own little work of art. There may be a killing involved, but there is also homage being paid.

Danny takes pride in using found materials; each trap is a testament to its locale. He crafts one cubby out of a large blue plastic milk crate he spots on the side of the road. He chops out the handles and inserts a big Conibear bear trap, then tilts the carton on its side so that the trap is upright. A dab of lure, a piece of moose meat for bait, then the disguise, a meticulous covering of brush. At a metre and a half you can't tell there's a trap there. Add several centimetres of snow and you'd never find it again if you didn't already know it was there.

At another set Danny moulds a piece of cardboard over the trap, like a Quonset hut, to build the cubby—"an old trapper showed me how." He stops to fashion a pole trap in one spot, cutting a 1.5-metre pole, 7.5 centimetres in diameter, and setting it into a notch in a tree at a 45 degree angle down toward the ground. Zeroing in on the bait, the marten will scamper up the pole, through a cardboard tunnel fastened to the pole and right into the trap.

"I got that from the trappers' course. I like to drop in each year to get new ideas. It's also an opportunity to socialize with other trappers." There's no Henry's Garage near Danny.

Farther along the line, he picks up a red five-gallon oil can gathering rust on the side of the road and cuts a hole in it to create another cubby.

"I like to work with what's at hand. If there's willow in an area, I'll use willow. It looks right." And if it looks right to him, he reasons, it will look right to the animal. It's better to use man-made bits and pieces that have been lying around for a while than alter the natural setting. Danny won't break off branches or pieces of brush next to the trap in case the animal notices the disturbance.

It doesn't take much ingenuity or trickery to catch the unwary marten. They don't learn from previous experience. Like dogs that will go after porcupine again and again, no matter how painful the inevitable outcome, marten will return for second helpings despite recent near misses. Even so, Danny personalizes each trap, going to considerable effort as if the beautiful little creature were as shy and elusive as a Tasmanian Devil.

Danny has little trouble with wolverines, though the terrain is very similar to Poncho's Tombstone Mountains line. David idly wonders, while watching Danny labour over a trap, if Poncho's expansive personality and willingness to play the game, his anger and joy at the twists and turns of trapping, actually attract wolverines, as if they sense a kindred spirit. Perhaps Danny, a quieter soul, doesn't provide the amusement value.

Only once along the line has a wolverine messed with one of Danny's traps. He stands looking at it for a while, then unemotionally goes to work building a more sophisticated trap bolstered by two snares right in the path of the wolverine's route coming toward and leaving the trap. On reflection, he doubles up on the exit snare, placing the second two metres behind the first, reasoning that the wolverine might be a bit careless on the way out. If the animal continues to elude him, Danny gets serious, boiling the wolverine traps to remove human scent and using clean gloves to build the set. Then he takes dog urine and spreads it all over. "The wolverine doesn't seem so careful after that."

Danny particularly enjoys the challenge of trapping lynx. "They're very shy, but they're curious." And we know what that does to the cat. Danny sets the lynx trap by nailing a piece of wolf hide, dabbed with castor, to a tree about a metre off the ground. "I don't know why but they pick a particular tree to scratch and piss on. Looks like any other tree to me. If you find one of those trees, you have to be careful or you'll catch every lynx in the area. You don't want to catch them all."

The scrap of wolf hide catches the lynx's attention. "Usually the scent pulls them first. Then they see the hide. They're curious and it draws them in." Then Danny lays out a rubber-padded leg-hold trap about lynx stepping distance from the wolf hide. Lynx usually won't put their heads into a big Conibear because of their ear tufts.

Danny painstakingly crafts the lynx set, seeding the approach area with upward pointing branches to guide the lynx toward the trap. "They don't like walking on the branches.

"This trap has rubber teeth. It's legal for lynx," Danny explains in response to David's query about use of the leg-hold, which he thought had been banned. Animals don't die outright in these traps but they don't suffer the terrible pain of the steel teeth in the old leg-holds. Conscientious trappers will check the line more often if they're after lynx. If they've caught one and it's still alive, they shoot it.

"One big thing about rubber leg-hold, if you snap it on your hand it doesn't hurt."

David picks up the trap dubiously and tries the powerful spring.

Danny lets it snap shut on his hand but can't quite smother a yelp of pain. "Well, it hurts," he amends, "but you won't break your hand.

"Times change. You've got to change with them. A lot of trappers were bitter when the animal rights people forced the banning of the leg-hold trap. I actually like the little Conibear better. It's lots better for marten. And the big one is great if you can get the animal to go in them. The only thing I worry about is that they may ban rubber leg-holds. They're the only thing other than snares you can catch lynx with."

DAVID IS SCHEDULED TO be with another trapper the next morning, Saturday, at Pelly Crossing, eighty kilometres south of Stewart. Dorothy assures him that there won't be any trouble finding a ride—there's a flotilla of cars and trucks heading to Whitehorse every weekend for shopping, visiting, sports competitions and haircuts. A few phone calls, and a ride is found in a car driven by a couple of sleepy young guys with not much to say.

David expects Pelly to be little different than any of the other tiny settlements in the north. Barely larger than Stewart, the town is home to three hundred and fifty Selkirk Indians, a scattering of whites, a gas station and an attached convenience store. Then, just north of Pelly Crossing, as the road bends toward the Pelly Bridge, a sign leaps out: *Penny's Place: Espresso, Ice Cream, Burgers, etc.* Things are looking up, David thinks. Espresso isn't exactly a staple in Yukon outposts. Sadly, Penny's Place is boarded up until next summer.

The Van Bibbers are pretty much the royal family of trapping in the Yukon. Ten of fourteen children are still alive, all of them seventy or over. Linch Curry, at seventy-two, is the second youngest.

The two heavy yawners drop David off at the back side of an unprepossessing mobile home set in a cluster of buildings: an old log house, several sheds and a greenhouse. But as he walks around to the front door, the panorama of the Pelly River valley unveils itself. David is stopped in his tracks by the sight, and as he stands admiring the view he's serenaded by three sled dogs sitting atop their houses.

The front door cracks open and a very short, very lean woman with dark, frizzy hair sticks her head out and gives him the full measuring-up.

"So that's what you look like," she pronounces. "Don't look like a writer to me." From inside comes a muffled shouting. "Guess you'd better come in," she says in the manner of one just making up her mind whether to send him packing or not.

Ira Van Bibber, patriarch of the Yukon clan, was born in Charleston, West Virginia. One of six boys, he and two of his brothers set out in 1898 to find gold in the Klondike. Most of the land was staked by the time they arrived, so they did a little of this and that, packed brandy over the Chilcoot Pass, cut wood and trapped.

Ira, who bore a striking resemblance to a young Jimmy Stewart, was a big, hard man—well over six feet with huge hands. Everyone remembers his hands. He settled at the junction of Pelly River and Mica Creek, now Pelly Crossing, then an utter wilderness—the nearest settlement, with two trading posts, was Churchill, a full day's walk. Linch still lives on the homestead with her husband, Bob Curry. It's a wonderful spot, perched on a high bank with the wide swoop of the Pelly running in front and the smaller Mica Creek curling around beside, giving Linch and Bob water on three sides of their mobile home. Framing it all is an escarpment to the south that holds the Van Bibber family cemetery.

The uninhabited log house was the family homestead, but it's not the original—that one burned down years ago when two of the siblings had a disagreement about whether brown paper would burn. It did, and the house went with it. The replacement home, actually the third homestead, is now a storage shed. There's a rough plywood addition to the mobile home that looks a little slapdash from a distance because it's unfinished on the outside. But inside it has been carefully and meticulously crafted—Bob built it. He's the guy people call when they want something fixed in the area. While David visited, he made a late-night furnace call for a friend and ended up replacing the fan motor.

Called Mother, Missus, but mostly Shorty, Linch's mother, a full-blood Northern Tutchone Indian, was a joyous person who lived to the age of 103 though she worked like a coolie her entire life. One family picture is particularly striking. Ira is lounging on a hammock reading the paper while his wife is industriously mending a fish net. On her face is a magnificent smile. She gave birth to fourteen children, three more were stillborn; there are now sixty-three grandchildren. "Mother was pregnant sixteen straight years," Linch says with amazement. "I don't know how she managed. Looking after the kids. Keeping house. Cooking. Tanning. Making clothes. When we went fishing she made the nets.

"Father was lucky," ruminates Linch. "The first two were girls. Father delivered the babies until the girls were old enough to do it."

Ira ran the family firmly and things had to be just so. "If Father was angry and sent one of the boys out to get a switch, they'd always come back with a club. And Father would use it." Ira's offspring weren't so much children as a work crew. When they built the cabin, the kids cut the logs, dug holes, whatever was needed. By the time they reached adolescence, they were capable of handling every adult task from minding the garden to skinning the kill. Ira liked order; the family needed it with sixteen people crammed into a small house. "We had to wash our face and comb our hair before every meal," smiles Linch.

Short and wiry like her mother, Linch sports a fuzzy perm that frames a face creased by lines of significant character. Her husband is also short but very white with a head of snowy hair. Linch still runs a trapline as extensive as Poncho's every winter, fishes commercially in the summer and brings down a moose every fall.

Linch started trapping when she was five or six, running lines in the vicinity of the house. She brings out pictures. There's a tiny child, warm brown face of a doll, shouldering a backpack almost as big as herself. "I couldn't open the traps with my hands. So I'd shove them open with a stick."

Linch learned a little more of the man's way than her older sisters. "Father ran out of boys. So he raised the last two girls as boys. We'd trap all winter. Squirrels, weasel. Little stuff. Snare rabbits. Father would buy us a big bag of candy in the spring.

That was our pay." One winter a proud Linch bagged four hundred squirrels.

School was also dealt with in the Van Bibber way. In the fall, the family cut down enough trees to make a large raft. Whichever school-age kids could be spared floated four or five days down river to Dawson, the time depending on the speed of the river. "'Why buy a steamboat ticket when the water runs that way?' That was Father's attitude." Linch never went to school but five of her siblings rafted in for "a bit of learning." Her brother Alex, then thirteen, was the captain. Today, at eighty-three, he's still the uncrowned king of Yukon trapping. In Dawson, the children sold the wood for fuel and used the money to pay for school, "but mostly candy," laughs Linch. In the spring they hitched a ride back on one of the steamboats.

The school, "just for breed kids" in Alex's words, was run by the Church of England. Room and board and a smattering of learning cost $25 a month. One of Linch's sisters, Helen, came down with tuberculosis in Dawson and died at 14. Ira Van Bibber never forgave the school. He pulled the children out and refused to let any of them attend again.

"After we were eleven or twelve, we were pretty well adults. Could shoot a rifle, so we'd go out on our own. We'd be gone for a week or more. Older brothers had long traplines. Each person had their own traps, hut and trails. We trapped everything. Fox, coyote, lynx, wolverine, wolf."

Early teen photographs of Linch are striking. She's still tiny and slender but now the bold sharp facial planes of her native heritage are evident. Her long hair is jet black and she wears heavy bush pants topped with a bright red checked bush shirt. She's quite beautiful but utterly lacking the self-conscious look of most children on the threshold of adulthood. Her gaze is confident and

261

her stance relaxed as she hefts a well-used 30-30 rifle which nearly dwarfs her. At her side are heavily laden dogs. "We used pack dogs for everything. Pulling toboggans in winter, packs in summer. Hell, we even used them to plough the garden."

The day after David arrives, he spends the time sitting around and talking while Linch and Bob play cards. A steady stream of locals "happen by" to check him out. Linch and Bob's trailer is something of a community centre where people drop in for a cup of coffee at all hours to catch up on the gossip. David apparently has been a part of that gossip for some time.

Before he arrived, there was a great deal of discussion about what he'd be like. One faction, led by Linch, thought he'd be a "pale-faced, long-haired" aesthete spouting poetry. The other faction, led by Bob the Cop (an RCMP officer), seemed to think he'd be some kind of bionic computer nerd. Neither seemed to be expecting much of anything more than a little entertainment. They seemed quite startled, and even discomfited at first, to discover that he is sizeable with a decent pair of well-padded shoulders and could handle himself outdoors.

Seeing Linch play killer gin rummy with Bob, it's easy to imagine her hunched over a lantern in a low-ceilinged line shack at 60 below whiling away the hours while snowed in, playing to the death.

"Hate cooking. Hate housework," Linch says vehemently. "I'd rather spend days in the bush than thinking about washing a dish."

Bob chimes in. "She takes off at 30 below—all by herself. I got smart this year. Pulled her out before she decided she wanted to get another moose. Doesn't matter if I worried anyway, she's still going out. Keeps a guy on his toes."

It's an unfortunate reference. "Bob tell you what happened to his toe last year?" Linch asks slyly. Bob's hearing aid suddenly isn't working as well as it was a minute ago.

"We went up river to get a moose. Get one every year. Took one of the local RCMP officers along for the boat ride. Old fool shot off his toe as he was getting out of the boat."

"Made me drive the boat all the way back," Bob interjects plaintively, his hearing aid suddenly working just fine. "Sore foot and blood everywhere."

"Old bugger was going into shock," Linch growls. "Didn't want him to go into shock so I made him drive. Had to keep hitting him to keep him awake."

Bob makes a feeble protest, but Linch cuts him off abruptly. "The Mountie's lying down in back bein' sick at the sight of Bob's toe shot off. Don't know what he'd do if he ever saw anyone really hurt. I just about had to club him with the rifle to make him help me with the gas when we run out."

David is there to talk trapping, but he's curious about the other part of Linch's life. She's both shy and eager to talk about her art. "It's the last thing, the tail end of everything—my painting." She's very apologetic about her work. Everything is "not finished" or "needs adjustment." In another life, she confides, she'd like art to be the first thing.

Linch's painting is accomplished if unschooled, with robust colours and clean lines. She likes to paint on things: real things, useful things. Gold pans are her specialty—from full-sized, about forty-five centimetres across, to ten centimetre miniatures. First she paints the pan a solid colour—she's partial to blue. Then she paints a scene in the bowl of the pan—a snowbound trapper's cabin, a mountain scene, a riverboat. In one a trapper is seeing to his dogs; it's almost surrealistic as the dogs seem to flow right into the landscape. Another trapping scene is a minutely detailed cabin set deep in the bush with hoarfrost-laden trees, looming mountains, a large food cache on stilts and dogs panting. There's also Robert Service's cabin, the Yukon cliché, but brought alive by Linch with vibrant yellow logs. Her animal scenes are powerful and authentic, wolves howling at the moon, caribou hoofing across the snow.

Linch also paints on hides and saw blades—from 1.5-metre crosscuts to wood saws with 30-centimetre blades. And these have found a modest international market. A woman from Paris placed an order two years ago, paying in advance, then picked it up this past summer. Linch has set aside a small pair of moose antlers to paint and recently she's begun painting on rocks.

When David takes a walk with Linch, she points out all the things that are worthy of painting or being painted on. She's forever picking up rocks and peering closely at them, "lookin' to see what's in it." She bends to retrieve a smooth flat stone and shoves it at David. "What do you see in it?" David stares hard.

"Nothing," he replies apologetically.

"Neither do I." She tosses it away.

The works David likes best are the simple domestic scenes. A group of women chattering and looking after children while they're stretching hides. The routine comings and goings of a household, the rhythm of life in the north.

IN THE EVENING Linch and Bob's son, Wayne, and daughter-in-law, Sandy, invite David to dinner. The TV is on when they arrive. Greetings are barely made before Linch and Bob hustle over to the television and immerse themselves in *All in the Family*, *Gunsmoke* and *Bonanza*. They don't budge, even to go to the bathroom, until it's time to go. Satellite television. Linch and Bob get only three stations with their antenna. Later, David asks Wayne if his parents are hard to buy presents for. "How'd you know?" he responds, with a helpless shrug. "They've got everything they ever wanted."

David nods toward the TV. "Try one of those." Wayne's face lights up.

From the outside Wayne and Sandy's aluminum trailer looks like any other stamped out by the millions. But they've transformed the standard, constricted, mobile home interior. It has character and charm and makes you want to stop and look into the corners to see what's there. "I designed it to maximize the feng shui," says Sandy, a short, dark-haired fireplug of a woman, watching David gaze around appreciatively. Feng shui is not a phrase David expects to hear while sitting down for a moose roast in a double-wide at Pelly Crossing, Yukon. Whatever the tenet of that philosophy, Sandy has nailed it. David is in the presence of style and grace—not a transplanted, self-conscious down-south version but a unique Pelly Crossing version. As David discovers Yukon feng shui, he also solves the mystery of espresso at Pelly.

Sandy started Penny's Place two years ago, at almost the same spot her mother-in-law had once pitched a tent and served coffee to those making the crossing of Pelly River. It's also where Linch met Bob forty-five years ago.

"I spent $2,000 on the espresso machine to show people that Penny's was different, that it wasn't just some greasy spoon with oil-can coffee." There's another little twist at Penny's—the outhouses. Other than their size—they're almost as large as Penny's itself—they look like any other pair of one-holers you'd find in the north. But these ones give reluctant visitors a pleasant surprise. They're plumbed with running water. "We get a lot of comments out of that. A lot of laughs. A lot of repeat business too. And a lot of pictures." There's a pause as she makes a mental note. "Maybe we should start selling film." Right now, despite the fancy outhouses, Penny's is basically a roadside stand serving hamburgers, chicken and veggie burgers, fries, muffins and espresso, but there is no doubt in David's mind that it will be much more one day—and all done with Yukon feng shui.

Wayne is a dark-haired, handsome man, with a slender, powerful body. His native heritage is etched forcefully on his thin, angular face. Like Bob, he can drive anything and fix anything. His little of this and that has included trucking, operating heavy equipment, trapping and hunting. He owns the only plane sitting on the Pelly airstrip and sometimes takes parties out to the bush to hunt or fish, but he can't charge for the air service because he doesn't have a commercial pilot's licence. "I took out a guy who won the 649. Took three trips for all his stuff. One just for his drinks."

There isn't enough snow to properly set out the trapline, but Linch has laid out a few so David will have an idea how they do things—"same as everybody else," of course. On the way to Linch's line, they get a glimpse of the Pelly River, a branch of the fabled Yukon River, the scene of toil and hardship, the path to riches and ruin. It looks gentle from a distance but up close it's swift and studded with fists of granite—steamboat killers.

Pale winter sunshine doesn't change colour much. The landscape is enveloped in shades of bleak. Still, the shadowy hues provide a contrast to the blue sky—an aura that brings the hoarfrost clinging to everything into sharp contrast.

Outdoors is treated like a giant spare room—things not used, things broken or outgrown, are stuffed into its vastness. When the Alaska Highway was being constructed through the Yukon in the 1940s much of the heavy equipment was too used up to be salvaged; it was just left where it was last needed. It's all still there, ghostly columns of crumbling earth movers sitting silently, shoulder to shoulder.

But when you leave behind the marks of civilization, Yukon's glory unveils itself. Gone are the piles of unburned slash on the side of the road, gone are the rusting hulks. There's only nature. David drives northeast with Linch and Bob, off the main road and toward the trapline. At first the timber is stunted and spindly; the poplar look like they headed in different directions for each year of growth. There are burns here and there; sometimes every bit of growth has been razed right to the ground. In other places the spruce stand like blackened spears, the branches gone. As they drive deeper into the bush, the timber establishes a presence. The trees aren't Carmanagh Valley–sized, but after the puny growth near the main road and river bank, they seem impressive.

Linch's sets are meticulous, every trap just so. The marten boxes are mounted on trees a uniform distance from the ground "to keep the squirrels and mice out." For an artist, there's little artistry here, but her work is clean and precise with thought given to making the job more efficient. The marten boxes are designed to fit into each other for easy transporting and storage. Linch surveys the first set.

"It's the bush. I'd still go out even if I didn't trap. One year I didn't trap but I still went out in my skidoo. It fills time in. Everybody has a hobby. It's not the catching, it's the being out."

For Bob, every trip on the trapline, every animal shot, is a trial. He's the kind of guy who's forever finding injured animals on the side of the road and nursing them back to health. "I call him

Greenpeace," Linch jokes. If he could find a way to befriend a wolverine, he probably would. "I have to shoot them right away or I start getting to know them," he says of his annual moose-hunting expedition.

"If there's a missing dog around, everybody comes here first, knowing Bob will be feeding it," Linch laughs with mild derision. But back at their house, David overhears her giving Bob hell for neglecting to feed a whiskey jack that has taken up residence.

"Tell him about the wolverine," Linch urges in the same tone she used when she introduced the shot-off toe story.

Bob was one of the first truckers up north in the 1940s. On a Keno-to-Pelly run, he hit an animal on the road. "Didn't know what it was . . . little bitty thing. Dead as could be. Picked it up, threw it in the back, thinking someone could tell me what it was."

Bob drove for a couple more hours before pulling into the transit garage. For a while he shot the breeze with a bunch of drivers around the wood stove, then headed for the bunk house, completely forgetting about the dead animal.

"It came alive. Guess it was just stunned," he recalls a little sheepishly. "It just about tore that garage apart. It looked like an elephant had been running around the walls. The guys spent half the night hiding in the cab of a truck before it smashed through a window . . . first wolverine I ever saw . . . little bitty thing."

Bob may not like the killing but he loves his collection of old guns. "I don't really need nineteen guns but I like guns. Like having them around." They're as carefully organized and cared for as his workshop and everything else he does.

For all Bob's talk about how stubborn Linch is, he could give a mule lessons in wilfulness. He insists on driving David to

Whitehorse. After a lengthy argument about whether he's going to let David buy him some gas for his truck, he finally relents. Then he sneakily fills it only a third of the way, thinking David won't notice. While Bob is inside having a coffee, David, even more sneakily, fills it all the way up. The wily old bugger doesn't catch on.

CHAPTER FIVE

WEST

THE BERRY KING RISES every morning at five to walk alone in his fields. Sometimes he moves quickly, almost marching. Other times he meanders, bending to pick a raspberry, rolling it in his fingers, marvelling at its perfection or frowning at a nearly invisible, dusty covering of powdery mildew. His eyes slide across his domain, flicking from irrigation ditch to hillock and coming to rest on a covey of tractors parked in the corner of a field, seeming to commune with one another as the sun pulls itself up and over the coastal mountain range.

On some mornings, light fires the landscape, bringing a particularly weedy blueberry field into sharp relief. Another dawn and heavy clouds with a fog frosting flatten the fields into a grey palette, making bush, hedge and bog recede. Though roads and houses, barns and sheds speckle the fields, there are moments when it appears to be all his, as if he could keep on walking and never come to the end of what he has created and nurtured.

But something else occupies his mind most mornings as he sets out, letting the day dictate the tone and pace of his walk. It is a luxurious time; he savours the precious moments spent with his god, a deity foreign to most Canadians but to the Berry King present in everything, active everywhere—especially on the land. "I can worship any place. But when I'm walking in my field in the morning I feel closer to God than anywhere."

"I live in myself. I don't look over my neighbour's shoulder. When I go out driving to one of my fields, that's all I think about—what is going on in that field. When I come back, all I'm thinking about is my home and family. I mind my own business. I keep a low profile."

But keeping a low profile isn't really possible for Rajinder Singh Lally. He is a Sikh, surrounded by a sea of white faces. And he and his countrymen are rapidly gobbling up much of the farmland in the Fraser Valley. He arrived in 1972, soft-handed, empty-pocketed and ignorant of the land. In the time it took his sons to grow into teenagers, he went from labourer to landowner. Today, with more than 200 acres of mineral-rich dark soil under cultivation, he is one of the biggest berry growers and packers in the country.

* * *

271

MOST CANADIAN SIKHS have arrived since the partition of the Punjab in 1948, but the first came much earlier. A handful of diary entries from the gold rush refer to dark-skinned Indians working in the rough camps that serviced the fortune seekers. And there are reports from the 1850s that an Indian flute player provided an exotic element to a touring American theatre company. Whether they were Sikhs, Muslims or Hindus, no one knows—to white North Americans, all East Indians were the same and invariably referred to as Hindus.

In 1897 the Sikh Lancers and Infantry regiment were sent from the Punjab to perform at Queen Victoria's Diamond Jubilee celebrations in London. They returned home via Canada, travelling on the CPR from Montreal to Vancouver. Many of the soldiers were farmers who had been forced off their small land holdings by a combination of high British taxes and poor economic conditions. They were stunned by the vast openness of the prairies and the abundant game, marvelling at the enormous Rockies with their glaciers and fast-flowing rivers, but they were most taken by the Fraser Valley, which reminded them of the Punjab's wonderful farmland.

Some believe a sizeable portion of the regiment deserted when the train hit Vancouver, which may account for the fact that there were Sikhs here before the first "official" immigrants arrived. Border crossings were informal affairs in the early 1900s, and any number could have come north from Washington State without appearing in the government record books. The first official Punjabi immigrants began arriving in Vancouver in 1900, and by 1906 the population was around five thousand—most of them decorated ex-soldiers of the British Indian Army. Though they were intensely suspicious of the ruling Raj, they had grown accustomed to a measure of British tolerance and respect after proving their loyalty and ferocity on the battlefields of Burma, India and China. The Sikhs expected the same of their new country, a British colony. They were in for a rude awakening.

The local citizenry, overwhelmingly white, were already none too pleased with the "Japs" and "Chinks" who preceded the Sikh "rag heads." The hostility wasn't just racial but also economic, with competition for work a major factor. As British Columbia slid into a devastating depression in 1907, tensions between the whites and "Orientals" escalated with the formation of the Asiatic Expulsion League, with chapters in Washington and British Columbia. The organization's theme song was "White Canada Forever."

This is the voice of the west & speaks to the world,
The rights that our fathers have given.
We'll hold by right & maintain by might
Till the foe is backward driven.

We welcome as brothers all white men still,
But the shifty yellow race,
Whose word is vain, who oppress the weak,
must find another place.

Chorus

Then let us stand united all
And show our father's might,
That won the home we call our own,
For white man's land we fight.
To oriental grasp and greed
We'll surrender, no never.

273

Our watchword be God save the king.
White Canada Forever.

Dedicated to stopping Asiatic immigration and expelling those already in Canada, the league was particularly incensed by the Sikhs, whom they found less deferential than the Japanese or Chinese.

"The campaign against the oriental labour has taken on a new and sinister turn in this city, Vancouver," the *Globe* reported during the anti-Asiatic riots of 1907. "Last evening a gang of men from Bellingham across the border of America-Canada came to Vancouver and organised a parade with the intention of making trouble. There were some 30 of them and they were reinforced by a large number of hoodlums who began to raid the stores and assault the orientals."

The Sikhs fared well with regard to property damage, because they didn't own any, but many were viciously beaten and had their turbans ripped off. Emboldened by the riot, the league gave expulsion notices to twenty Sikhs who were laying track for a railway company in Marysville, Washington, just across the border. They had a month to leave the country or suffer the consequences.

The twenty, mostly former officers in the British Indian Army, bought rifles and, as the deadline approached, dug foxholes, preparing to stand their ground. On the appointed day a thousand armed men showed up to evict them. The Sikhs' erect and confident military bearing, coupled with their rifles, bandoliers of ammunition strapped over their shoulders, and ominous swords, called salottars, caused an uneasy stir in the crowd. The evictors shouted and threatened but didn't move forward. At first the Sikh leader, Bhai Vir Singh, tried to discuss the situation with the league officers, who greeted his overtures with silence.

Then a flurry of stones hit the Sikhs. They surged forward easily, felling the front row of the crowd with their salottars. The crowd took to their heels and the Sikhs gave chase, harrying them through the streets.

ONE SUMMER, DRIVEN by a passion to acquire a loden green sleeping bag lined with red flannel, Alison, thirteen, got a job picking strawberries in Nova Scotia's Annapolis Valley. The 6:00 a.m. pick-up was at the post office near the entrance to the airbase. Every morning a severely dented truck hove into view with twenty or more workers hanging out of the back. An elderly gentleman, wearing a dark grey turban and what looked like pyjamas, drove the picking crew to the fields and back every day. For three weeks he didn't say a word to or even look at Alison. She tried, unsuccessfully, not to stare at his beard, which seemed to be growing into the hair beneath the turban. He seemed at once sinister and holy.

One day toward the end of the season, the pickers were dropped off as usual at 3:30 p.m. near the post office entrance. It was pouring rain, the kind of rain that pummels your skin. The workers bolted into their cars, and Alison sloshed over to her bike, which she rode to the rendezvous every morning. The rain came in great washes, almost knocking her over and whipping the bike out of her hands. Suddenly the bike magically levitated. The turbaned man lifted it as easily as if it were a tricycle and deposited it in the back of the truck. "I will drive you home," he said gravely.

275

Alison's mother had given her the usual warnings about strangers, but as she had blithely ignored them all in the past there seemed to be little point in starting to pay attention now, especially since she'd driven with him to the fields every morning. Besides, it was raining extremely hard. The truck drove past streets of nearly identical PMQs—private married quarters—and the silence in the cab stretched into minutes. "My father has a Gurkha knife," Alison said, referring to the traditional Hindu fighting sword.

The man turned to her and smiled. "I am a Sikh." He pronounced it "sick." She decided to say no more. If the man was ill, he surely didn't want to talk.

David met his first Sikh at Christmas when he was five or six. Victoria, British Columbia, during the mid-fifties was about as white as it got; still is for that matter. Aside from the ethnic splash provided by a small, very quiet Chinese community clustered around Government Street at one end of downtown, the entire city was uniformly pale and Christian. That Christmas David answered a knock at the door of the family's sprawling Victorian home overlooking the broad expanse of the Olympic Mountains in northern Washington. Standing there was a tall erect gentleman, looking like he had stepped straight out of a Kipling novel. He wore a dark turban and a heavy but very carefully brushed beard and held a large paper bag in his arms.

What struck the young boy forcibly was the whipcord leanness of the man and his elegant, almost flowery, manner of speech. David assumed he was a maharaja.

The maharaja asked if David's father, "the good doctor," was at home. Loath to leave the door in case the man should disappear, David dashed off to summon his father. Jack Cruise greeted him as Mr. Singh, which David thought a wonderful name. Sing. Decades later he learned that all Sikh men took Singh as part of their names. Jack Cruise and the dark stranger had a conversation that was full of apologies for disturbing the family countered by many assurances that he wasn't.

Eventually the man handed over a bag, a "small offering" he called it, filled with fruit, jars of a jam-like paste and something thin wrapped in waxed paper. The jam-like stuff didn't taste like anything Kraft put in their jars, and the wrapped parcel contained thin pancakes that were exquisite when lavishly spread with the sticky filling.

It was in the time before medicare, and the good doctor, like many of his profession at the time, believed that you looked after every single patient regardless of what they could pay. He removed cataracts from both of Mr. Singh's eyes—literally opening them and giving him a precious, life-long gift. At home in the Punjab he would have gone blind.

We didn't set out to write about Sikhs at all. We were intrigued by migrant farm labour. The songs of Woody Guthrie and the books of John Steinbeck made us wonder if families still travelled the country, sowing and harvesting. It was an school friend of David's, a high official in B.C.'s agriculture business, who steered us in a different direction. "You know," he said after a conversation covering everything from apples to barley, "the most interesting thing going on in B.C. agriculture is the Sikhs. They've basically taken over in the Fraser Valley. They're amazing, really amazing. But they're very secretive. You'll probably never get anyone to talk to you."

Once you shake off the last of the lower mainland's high-rise and shopping mall developments on the way out of Vancouver, the Fraser Valley unrolls before you like carpet, more lush with every kilometre. It's dawn and the fog and clouds have settled in, weaving around the trees, creating a screen of white and green. A good thing, too, as the uninterrupted sight of the mountains that encircle the valley is almost overwhelming after the depressing suburban sprawl. Then, just outside Abbotsford, about an hour's drive from Vancouver, the glaring lights of the Fraser Valley Auto Mall smack you between the eyes, a reminder that Mother Nature still comes second.

As the gloom drains down to the horizon, the queen of this particular panorama teases and taunts. She pokes up here and there, a purple shoulder, a shaft of white, then disappears behind the thick stands of conifers lining the highway. Suddenly she strips, drops all artifice and flings herself at you. Mount Baker. Like a Rubenesque woman she's an embraceable sight as she sits rimmed by lower hills crouching as vassals at her feet. Her skirt is snow, her curves are glaciers.

Abbotsford is as plain as Mount Baker is dazzling. The town's founders and subsequent planners could not have created a place more at odds with its surroundings. It looks like something designed by a committee of Burger King executives who felt uncomfortable with Mount Baker's glory and decided to try to tone it down. Nothing fits or connects; there's no real town centre, no sense of age or history, only one mall after another and streets of architecturally dull houses.

A number of places in Canada lay claim to having the richest and best farm land—the Niagara Peninsula, the Red River Valley, Vancouver Island's Saanich Peninsula. Come to think of it, after criss-crossing the country, we uncovered such pride of land in every province. But no matter how vociferous the contentions from other parts, it would be very hard not to award the trophy to the Fraser Valley.

The growing season is the longest in the country, two hundred frost-free days most years. The broad and deep Fraser River provides a backstop during dry spells, and everywhere you go irrigation ditches and dikes seam the land. Though the valley is only a tiny slice of the massive province, almost half of B.C.'s farms are nestled among the great mountains here, generating more than fifty per cent of total farm revenue. The valley's aspect and location could easily have been its death knell. Its beauty, climate and proximity to Vancouver, where development waxes and wanes like a teenager's moods—giddy and thoughtless full-frontal assault one minute, sullen retraction the next—might have sealed its fate.

But every now and then a political shaft of brilliance blesses an area. In 1973, with farmland disappearing at the rate of 6,000 acres annually, most of it consumed by Vancouver's suburbs, the fledgling New Democratic government established the Agricultural Land Reserve, sheltering nearly 5 million acres, much of it in the Fraser Valley. Bitterly controversial, the ALR requires an intense public hearing process before even a sliver of land can be reclassified. Though the intent of the ALR has, at times, been bent under enormous pressure, no government has dared to rescind it.

RAJINDER LALLY, the Berry King of the Fraser Valley, is over six feet tall, medium heavy set, with the brooding eyes of a Valentino. He seems to take up far more space in a room than his dimensions warrant. A bull-like power radiates from him, but it is benign, non-threatening, almost fatherly.

Rajinder's drive, coupled with the efforts of his Sikh workers, has made him a force in B.C.'s berry industry. He grows raspberries, blueberries and cranberries on his 200 acres. His packing plant employs fifty people at the height of the season and is the second busiest in the province. And now he's working on a

$40-million project that will make him a major player in the greenhouse business.

Rajinder is quick to smile, but his habitual expression is aloof pensiveness; he's thinking, weighing. He was born in the small northern Indian village of Jalandhar Nangal Shama. The Lally family was comfortable but far from wealthy. "In India it was a very relaxed life. One family member would work and the rest would live off that person." Rajinder smiles and glances at his hands, once relatively idle; he actually doesn't say he was one of those living off the family, but his face does.

Rajinder's father was a cashier for a bus line. He had a little land on which he grew wheat, corn and sugar cane. Rajinder has the first year of a master's degree in Punjabi. He might have become a teacher or a poet. He had a flair for imparting knowledge—still has—and a fascination with languages, not just the aggregate of vowels and consonants, but the soul and origins of the sounds that define a person's heritage, class, education and prejudices.

Rajinder was jolted out of his comfortable life by a growing awareness of his father's aging. "I am an only son. I became responsible for my four sisters and especially for my mother. In India there was no work for me." On August 13, 1972, Rajinder arrived in B.C's interior. Twenty-seven years ago tourists had only just begun to discover the rugged heart of the province, and most settlements were working towns with no pretensions, busy on Saturday afternoons with miners, cattlemen, loggers, farmers and their families coming in for the week's supplies and a haircut. Merritt was like that.

Rajinder's sister and her husband had been living in Merritt since 1969 and they sponsored him for immigration. Growing up in a pleasant Punjab village, blessed by a gorgeous climate with three full growing seasons and accustomed to ample leisure,

Rajinder Lally had worried about very little in his twenty-two years of life. But in the first half of 1972 he worried a lot. Though well-educated, possessing all his teeth, free of disease and having no criminal record, he had no reason to think Canada didn't want him, but still, he worried. "Then I got called for a medical. I knew then that I had passed. Immigration scores you out of one hundred. They gave me seventy-eight."

The turbaned young man arrived in Canada with the standard few dollars in his pocket and little experience. "I'd never done any physical work in my life before I came. I went to school, I came back. That was all," Rajinder says, bemused by the life of leisure he once led. His sister, who had been warned that her brother was lazy and spoiled, told him that "I had hard work ahead and if I gave up it would be shameful for her in this society."

Avoiding his sister's scorn was a serious matter. Rajinder went to work at a local lumber mill owned by a Sikh, where more than half the employees were from the Punjab. Rajinder loaded boxcars by hand, repetitive, back-breaking work—short of pickaxing coal seams a kilometre underground, little could have been more exhausting.

One board foot heaved onto a boxcar put a penny in his pocket. The only limit was his own strength. Together with his workmate, another young Sikh, Rajinder loaded wood until they ran out of boxcars or lumber. "It was good because we could come back after hours and work. It didn't matter as long as there was wood to load."

Rajinder was surprised by how much he could do with his body. He and his workmate could load up to three cars a day, each holding 35,000 to 40,000 board feet of lumber and netting them about $90 each. A typical non-union labour job at the time paid about $4 per hour.

Soft but not overweight when he arrived, Rajinder dropped from 184 to 130 pounds in four months. In his first month he discarded his turban and cut his hair. "I found it impossible to keep my hair, turban and beard clean. All day I was fixing my turban. I would bend down and it would fall off. Then I would have to stop working and adjust it. As well, many other Sikhs, including my brother-in-law, weren't wearing one. It just seemed easier."

Rajinder shrugs slightly when he speaks of this decision, as if he had made the choice between wearing a plaid shirt or a plain one. "I made a quick decision. Sometimes I regret it. But there are other means of honouring God." To many Sikhs, discarding the turban is a sensible concession to their new country; to others it is a betrayal of the essence of their religion. For Rajinder it was a pragmatic choice, physically and socially.

The turban is a lightning rod for resentment, fear, prejudice, racism—the dark, nasty bits in our souls. Even in India it forms a racial and caste line, as most male Hindus and Muslims have long ago abandoned headgear. Without it, in a multiracial community, a Sikh can blend in . . . if he wants, passing for a southern European, a Mexican, even a Jew.

SIKHISM IS A YOUNG faith centred on the family and the land. There are only twenty-five million Sikhs worldwide, a tiny group compared to Hindus or Muslims, with an ability to incite animosity out of all proportion to their numbers. Sikhs are often called, with both derision and admiration, the Jews of Asia. Their religion is just half a millennium old and based on the teachings and interpretations of ten gurus whose message is surprisingly simple. Nanak, a Hindu born in 1469, became the first guru. As a young man he preferred studying the works of religious scholars to helping with the family business. He pestered wandering Muslim and Hindu holy men by pointing out inconsistencies in their religions. Nanak blamed the historical oppression of Punjabis on the arrogant intolerance of the two dominant faiths.

Nanak did little to make his family proud. He wasn't interested in family affairs and often gave away his money to the poor. Though apparently content enough with his arranged marriage and two sons, he abruptly abandoned them one day for a life of wandering, meditation, fasting and prayer. He concluded that his mission in life was to bring Hindus and Muslims together, and that it could only be accomplished by a man of the people, rather than an ascetic priest preaching esoteric religious tenets.

Nanak attracted two followers: Bala, a Hindu peasant, and Mardana, a Muslim musician. Together they travelled from one village to the next, across thousands of kilometres of the vast country. Nanak spoke his sermons in verse, accompanied by Mardana on a lute. Entertainment remains integral to the religion. The most popular Punjabi singers sing hymns in temples against a musical background of ancient acoustic and modern electrified instruments.

Nanak called himself a teacher, or a guru, emphasizing that he wasn't a god on earth, nor kin to any deity, nor even a pipeline for divine prophecies. Love each other first, he taught, if you want to love God. He criticized Hindus for their meaningless rituals and systematic discrimination against lower castes and women. He was even harder on the Muslims, whom he denounced as intolerant fanatics.

Sikh writings describe Nanak as a man of "gentle ways, possessed of a kindly sense of humour" who embarked upon a crusade "without any anger, violence or recrimination." Gentle and kindly though he may have been, his teachings were body blows to Hindus and Muslims and his humour was a deliberate irritant.

As part of their religious observance, Hindus stood on the banks of the Ganges and threw water into the river as an offering to their departed ancestors. One day Nanak stood on the great river's edge and began throwing in the opposite direction. "I am watering my fields," he announced to the curious. "If you can send water to the dead in heaven, surely I can send it to my village in the Punjab!"

On another occasion Nanak "happened" to fall asleep during prayer with his feet facing Mecca. An irate mullah kicked him awake, loudly abusing him for his sacrilege. Nanak's response could be roughly translated into today's street jargon as: "Yo brother, if you think where my feet are pointed be dissing your God, be my guest to move them yourself."

Nanak's utterances were the day's equivalent of the perfect photo op coupled with an exquisitely repeatable sound bite. Word rippled far ahead of Nanak's travels, and at each village he was greeted by people eager to hear this provocative young guru. His notoriety, along with his simple and entertaining message, had wide appeal and attracted disciples called shishyas. Nanak returned to his family to live out his twilight years in the village of Kartapur, where the first Sikh temple was built. It became known as the gurdwara, gateway to the guru.

In addition to pacifism, the central tenets of Sikhism are caring for and nurturing family and community. The body is to be respected and only wholesome food should be eaten. Smoking and drinking are considered unwholesome. Though there is no specific prohibition against meat, many Sikhs are vegetarians. Hard work is a way of honouring God, and nature is a vital part of God's domain; hence the Sikhs' passion for farming.

Tegh Bahadur was the ninth guru, more important for the way in which he met his fate, and the impact it had on his son, than for his teachings. In 1675 Tegh was ordered by the Mughal emperor in Delhi to renounce Sikhism and convert to Islam. Either Tegh claimed to know, or the emperor believed Tegh knew, a technique that would protect his neck from the blow of a sword. The emperor thought he'd try it out and see. Before his execution, Tegh wrote a message on a piece of paper and tied it around his neck. He was just as cheeky as Nanak. "Sees diya pur sirr na diya"—I gave my head but not my secret.

Sikhism and India would never be the same. Gobind became the tenth and last guru, at the age of nine. In addition to being steeped in the writings of his predecessors, he was, despite his youth, educated in the arts of war. "When all other means have failed, it is righteous to draw the sword," he proclaimed, in stark contrast to Nanak and the other eight gurus.

Gobind likened his followers to sparrows. Teach them how to hunt the hawk, he instructed, "and one man to have the courage to fight a legion."

In 1699 Gobind put together an elite fighting force, the Khalsa —the pure—that became the cornerstone of the militarization of the Sikhs.

To solidify their unity, Gobind baptized his Punj Piyaras, Five Beloved, and gave each man the surname "Singh," meaning lion. Thereafter all Sikh men took Singh as part of their name and all Sikh women include Kaur, meaning princess.

Gobind made his warriors swear an oath: they must never cut their hair or beards, they must wear a comb in their hair as a reminder of the importance of cleanliness and tidiness, include in their garb shorts—emblematic at the time of warriors—and encircle their wrist with a steel bangle as a symbol of poverty.

His warriors were to carry a sword, called a kirpan, at all times.

Gobind was no military genius and spent his military career mostly in retreat. After his death at the hands of his Muslim retainer, the Sikhs transformed themselves from farmers into fighters, incurring ever greater wrath in the process. At one point, the Muslim governor of the Punjab ordered the execution of every adult male who had long hair and a beard. Historians, in describing the carnage, likened the plains of the Punjab to a bowl of blood.

THOUGH RAJINDER RARELY attends temple and doesn't rigidly follow all Sikh traditions, he considers himself a religious man. He's well-versed in Sikh history and studies the bible, the Granth Sahib, whenever he can. "All you need to know to live life as a good Sikh is there," Rajinder says. "I read it every day. I've read it through many times. There are many lessons there—for all of us." One of his most prized possessions is an extremely rare miniature Sikh bible given to his grandfather by the British when he joined the army. He's added a special room for worship on to his house, with an altar, symbols and bible, so his mother can worship in comfort. The room is open to his workers, who often can't go to temple during the busy season.

After his first year in Canada, Rajinder had $10,000 in the bank. He'd also managed to send $2,000 back to his mother in India and pay his sister $80 a month for room and board. First he bought a $32,000 duplex with $8,000 down and rented it out to pay the mortgage. Over the next six years, he put every penny of his savings into more duplexes and land. But Rajinder didn't intend to be a landlord or real estate developer; the houses were a means to an end. "I will work for myself. It was always on my mind, even when I was working in the mill making good money. I liked farming. In one corner of my mind it was always there."

Like any business story, there's a touch of inspiration, a bucket of perspiration and a dollop of luck. When Rajinder sold his duplexes in 1978, British Columbia was in the throes of one of its many real estate booms. He wasn't going to find the Punjab in B.C., but the closest he could come in climate and growing conditions was the Fraser Valley, where there was already a substantial Sikh community, mostly working as farm labourers. At the time raspberries were the most lucrative crop and world prices were at record levels. "I'd never eaten a raspberry. I'd never even seen a bush before," he admits with a chuckle. "Same with blueberries and cranberries; I'd never seen them before either. I didn't have any idea what to grow. But at the time you could make a very good profit from raspberries."

He was half right. In the Punjab a family could live well on the five acres Rajinder bought, but that amount of land hardly merits hobby farm status in Canada, even in the rich Fraser Valley. "I never considered all the details." He had recently married and planned on moving his young family to Abbotsford to begin a new life as a farmer. The missing details meant that his young wife had to manage the farm by herself and eventually take a job to keep it going. Rajinder spent the next three years commuting from the mill in Merritt to Abbotsford until he'd saved enough to buy more land.

The story of Rajinder Lally is not a succession of astute moves, carefully planned and precisely executed. He's quick to laugh about his mishaps, but it isn't a sheepish laugh, a regretful one or even the laugh of a man who has learned a hard lesson. Rajinder's decisions are intuitive—gut feel. He is confident that native ability coupled with hard work will carry the day. "With God's grace," he's fond of adding.

IF YOU COME TEARING over the big hill from Abbotsford, on the road that swoops down across the Matsqui Flats on its way to the Fraser River, you can easily zip right on by the Lallys' Gladwin Farms. The house is like any of the neighbours' semi-rural, semi-suburban bi-levels, close to the road with a small front yard. There are various outbuildings, surrounded by fields of blueberry bushes. Except for the distinctive mountain backdrop, it looks like many places in Canada where suburb meets country.

It's hard to believe that this is the second busiest berry packing plant in the province, pumping out millions of kilograms of berries every summer.

From the outside, the plant looks like an oversize garage. Inside there's all the intensity and bustle of a big job being done in a small space. Forklifts hum and beep, conveyor belts rattle, pallets groan with the weight of the berries, and wooden boxes smack together. But there is something odd about the scene. No people noise, despite the number of bodies crammed into the shed sorting, picking, packing, lifting. No shouts slice through the throb of the separators, no chatter, only brief, matter-of-fact comments, all work-related. On his first day with Rajinder, David stands for long periods watching the assembly lines and never sees lips move.

Most of the field workers are men; most of the packers are women. Fifty of them work at four lines, separating the best blueberries for the fresh and frozen market; the culls are sorted out for juice. There's $50,000 worth of machinery on each line—a separator, conveyor belts and a labeller. Everything is crowded together with not a single wasted square centimetre. Three propane-powered forklifts weave in and out with crates of berries; they run silently, except for the odd screech of tires, the faint whirr of hydraulic lifts and the ever-present backing-up beep.

At the height of the season, the plant goes full steam from 7:00 a.m. to midnight every day for ten to twelve weeks straight; first raspberries, then blueberries, then cranberries. And there's a month of work packing bulk Japanese oranges at Christmas.

Rajinder Lally has an ace in the hole that any businessman would kill for—his countrymen. The same clannishness that can provoke animosity gives him a huge advantage over his fellow farmers. In addition to the sheer back-breaking work Sikhs are willing to shoulder, they accord Rajinder a special authority impossible for a non-Sikh owner or boss to command, that of a father figure combined with the almost mystical, natural authority of a religious and cultural leader.

To some it's paternalism pure and simple, and to white growers who are competing with him, it's an unfair advantage incompatible with a democratic society. "Look, I've got nothing against Sikhs," rails one grower. "I hire them when I can get them, which isn't too bloody often. But that guy Lally runs a little feudal kingdom over there. I don't know exactly how he does it, but he plays it for all its worth—and it's worth a bundle. You can't compete with him."

There is something going on at this plant and in his berry fields that goes far beyond workforce and employer. There is a community here. Grandparents or older parents work as pickers, while their granddaughters and daughters work in the plant. Many have been with the Berry King for more than a decade. Every year a few new ones come in to take the place of those who have bought their own land or taken full-time jobs elsewhere.

Usually they're related to some employee, past or present. Rajinder uses four buildings on the property to accommodate as many as forty workers who don't live in the area. Traditionally turbaned and sari-ed Sikhs, modern Sikhs, families and single people live in close, harmonious quarters during the intense harvesting season. The houses are a little ramshackle but meticulously clean.

David has been with Rajinder for only a few hours, but as he shows him around the houses, he introduces him as a friend to everyone they meet. Cooking is communal, and over the long day luscious smells are constantly in the air. The cooks stop to chat, imploring David to sample tea, pappadams, chapatis, curry—whatever is on the go. They don't hide their disappointment when they can't tempt him.

A summer job picking or packing is not the kind of work that would encourage too many white people to return year after year. "It's not a lot of money per hour, just minimum wage," Rajinder agrees. "But you have to look at it the way the Sikhs do. We have a lot of husbands and wives picking, working together. Some grandparents as well. For a family unit that can be a lot of money in a few months. That could be the down payment on a house, or enough to start up a business." Rajinder has a couple of families earning over $15,000 from a summer of picking and packing.

During the week David spent with the Lallys, two former employees came to visit, a young Sikh man and woman. They arrived just before closing on separate days and came first to Rajinder's office to give him their regards. The man is working on his engineering degree and the woman is enrolled in a graduate program. Rajinder already knew the details of their progress, but he listened appreciatively on each occasion as the visitor talked. Leaving his office, they waited patiently for the plant to close then hurried over to greet friends and relatives. There were smiles, warm greetings, handshakes and hugs. Such visits are commonplace.

THE FIRST SIKHS WHO came to Canada early in this century expected hard work, but what they found was little work of any kind. Canadians didn't want to hire the strange bearded men who didn't speak or read English. After the first year, things began to look quite desperate for the ragtag group of Sikhs who were now looking more and more like beggars every day. They couldn't find work and they had no money to return home. Living conditions were worse than the psychological ones. Most were impoverished, having spent their last rupees on the voyage. Few had adequate clothing, and the chill damp of the west coast was a miserable shock. The first arrivals found no countrymen to welcome them, and no temple or gurdwara for emergency shelter. Many slept out in the rough under trees, cocooning themselves with grass. In winter, they begged shelter in stables or animal sheds and considered the dung and urine a good trade-off to nights in the open.

Then Bhari Arjan Singh, one of the few Sikhs who spoke English, stepped forward. He approached a sawmill manager and made him an offer he couldn't refuse: a free test run of a Sikh crew. He then hand-picked twenty of the youngest, most vigorous men and told them their fate and that of those who followed lay in their hands—each one must do the work of several. White workers at the mill used push carts to move logs around the yard. The Sikhs hefted them on their shoulders and double-timed to and fro. Word spread about the Sikhs' extraordinary capacity for work and especially their willingness to take even less pay than the Japanese and Chinese.

Once the Sikhs had some semblance of community, they were

anxious to have a gurdwara. Arjan Singh found a site, negotiated the rent of $25 a month, collected from the men and then acted as priest. The gurdwara wasn't just a place of worship, but also a temporary residence for first time new arrivals.

No sooner was the gurdwara in place than complaints arose about how unsanitary it was. The authorities constantly shut it down for "health" reasons, allowing it to re-open a few days later when the charges couldn't be substantiated.

Another problem was what do with their dead. Traditionally, bodies were cremated on a funeral pyre, a practice that horrified white Canadians. Flaming corpses would terrify women and children, the outraged citizens protested. Dogs would also carry off the bones and burned parts of dead bodies. No amount of impassioned explanation could convince them otherwise. The Sikhs tried to assure the protesters that the intensity of the fire would completely consume the bodies with no leftover parts. And in any event, they weren't about to let dogs make off with the bones of their loved ones.

When the first Sikh man died, an emergency committee was hastily convened and met with various authorities who steadfastly refused to let "barbaric body burning" take place. Arjan Singh found a white undertaker who, for a fee, was willing to claim the body had been properly buried, in return for all future Sikh business.

A select group collected the body from the undertaker and, armed with a can of kerosene and a box of matches, forged deeply into the forest, not anxious to be caught conducting mysterious rites over a dead body. As they built a huge pyre, a moist snow fell, dampening the grass and wood. Soon they were ankle-deep in snow, with no kerosene, and down to their last match. Arjan Singh kept his head and painstakingly slivered a dry piece of wood.

They all held their breath while he struck the last match, it flamed and the pyre caught.

Just as they'd nursed the fire into a roaring blaze, two heavily armed white hunters wandered into the clearing and warmed themselves by the fire. The Sikhs were paralyzed with dread. "Why such a big fire?" enquired one of hunters. Suddenly no one, including Arjan Singh, could speak a word of English. Puzzled, the well-warmed hunters bid the strange group goodbye and went on their way.

Eventually the authorities allowed the Sikhs to rent a section of the cemetery for $20 annually. If they erected a five-and-a-half-metre wall on all sides to protect innocent women and children and keep the dogs at bay, the Sikhs could undertake cremations to their heart's content.

AS DAVID LOUNGES ON the periphery of the plant, making notes and sampling fat blueberries, a local Sikh grower with a medium-sized farm drives in with a truckload of berries for packing. The plant is off limits to growers unless they are with one of the family members, because the area is small, equipment is moving constantly and any intrusion is a distraction. The rule isn't much of an imposition, since you can easily see everything by standing outside and there's always a family member around. Even so, this grower wanders around inside the plant. One of the younger supervisors, a slender attractive woman in western clothes, politely informs him about the regulation. He snaps at her, indignant that a mere worker, and a woman at that, should have the effrontery to ask him to leave.

Rajinder sees the incident developing and quietly confronts the outraged grower, who is puffed up like a pouter pigeon. When the man won't apologize to the woman, Rajinder firmly tells him to leave the property and not return—ever. For a moment the man stares in disbelief. Then his body turns rigid as if he is about to strike. Nothing changes in Rajinder's posture or demeanour, but his soft eyes turn from limpid and concerned to hard and forbidding. The man slinks away.

Three times during her breaks, the young woman comes to Rajinder and apologizes for causing the company the loss of a grower. The first two times Rajinder gently reassures her, "It is not your fault. You must not concern yourself." The third time an edge creeps into his voice. "What kind of man do you think I am that I would let him speak to you like that? You did what I told you to do. That man is no longer welcome here and that's all there is to it."

Rajinder scrupulously follows the labour code in the treatment and payment of employees, but no white employee pool would work the kinds of hours he needs at the peak of the season, overtime or not, days-in-lieu or not. The Sikhs jump at the chance to work extra hours.

"If days off weren't the law, it would be difficult for me to force them to take a day off," he says. "They want to work. This way I don't have to force them to rest. Everyone needs a day off. And besides," adds the farmer-businessmen, "it keeps them sharp."

THE BLUEBERRY SEASON has just finished and the cranberry harvest is under way when Alison pays a visit to Rajinder. He is frantically busy with last-minute work on his new cranberry fields, but he's eager to show her what has been accomplished over the summer. They jump into his truck and drive a short distance to the far corner of a field adjacent to the plant. Just as Rajinder is explaining the complexities of the irrigation trench, a small vehicle pulls off the road onto the shoulder of the field. A serious-faced Sikh gets out—Worker's Compensation. He stands looking around and frowning, as if examining the wreckage of a tragic plane crash. The dance has begun.

The two men see each other clearly enough, but both feign otherwise. "We'll go over here," Rajinder says to Alison with a twitch of his lips. For the next few minutes, the two men circle slowly, gradually getting closer until acknowledgement can no longer be avoided.

"Hello! How are you?" beams Rajinder.

"I am fine," responds the WCB gravely. "But we have some problems . . . problems . . . yes, problems." The man rolls the word around in his mouth as if it tastes particularly good. There is no "we" in the "we"—"you" is what he means, but it is the way of such negotiations that one always starts off with the appearance of collegiality, if not congeniality.

"We do?" says Rajinder with tiniest emphasis on "we."

"I know the heavens will not fall here but a lady lost her leg recently on a harvester," the man states sadly. "And four people died on a farm in Hope." There's a faint insinuation that Rajinder is somehow responsible for the lady's leg and the unfortunate deaths.

Rajinder shrugs. "If the heavens fall, I don't mind. Hell's a different matter."

It isn't the response the WCB man wants. "What about the PTO covers," he presses, gesturing at the machinery in one corner of the field. "What can we do about that?"

Rajinder looks at the tractors as if seeing them for the first time, as if wondering how they got there.

"It's the same thing again and again." The WCB man shakes his head wearily. "It's all on computer now," he adds, somehow implying that Rajinder has a WCB rap sheet to rival a mobster's FBI file. "That man with a turban"—there were half a dozen working in the field—"I asked him where is the first aid kit. He didn't know. The old men don't know."

Rajinder says nothing and the man ploughs on.

"And they don't know your phone number. What happens if there is an accident? No first aid kit. No phone number."

"There is a first aid kit," Rajinder interjects blandly, making no move to produce it.

There is a brief standoff; each man surveys the field, pondering the next move.

"What about your phone number?"

Rajinder unleashes a big grin. "I have a hundred and fifty pickers. Do you expect them all to know my home phone number?" His smile falls away abruptly—the dance is over. The men draw closer, glance at Alison and switch to Punjabi. Their conversation finishes with a quick, hard clasp of the hands. As he gets into his car, the WCB man glances over at the workers as if expecting to see mangled bodies. Then he leaves.

"Are you in trouble?" Alison asks tentatively.

Rajinder laughs. "Oh, no, he's doing his job. Let's go look at cranberries." Later he points out that he always carries a cell phone and the number rings through to both home and office if he doesn't pick up. And that the supervisor of each of the crews also has a cell phone. "Some of these people are family," Rajinder says, noting that the supervisor of the blueberry pickers is his sister. "The rest are like family. He knows that. WCB knows that. But he's a Sikh, he has to push me."

*   *   *

RAJINDER'S SONS, RAJVINDER, seventeen, and Raminder, fifteen, are developing like two halves of the father. Turbanless, short-haired, running-shoed and T-shirted, they look like any teenagers, anywhere. They attend the local public school, and their rooms, though far, far tidier than the average teenager's, are full of boy stuff—sound systems, model airplanes, posters of cars. But the similarity ends when they step off the school bus.

Rajvinder has a big, open face like his father's; he smiles a lot and has opinions on every subject and answers to every question. And, like his father, his friendly open visage can turn menacing in a heartbeat. Where his brother is willowy, Rajvinder is oak-like; he'd be the perfect football noseguard. "Never interested me," he says cheerfully about sport. "I played a bit of street hockey, that's all. Never wanted to do more."

When Rajvinder, who's already slotted into the inside man role, speaks of farming, matters of the earth rarely enter his conversation. "You're not all boxed up with farming. Most kids do nothing in the summer, but me, I have two lives. I can leave one and go to the other. It gives you a break, it makes things interesting. People think of farming as dull, something you do because you're not smart enough to do something else. Besides, look at all the people you meet!" Rajvinder exclaims. "I meet more people in one summer—many different kinds of people—than most kids meet in their lives."

Rajvinder has absorbed from somewhere in the family tree a larger measure of caution than his father. He's also part of the new world and recognizes that self-respect may come from a job long held and well done, but respect and clout beyond the family require a broader horizon. "I would farm even if my father didn't," he says earnestly, "but it is important to have something to fall back on. I think I will get my bachelor of science, perhaps get a medical degree. Even if I don't practise you gain respect. It's important, the more you know and can do."

His mother, Sukhi, sitting silently in the background, interjects. "Farming is good, very good," she says softly. "But it is hard work, very hard. I would like him to do something else. To be able to do something else."

Raminder is fifteen, slim, tall and shy—as reserved as his brother is voluble. Nearing six feet, he moves with the athletic grace of his father and drives front-end loaders like Parnelli Jones. Once behind the wheel he does everything at full speed and with an unnecessary but joyful flourish. He plans to be the outside man when he finishes school, taking charge of anything that moves or grows.

It takes Raminder a while to find the words to explain why he likes farming. While his brother rattles on, gesticulating largely and smiling often, he sits on the couch in the family living room mulling over the question. Either that or he's waiting patiently for the visitor to go away and stop asking silly questions about subjects that are beyond a quick and easy evaluation. "I like the freedom," he finally says when Rajvinder pauses for a breath. "It's enough."

The boys work the same hours as everyone else during the summer, from 7:00 a.m. to late at night during the peak of packing, and have since they were twelve. In the winter they don't usually work after school, but if there's something to be done they quickly step in. The boys' work is not "helping." Helping implies a distance, a lack of ownership or responsibility. Helping may warm the heart but it carries no weight, no commitment. Rajinder's sons do not help.

In 1997 Rajinder sent them to scout around for a tractor. They found one they thought would do, asking price $20,000, and brought it to their father's attention. Rajinder went to the dealer and after talking money came away with the impression that when push came to shove, $18,000 was the bottom line. "I gave them a blank cheque and told them to get the best deal. They bought it for $16,000."

Farming encourages you to live every minute in the present, though the mind often floats into the future, contemplating more rain, better prices, less rain, new markets. Rajinder loves to talk about the future, and when he does, he is a little like a boy standing at a toy store window at Christmastime, dreaming about playing with everything he sees. But he also looks forward to a time when work no longer exists in lockstep with breathing.

"My goal is to have someone in charge of each one of my operations. I'd like to sit back a bit, give some advice to my sons and watch them take what I have done and expand it." His sons laugh when Rajinder's words are repeated to them. "Sit back?" queries Rajvinder. "I think he will just find something else to do. He will never stop."

Rajinder came to Canada as an adult, which gave him a certain strength to deal with the inevitable difficulties of being different, and a sense of perspective on how the shadings of skin colour and the orientation of worship can affect your life. He refuses to talk about any difficulties he may have faced other than to say, "This is a great country . . . we are all very fortunate . . . this is the best place in the world."

But he was far more concerned about his Canadian-born sons' ability to dodge the slings and arrows of racism, even in a community where the Sikh presence is a vibrant one and protected in some measure by sheer numbers. "I think when you're born in a place, it's more difficult. You grow up thinking you're the same, that colour and religion don't matter. It hurts more when it happens."

"When they went to school, I told them to mind their own business and keep a low profile. When they went to school, I told them they should be strong unto themselves. Don't look for trouble, just the opposite, but if trouble comes be strong."

Rajinder needn't have worried. The boys attend a mostly white school where they are known to be friendly and cooperative with the other teachers and students. They travel back and forth on the bus but take little part in the school life, after-school activities, clubs, sports or even out-of-school friendships. Their life is the farm.

On the surface, Abbotsford is a happily blended community of whites and Sikhs. At one of the malls along the endless commercial and retail strip, a United Nations of players and spectators crowds around the oversized chess game in the food court. At every corner you see the Punjab, sometimes oddly blended with North America. A Sikh woman in a gorgeous deep yellow sari bustles along, her feet clad in Nike runners. An ancient Sikh man with a towering green turban, white robes and tidy beard chats on a cell phone as his grandson, also turbaned, trots behind, jigging to the music from his Walkman, his baggy snowboarder pants dragging on the ground.

It is a careful relationship of Indian and white. The Sikhs are vitally important to the area, and most business people in the area recognize how much they contribute to the economy. On the other hand—and there is always an on the other hand—they are different. "Clannish," one woman operating an Abbotsford restaurant sniffs. "You never see them in here. I don't know where they spend their money. They've got their own everything, church, food, everything. They even hire their own. Just try to get on at one of those farms in the summer. Forget about it! You'd think that what the white people have isn't good enough for them. I'm surprised they even go to school with white kids. It's like we contaminate them or something."

Despite over a decade of violence tied to Sikh militants—shootings, bombings and power struggles at several west coast temples—the mixed schools in the Fraser Valley are fairly peaceable, unlike those in Vancouver's east end, where a veritable war rages among the various Asian groups. But some worry that as the Sikhs grow more prosperous and influential, the line between peace and confrontation may grower thinner. Rajinder, who spends a good part of his life in the white world, has found the delicate balance between blending in and retaining his identity as a Sikh. You work hard, remain true to God and try to do nothing to make yourself stand out or incite resentment. His sons walk the same path.

When Rajvinder turned sixteen, his father bought him, as a reward for hard work, a beautiful second-hand sports car. It's a lovely little thing, low to the ground and obviously built for speed. Rajvinder is completely enamoured of it. The first weekend he got the car, he drove it almost non-stop, but on Monday morning he rode the bus to school as usual and has every day thereafter. "It would draw attention to me," he says matter-of-factly. "I don't want that kind of attention."

DAVID SPENDS A LOT OF time in the yard near the plant, watching the dawn-to-dusk activity of truck drivers arriving, loading and leaving. Most of the growers delivering berries to be packed are local Sikhs and many drive their own trucks. Long-distance drivers, picking up packed berries for faraway markets, are predominantly white; most of them get in and out as quickly as possible, paying little attention to the blueberry crew. The odd time, a driver suffering from too many kilometres, too little sleep or too long away from the marital bed gets scabby about the loading procedure or having to do more than he thinks he should. Rajinder saunters up with a cobra smile and suggests they consider doing things the right way, the only way—his way. He always politely offers to let them pick up their berries elsewhere, not terribly appealing to a driver from New Mexico. Truckers who treat Rajinder's workers with courtesy drive away with boxes of berries for themselves and their families. The others leave with nothing.

A few are plainly discomfited to be dealing with Sikhs. "Fucking rag heads" or "towel heads," they mutter, sometimes loud enough to be heard by the workers. David wonders how cavalier they'd be if they knew anything about the Sikh warrior heritage and the religious tradition of carrying very serviceable daggers on their persons.

Rajinder shuttles back and forth across the driveway between his small office and the plant. He can keep an eye on his operation, be handy to the phone and accessible to the two young women who manage the office. It's a central point and all traffic must pass by. The rhythm of work is persistent and unending. The sweet fruit smell of crushed berries mixed with the sharp fumes of diesel thickens as the day heats up—warm waves roll up from the tarmac in the wake of truck arrivals and departures. The drivers who have never been to the Lally farm pull in and look around for the foreman. Inevitably, after casting their eyes over the yard, the turbans, the dark-skinned men and women, they settle on the only white face, David. Even if Rajinder, who exudes BOSS, is standing beside him, they often address David first, to Rajinder's quiet amusement.

"Must be the notebook," David says apologetically the first time it happens.

Rajinder's only response is a minute lift of his left eyebrow.

At midday a rail-thin, acned driver, who looks barely out of his teens, steams over and stands before David, his back squarely to Rajinder. The man's skin is so pale it makes his sprinkling of pimples seem ready to explode.

"Will you tell your *boy* there that I'm not loading my truck *by myself*," he demands in a distinct Texas twang. "The lazy fuckin' bastard won't help. What's he there for anyway?" The trucker punctuates his tirade by expectorating a greasy bundle alarmingly close to David's shoes.

David sees Raminder standing impassively at the back of the truck beside his forklift, waiting to get back to work. He's not angry or upset, he just has other things to do. David glances over to the father, who is casually enjoying the view of Mount Baker as if he didn't have a care in the world.

"Better tell him yourself," David responds. "He's the boss." The trucker's face grows as red as his zits. A hacking snort comes from Rajinder's direction, halfway between a laugh and a cough.

"The boss?" the trucker asks in disbelief.

"The boss," David replies firmly.

The trucker grumbles off. Normally the boys, or anyone else who is around, help with the loading—the faster they come and go, the better for everyone. This trucker hoists his pallets in grim and sweaty solitude. He reefs hard on his air horn as he pulls out, but even that sounds impotent.

Get-rich schemes are just as tempting to farmers as the average guy, perhaps more so because of the annual fight to break even. The promise of something that limits the uncertainty stretching from planting to harvest, or at least compensates for it with high prices or limitless markets, is hard to resist. Some years, farmers plant their seeds already knowing from world prices that the best they can hope for is break-even. And that's if everything goes well.

"I took my wife and sons to see Las Vegas," Rajinder recounts. "When I came back, people asked me how much we won or lost. I told them we didn't gamble, we only went to look. We gamble at home every day."

Some years the banker hovers like a plague at the door and farmers know there is absolutely nothing they can do to make the books look any better. Every now and then they'll hit it right— three cherries—and the money pours in. Small wonder that farmers might be susceptible to a scheme that promises to vault them into the bigs.

Ginseng was the scheme of the 1980s. Up and down the Fraser Valley you could see dark coverings, looking like Bedouin tents on the Wadi Rhum, sheltering the crop from bugs and frost. Prices soared; VSE stock promoters got into the game. The crop was in play, as they say in the market. But the reality is that the little guy never learns about the real get-rich schemes, at least until it's too late. Either that or he never has quite all the information. Ginseng turned out to be nature's version of a pyramid scheme. By the time the crop was ready to pick, there was so much supply the price was hammered through the floor—well below break-even. The only people who really made a killing were those controlling the seed or the promoters touting stock or land.

One could say that cranberries are the agricultural scheme of the nineties—a five-acre parcel can provide a comfortable living for a family, and there isn't another legal crop that can claim the same. The seductively beautiful fruit that teases with its rich, ruby colour, then jolts the taste buds with a powerful hit of sour, has always been a bit of an oddity. Early growers were indefatigable promoters, trading heavily on Native mythology to lend romantic allure or medicinal magic to the palate-puckering berry.

One story, reportedly direct from the natives themselves, features the cranberry saving the life of Richard Bourne, a Christian missionary who worked among them. Bourne somehow crossed the tribe's medicine man, who brewed up a spell, and Bourne suddenly found himself mired in quicksand. There he stayed for days, miraculously neither sinking nor weakening. Unknown to the medicine man, a white dove had been feeding the missionary with round red cranberries plucked from a nearby bog.

The berry was a panacea for Native people, who used it in poultices and dyes and as a welcome additive to bland pemmican. Early settlers used it to stave off scurvy and "to allay the fervor of Hot diseases." Not everyone was impressed. The author of a nineteenth-century report encouraging Americans to eat more French products bemoaned the barbaric eating habits of the New World citizens, which he blamed on "the eating of too much cranberry sauce."

Systematic culture of cranberries began near Boston in the early 1900s when Henry Hall transplanted cranberry vines into his backyard. Hall had established a salt works on low-lying land that was underwater in the winter and dry in the summer. Cranberries grew wild nearby, and Hall noticed that when sand blew on them they flourished. Despite the ridicule of his neighbours, he created his "cranberry yards." By 1932, the naturalist reported that his yields ranged from seventy to a hundred bushels an acre.

Cranberries became fashionable, and the culture of the berry rated articles in major newspapers and magazines. Then in 1959, an aminotriazole epidemic forced authorities to condemn the entire North American crop, the market crashed and the red berries fell out of favour. It took twenty years for cranberries to find their way back onto the charts. The health food industry fell in love with them first, claiming that the fruit had all kinds of powers, including the ability to reduce cystitis—a common female urinary tract infection. By the 1990s, foodies had elevated the berry to cult status. From mere juice and an accompaniment for turkey, it began popping up in everything from crème brulée to sausages, and the dried form, called craisins, was touted as tastier than raisins.

But there's a world of difference between bush crops like raspberries and blueberries and the bog-residing cranberry vines. In the first place, you can't just up and decide to grow them, planting them one year and harvesting the next. An acre of blueberries costs about $6,000 to get under way and you get a crop the second year. After soil preparation, irrigation, a flooding mechanism for harvest and purchasing the vines themselves, the bill to create a similar area of cranberries tops $28,000. Then you wait for three years to harvest the first crop. Ginseng looks easy in comparison.

Rajinder could find very little information about cranberry cultivation, or at least very little that did him any good. Nor were other growers in a hurry to educate him. "I read every book there is on cranberries," he explains. "They are excellent authoritative books. And they were all wrong. There was nothing right in any of them." The first year he lost half of his vines. "It was an expensive price to pay for knowledge," he says ruefully. "But I don't expect to have to pay again." Start-up costs for Rajinder's initial 28 acres of cranberries came to three-quarters of a million dollars.

Just to make matters a little tougher, you can't sell a single berry without a quota. The industry is tightly controlled, and the small group of good old boy cranberry growers in the Fraser

Valley weren't in any hurry to admit newcomers, especially Sikhs, low-cost producers who were already growing eighty per cent of the raspberries in the valley and seventy per cent of the blueberries.

At first Rajinder was stumped. Obviously there was no point in growing cranberries, no matter how potentially profitable, if he couldn't sell them. "I thought I was beaten," he admits. "But I finally found a loophole. The quota itself couldn't be bought and sold, so I couldn't get it that way, but if I bought land, the quota passed with it. After I did that, they closed the loophole, the next day I think. But I was in and there was no problem after that."

Led by Rajinder, Sikhs now grow twenty-five percent of the cranberry crop and their share is rising fast.

"ISN'T IT BEAUTIFUL?" Rajinder sweeps his hand over the watery field. Swaths of red, orange and yellow bob and ripple in a stiff breeze. "See how neat it looks?" He stops his car on a dike separating two fields. The morning air is thrumming with wind and machinery. A 100-horsepower pump is sending eight thousand litres of water a minute into what is now officially a bog. Faintly, in the background, is the beating thump of the harvesters, which look like a cross between a large rototiller and an old-fashioned water wheel. They flush the cranberries off the vine, allowing them to float to the surface. Green and yellow booms corral them, where they sit in herds of brilliant colour until they are sucked out of the bog and deposited in a truck. Added to the symphony of hue and sound is the stately convoy of three elderly Sikhs walking slowly along, guiding the harvesters. "See that man? He's sixty-five years old. Look at his beard, it's all white. Quite a picture isn't it?"

The three men, traditionally dressed, wade knee-deep in water through the bog. Staggered slightly, one behind the other, they churn up the berries from their resting place. All of them are wiry and nut-brown. A few paces in the rear, a clean-up man wields a rake, going after spots the machines may have missed. There's a sleepy, relaxed rhythm to their movements, belying the tough, cold labour of hour after hour in the bog. From the banks, Kevin Giles, a graduate student about to become Rajinder's full-time crop monitor, watches their progress. One of the men trips, dipping his buttocks in the water. Kevin roars with laughter and the other two join in. Rajinder leans against his truck, smiling. It seems as good a time as any for a break. As the three men trudge to the bank, Kevin spots Rajinder and waves him over. But the Berry King is speaking of God now and he isn't about to be budged just yet.

God is as intriguing a topic to him as the endless challenges and confounding variables of farming. The cranberries have made him think of God.

"This is my field, my cranberries, my workers. But I can't be proud about it, not too proud anyway. Soon you will be saying, 'Hey, I'm great! I own thirty-five acres. What do you own?' How then do you know where to stop, how do you know the point where pride becomes a dangerous thing?

"God created this, not me. God created a divine light. The earth is a creation of the divine light. The sun and earth created nature and nature created everything else."

Rajinder has been enumerating the points on his fingers, pausing now and then like a teacher with a student, earnest in what he says, anxious that Alison understand. Somehow it seems right for the agnostic and the Sikh to be standing on a dike in the Fraser Valley, backs warmed by the morning sun, faces chilled by the quickening breeze, discussing God.

"When you go to the superstore they will sell you no-name brands. There is no no-name God. God is God—to me there is only one."

For at least six months of the year, the Berry King's work takes up every day of the week, leaving little time for formal worship. He goes to temple when he can, but he spends more time with God outside the walls of the gurdwara. "You don't have to do certain things to feel God. It's in the nature, in the land. You can feel it everywhere. Don't you think?" For a moment there is silence. Alison has been lulled by the rhythm of his voice, the sun and the fresh air. She starts when she realizes he is waiting for a response. Rajinder crosses his arms and stares out over the bog, giving her time. A lifetime of religion for Alison consisted of three weeks of Sunday school, one funeral, one wedding and a picture of Jesus, looking a lot like Cat Stevens, that her sister had kept beside her bed while growing up.

"It's very simple when you think about it," prompts Rajinder. "The land and God."

THE AMIABLE AURA INSIDE the Mission Gurdwara, half an hour from Abbotsford, is like a Saturday morning farmers' market in a small town—and as it turns out, a stark contrast to the atmosphere in Abbotsford, where a clash that day between fundamentalists and moderates results in a stabbing. Rajinder chose the Mission temple because he feared a confrontation was imminent.

There is segregation inside the temple but it seems to be a comfortable division between men and women and not absolute; some couples and families sit together. They all remove their shoes and cover their hair. Cloth handkerchiefs are provided for those who don't bring their own.

David catches himself staring at the vibrant hues of the women's saris as he might during a chance encounter with a flock of butterflies in a field. The colours are glorious and the sight of a group of them chatting together lifts the spirits. It's a stark contrast to Christian churches where sober shades make the whole business of paying homage to God flattening before you even walk in the door.

The Sikh men are lithe and upright, even the most elderly. They walk with unusual pride and athleticism. The women seem far more beautiful than they should be. Perhaps it is the surroundings or the healthy warmth of their skin tones but everyone is imbued by a kind of glow. David wonders if they feel it or if it is just the observation of a stranger.

They walk into the area of worship, stopping to bow in front of the altar. It's a tradition that has grown up over time rather than one that has been prescribed. A few days earlier, David had asked a cheerful, gnarled old Sikh gentleman if he should bow. "If you feel respect for the religion, bow. If you don't, don't," he smiled broadly. "No one will use their dagger on you."

The altars are more or less ornate, depending on the temple, but they all contain the basic symbols of the Sikh religion— swords, kirpan and deadly metal throwing circles—legacies of the tenth guru. At the front of the altar is a long wooden box where donations are placed after the service—the donations support all the efforts of the temple. The Abbotsford temple brings in about $100,000 a month, while the Surrey temple raises approximately $60,000. Some Sikhs point to those two healthy figures as motivation for the recent disruptions at the temples—control of the money, not service to God or devotion to the Punjab.

Behind the altar is a raised area where the Granth Sahib rests; the huge bible contains more than six thousand verses. It is a revered item, handled carefully and treated with respect. Each night it is put to bed to "rest" until 5:00 a.m. Sometimes the bed is very elaborate, with brass head rails and frilly, gaudily coloured wraps making it look like a nursery where a pampered baby is being put to sleep. "I don't have any time for that," Rajinder admits. "It's pure ignorance, but it's not hurting anyone, so it doesn't matter."

The service begins with the priest reading sections from the Granth Sahib. It is an unusual pleasure to listen to a sermon in a language you don't understand. You concentrate on the cadence and flow, trying to sense meaning from emphasis and tone. Not having to absorb lessons or information leaves you free to contemplate the people and surroundings. There's also music and singing, the voices lyrical and rich in the rolling Punjabi tongue.

As integral as the land and nature are to the Sikh religion, so the kitchen is to the gurdwara. After the service, a meal is served and anyone from the community is welcome. Every temple has entrances at all four points of the compass to symbolize its openness. If you join them for a meal, you'll leave with a stomach full of Punjabi food at it's most basic. No one brings fancy food to the temple, so the humblest worshipper with the plainest offering is on the same footing as the richest.

In the dawn of the religion, chairs were forbidden in the gurdwara because there wasn't enough money to buy them for everyone, and it was important that no one be seated while others are eating on the ground. It was simply an issue of equality. Kitchens in Canadian gurdwaras have always had chairs. "I still believe in the traditions, or more specifically the intent of the traditions, but I don't want to go back five hundred years," says Rajinder bluntly. "When I go to temple I sit in a chair."

* * *

ONLY A FEW CAUCASIANS work in Rajinder's various operations. One of them is Tom Stearns, a short, wiry, emotional spark plug of an Englishman with a boyish demeanour. He spends ten weeks or so a year with Rajinder and the rest as a sales executive with his primary employer, B.C. Tree Fruits, which is owned by the four largest Okanagan packers and has branched out in recent years from apples, the main Okanagan crop, to handle berries. The organization serves as a marketing conduit, using its vast contacts, experience, clout and customer base to sell berries, in return for a commission and off-season employment for people who might have to be laid off otherwise.

Stearns grew up in London, steeped in the stereotypes and prejudices against East Indians, especially Sikhs. He called them Pakis, thought they put butter in their hair and believed they didn't wash regularly. "I'm embarrassed to think about it," he admits.

The Lallys extended what they considered normal hospitality to Stearns. "The astonishing thing is that I've been accepted as part of the family from day one and I don't think any other culture would do that. For sure no Canadian would do that."

"Rajinder has such a standing in the Sikh community here that for many all he has to do is suggest something and they will do it. Many come to him for guidance. He's like their father. He looks after them. I've never even seen a hint of anger from him." Stearns laughs a little sheepishly. "At first, because I didn't understand the language, I thought they were mad at each other all the time!

"I've never seen harder working people. I've been in a lot of packing plants and I've never seen anything like it. No complaints, no tension. No one's late. No one carries on. No talking. We had some white kids work here when I first started. They didn't last two days. I myself wouldn't work seventeen to eighteen hours

312

a day. But when you work as a family, it makes a difference. The family is everything, and everyone seems to be directed to the family prospering as a whole."

A typical day for Stearns in his Kelowna office would run from 8:00 to 4:15. At Lally's he stretches it to 6:00 p.m. "I feel guilty when I leave."

Another white man in Rajinder's operation is Jack Wessel, who was general manager of the B.C. Federation of Agriculture for twenty-five years. He has no official title, but Rajinder frequently refers to him as "my partner," though he has no financial interest in the company. The best way to describe Jack's role is *consigliere*, an advisor.

If you had to sum up Jack Wessel in one word, it would be wily. Rajinder watched Jack for many years and was impressed with his ability to effortlessly sashay and sidestep his way through the bureaucratic labyrinth.

Like many entrepreneurs, Rajinder isn't a natural detail man. Jack is master in that realm. He's not comfortable unless all the *t*'s are crossed and *i*'s dotted. Jack has no problem cutting a corner if it means extra profit or the solution to a problem, as long as it doesn't create worse problems down the road. But he's quick to point out that such corner cutting is possible only because the *i*'s and *t*'s are taken care of.

Another important function Jack performs is providing a white face when a dark one will stand out, which happens more often as Rajinder's dreams get more ambitious. Rajinder is a congenial, interesting man who strives to blend in even to the extent of taking an occasional drink. "But don't ever let him pour you a drink," warns Jack. "Christ! He doesn't know the difference between the mix and the alcohol. After one of Rajinder's drinks, you won't be walking away, I can tell you that." But there are places where no amount of congeniality and ability will provide an entrée.

Jack tries to protect Rajinder from the pitfalls of his dreams, which, if he follows his trusted seat-of-the-pants formula, could break the Berry King. The two million kilograms of fruit that go into his packing plant and come out packed for market make him the second-largest and lowest-cost packer in the province. But he's at capacity, and then some. The only way that he could crank out a single extra kilogram of berries would be to engineer another few hours of daylight.

The efficiency of his operation has become Rajinder's conundrum. Pushing his plant, his employees, family and equipment to capacity is extremely profitable—so profitable that it's tempting to let change fall farther and farther back on the agenda. Being a low-cost producer allows Rajinder to penetrate markets that competitors can't get near. He takes great pride in being able to make a profit shipping blueberries to Minnesota, the largest producer of the berry worldwide.

But the Berry King is bursting at the seams. The yards aren't big enough to provide adequate storage, so he's always doing an elaborate dance, moving containers of packaging around constantly in order to get at one thing or another. With little storage, they often run short of packing materials.

The dream is a $40-million state-of-the-art greenhouse and packing plant, designed to provide fresh sweet peppers to Vancouver and the rest of the Pacific Northwest. The risks are huge. To get the financing, Rajinder is using his entire existing operation, worth approximately $6.5 million, as collateral. If the plan works, he'll branch out with another greenhouse in northern California, so he can supply the market year round. If the figures hold up, he will repay the loan in five years, with a thirty to forty per cent return thereafter.

It's the *ifs* that worry Jack, a self-described born worrier. He takes Alison for a drive to show her the rest of Rajinder's fields and stops abruptly at the edge of one planted with blueberries. "Rajinder and I have this raging argument about weeds." He peers at one bush. "I know you've got to control them but I worry about what that chemical stuff is doing to the bushes."

"What does he say?" asks Alison.

Jack frowns. "He tells me not to worry!"

When Jack agreed to come and work with Rajinder, he was excited about the entrepreneurial opportunity. "My job was quite stressful. You're trying to represent the industry, but it's hard to make changes. You may know what's good for the industry, but you can't do it. I told Rajinder I want to enjoy life more and work less." He snorts. "So the first morning he phones me at six o'clock and says how come you're not here! I nearly had a heart attack. I had no idea about his hours. He covered it up nicely."

He drives south toward some raspberry fields on the gravelly "bench" land that Rajinder leases close to the border. "This guy's a donkey." He gestures at one rundown farm. "If blueberries are ninety cents, he wants a dollar. Oh, I've got to get some gas," he mutters looking at the dial. "Rajinder and I own a small plane and I filled it up this morning. Cost me eighty-five cents a litre. I nearly had a heart attack!"

Part of Jack's job is to troubleshoot the financing of Rajinder's expansion. "Farmers have really shot themselves in the foot. They'll sell land and because Dad paid ten bucks an acre they're happy with forty. But you've got to look at it differently. What is the land's real value? I don't care what the land next door is worth or what you paid for it. What can it generate? The average land price might indicate your farm is worth two million, but I think it's worth four and a half million if it can earn the income. That's what you've got to lay out to investors. Can it generate the income?"

He swings into one gas station but pulls out when he sees the price. "Fifty-four cents! Yesterday it was fifty-two! We'll get a better price.

"Rajinder is always crying like crazy about his taxes. I like that. I tell him my goal is to hear your taxes are too high. Then your land's valued at what it's worth."

Two more gas stations, and the warning light has been flickering for some time. Jack drives along Zero Avenue, which separates the United States and Canada. "I really get a kick out of coming here in the summer," says Jack. "At lunchtime everybody stops to eat. On one side of the road it's all Mexicans eating tacos and things like that. On the other side of the road it's all Indians eating their food."

After four gas stations Jack gives up and pays fifty-four cents a litre. "At least they serve you for that," he grumbles. "The trick about farming is you've got to make it more profitable. With Rajinder's greenhouse plan we're not just building a farm, we're building a business."

On the way back to Rajinder's, Jack suddenly asks, "Rajinder ever tell you about the dog?" Alison shakes her head. "Well, this just shows you what I've got to deal with." Jack goes on to tell of a stray dog that wandered onto the farm and stayed. "It just moved right in and the boys are feeding it, so of course it's not going anywhere. It's having a good time!

"Late one evening, around Christmas, Raminder was helping a truck back into the yard when a car whipped around it and hit the dog. Raminder, who loved the dog, was distraught, but the animal had disappeared, so Rajinder went out with a flashlight and searched but couldn't find the dog. Two days later the battered animal dragged itself into the yard. Rajinder wrapped a blanket around the poor creature and took it to the vet. The dog was a mess, broken this and that, really serious. Better to put him away. It was going to cost $2,000 to fix it."

The next day Jack went to the farm and everyone was happy. "Please tell me you didn't say fix the dog," Jack pleaded. Rajinder just smiled. "Why would you do that? We have no money! It's a stray dog!" For two months the family nursed the dog back to health and it now has a place of pride in the yard. Jack rolls his eyes. "It cost $1,800. I can't stand dogs!" Then he sighs, "But that's Rajinder for you."

THE LALLYS LIVE IN THE HEART of Canada's little Punjab; it's where the majority of Sikhs who want to work the land have chosen to live. Less than half an hour farther west another Sikh family, the Bains, have carved a place on the land. Where most other Sikhs today farm berries and market crops, they have milking cows. Where most Sikhs have gravitated toward a community of their own, they have chosen the relative isolation of a town populated by whites and native Indians.

THE AUCTION BARN on the highway between Abbotsford and Chilliwack has the look and feel of a carny convention. It's gloomy and grubby but hopping. Against a background of bawling, mewling and mooing, farmers hail each other, stop by stalls and holding pens for a chat, all the while eyeing what's available for sale.

"Hey Fred, what kind of junk are ya unloading today?" a man hollers across the concrete alleyway. "Son of a bitch, May, I keep hoping you're gonna leave this guy and settle down with some quality!"

May pulls at her over-black hair, left ten minutes too long on the perm rods. "You making an offer, Donnie?" she queries in a voice with the volume and pitch of a tugboat whistle. Donnie grins and ducks his head, his "over-my-dead-body" expression clear to everyone but May.

A striking woman, tall and glamorous, with highly polished talons and a cascade of red-gold hair bobbing down her back, walks pouting behind a young Fabio lookalike with skin-tight Roper jeans that leave little to the imagination, gratifyingly so, judging by the smile on May's face when he passes. The pair are wearing matching blue and black cowboy boots with the kind of rippled, pocked leather that could only come from the hide of an alligator.

Hard on the heels of the chic couple, a family shambles in dressed like hobos, stetsons bleeding oily stains halfway up the crowns, plaid shirts untucked, beards poorly trimmed and ancient boots ready to give out at the seams. The mother, thin and grey with a well-sucked cigarette butt attached to her lip, is encased in polyester knit. Despite the warm fall day, it's tomblike inside the hall. "Go git yer mother her jacket," the father orders one of the sons. He slouches off to the parking lot, stops beside a rusted Ford pick-up and fumbles for his keys. Keys found, he turns and opens the door of the next vehicle, a Mafia-black, late-model Mercedes.

Gurdeep Singh Bains—Gurts to his friends—breezes in. Well over six feet, with handsome, virile looks, he doesn't half stand

318

out in his bomber hockey jacket and dark blue turban—the colour favoured by Sikh warriors.

Gurts was up at dawn ploughing a field near his house. The long, slow, gorgeous fall is about to end and rain is on the way. He's been ploughing like a fiend for several days, trying to get the last of the fields turned over before mud overwhelms everything. Just before eleven, he flew into the house, making the kind of noise a hungry kid would after a little league game, flung himself onto a bench seat in the small kitchen and began shovelling food. Sarbjit, his Malaysian wife of six months, is as serene as Gurts is energetic. She filled his plate several times, marvelling at his capacity.

"Have you ever seen anything like it?" she asked Alison softly, not troubling to disguise her pride.

"Let's go!" Gurts shouted as the last forkful disappeared, hauling on his jacket before he'd finished chewing.

Gurts drives with the same intensity as he eats and ploughs. "Look at that!" he growls as a big sedan pulls out leisurely in front of him. "Some people just want to get themselves killed." It seemed to take only minutes to arrive at the livestock auction yard twenty kilometres down the highway.

The parking lot is starting to fill up when Gurts drives in. Every manner of truck is there, from downtrodden workhorses on up to diesel double-wheelers with massive chrome bumpers, gooseneck connections and cushy leather-seated cabs. "The nice ones belong to dealers," explains Gurts. "If you're ever at an auction and a dealer starts bidding on a cow, just quit. They start jacking the price up back and forth between them, and if you're in there suddenly they stop and you get stuck paying thousands for something worth a hundred bucks."

The auction ring is surprisingly small, with steeply banked benches in a semi-circle around a sand pen. Gurts's long legs propel him up the stairs two steps at a time to find a seat halfway up. His is a single turbaned head in a sea of stetsons and baseball caps.

"First thing you've got to find out is what's wrong," he instructs Alison. "If they're good cows, why are they here? Maybe they kick. Maybe they can't have calves any more."

The first cow charges into the ring, scooting madly around the perimeter as if trying to evade a deadly predator. "December 7, '97, freshed, bred September 17th, due June '99," intones the auctioneer. Cows need a holiday from the work of being milked twice a day. Freshed means a cow has just had a calf and is ready to be milked again. The auctioneer lists her milk output for the last three months. "July, 34.4 kilos; August, 27.7; September, 25.9. Okay ladies and gentlemen, she's a fine one." And away he goes in the auctioneer patter.

Gurts shakes his head. "Look at her bag. She's heavy in the front, light in back. You want the bag even, 'cause when you milk her the machine will start making noise and short out. That all takes time to fix, and if you've got a hundred cows you don't want to be messing around with one."

Gurts leans forward, elbows on knees, following the bidding intently. The price climbs and climbs and with each new bid he clucks, "Jeez, I should have brought some cows in. Look at the prices!"

A small group of dairy farmers sitting a few tiers down are also watching the bidding closely. They are from Point Roberts, the tiny bit of America stuck on the end of Delta just outside Vancouver. They are here to pick up six replacement cows—good milkers to see them through the next few months. They've come from an auction the day before in Washington State where "cows with two teats fer chrissakes" were going for the same price as those selling in Abbotsford. The U.S. dollar makes buying here infinitely more desirable. They are arguing mildly among themselves as the bidding progresses. The cow with the lopsided bag eludes them.

"Shit! Goddamn it, Dwight. I tole you ta take her up ta $250." The man's wife prods him hard. "Watch your mouth, Gerry, there's a priest or somethin' behind us." They stop bickering for a moment and steal a look at Gurts, who is oblivious.

"See this one?" Gurts points to a cow just entering the ring. "Her teats are sticking out to the side. When she freshes again she'll get mastitis." The Point Roberts gang bid determinedly and in twenty seconds become owners of the cow with teats like wings.

At that moment Gurts's parents, Darshan and Giani Joginder Singh Bains, arrive—sweep in is more like it. A few heads nod in friendly greeting. Mr. Bains acknowledges them with a cursory wave. Darshan is a tiny woman. Though frail and bent with arthritis, she walks with regal grace, tossing off a queenly smile to those she recognizes.

A hornet buzz of discontent stirs in one corner.

"I always pray he won't show up," groans Harvey, a regular, who wears shrewdness like an overcoat. "When I see that turban coming round the corner I think, oh christ, no deals today. He's screwed up more things I've had going than I can tell you. That man can spot a broken bolt a mile away. Maybe it's an Indian thing, I dunno, but he can look at a piece of equipment and just seems to know."

"I think it's creepy," pipes up his companion, who resembles Mickey's friend Goofy, but shorter. "You see him start bidding and people quit. They don't want to go against him or something."

"Nah, he's just smart. Smarter than us, I bet. I never seen him take a loss on nothin'."

Most Tuesdays, Thursdays and Fridays, Mr. Bains sets out for either the Abbotsford or Chilliwack auctions. Often he merely watches, storing information away for later use.

"It's an art, really," observes Darshan. "You need a sense of people to do well at an auction. You need to know how they bid, what they bid on, all of that. You've got to know psychology. Mr. Bains is pretty good at it." She grins broadly at the understatement.

Gurts attends when he can. He loves the action and is frequently bemused by his father's wheeling and dealing. "Dad just loves to deal. I don't know what he'd do if he couldn't strike a deal over something."

Though his father could probably write the book on the art of dealing, he left his son alone to make his own mistakes. "Once I came to an auction and bought three cows. I got them home and I discovered they all had mastitis. Every single one! Can you beat that? How stupid! So I was just in a panic. Anyway I went to the farmer and he gave me my money back. Lots wouldn't. Boy, I was lucky." The lucky part is not that he got the money back but that he did it before his father discovered his blunder. There wouldn't have been trouble, a trip to the woodshed or anything like that. His father might even have laughed, enjoying the fact that his son still had much to learn. Gurts preferred that such amusement come at someone else's expense.

Darshan can't climb the steep stairs to join Gurts and Alison so she stands at ringside with her husband. Mr. Bains doesn't appear to be paying any attention as the cows come and go and the patter rises and falls with each one. He seems far more interested in the people in the stands, the dirt on the floor and the flies crawling along the ring supports. But every now and then his eyes flick to a cow on parade. By the end of the session, he can list off the price of every one, how much too much the successful bidder paid and why that particular cow was worth less than half.

This day Mr. Bains buys nothing, but there are plenty of other days. David, who's interested in such things, spent several pleasant hours discussing what he's picked up recently on those other days—three tractors, a twelve-ton closed-box truck, a couple of trailers, various bits of farm machinery—about $500,000 worth, Gurts estimates. "Of course, he didn't pay anything like that for them."

Mr. Bains describes every deal, what he thought the item would go for, what he actually paid for it and what's wrong with it, if anything. One of the tractors he got for about ten cents on the dollar simply had a loose bolt in the undercarriage. "I crawled underneath and saw it. The rattling scared the other bidders away. They didn't crawl underneath."

Mr. Bains calls his auction finds, enough to stock a small farm equipment dealership, "inventory." Most of it he will never use personally, but a tractor just might be the sweetener in one of his land deals.

CHILLIWACK SEEMS CARVED out of the Cascade Mountains surrounding it. On dull winter afternoons the shadows close in and a mist of foreboding invades the intimate streets of downtown. It looks and feels like a working town that has held on to the personalities of the great characters who have passed through: the miners, cattlemen, fortune seekers, adventurers—not a few of whom have lost their lives scaling the mountains or shooting the boiling rapids—loggers and Native people who have lived off the Fraser and Chilliwack rivers for centuries.

In years gone by, most visitors whistled on past Chilliwack, pausing only to marvel at the stunning vistas at all points of the compass, especially the rock faces that loom over the town. On they went down the highway, exiting near Bridal Falls, hopping across the Fraser and coming to rest at the venerable Harrison Hot Springs, until the mid-sixties a beloved family resort and a favourite destination for newlyweds. But by the 1970s it had become an aging dowager whose wardrobe was long past its prime.

Tourists are now discovering Chilliwack in its own right, prompting some tarting up of the fine old buildings downtown. But all the Mountain Equipment Co-op hiking gear, twenty-one-speed chrome alloy–framed bikes and Gore-Tex kayaking outfits can't disguise its real nature. Chilliwack is a town with a personality still powerfully linked to its past and a character dominated by people with stories to tell and secrets to hold. Try as it might, a sense of ordinariness eludes the town.

When Darshan's father, Giani Harnum Singh, chose Chilliwack for the family in 1948, they were the only Sikhs in the community. Even today, only a handful of their fellow Punjabis have settled in the area. When you are different, it's smart to blend in, and many Sikhs have done just that, especially in agriculture. Farmers are a conservative lot, no more or less racist than any other group, but glacially slow to accept newcomers—any newcomers—until they prove themselves, have some "living time on the land," as one of them told us.

Once you lay eyes on Mr. Bains, any notion of blending in flies right out of your head. As tall and erect as his wife is small and bent, Mr. Bains strides into a room and overwhelms it. His turban and immaculately groomed and rolled beard are at odds with his sweatpants, pullover and feet encased in scuffed sandals. His face is big and mobile—he would have made a great stand-up comic—and there always seems to be something going on behind his eyes that's three or four steps ahead of whatever is coming out of his mouth. During the days we spent with the family, we never heard Darshan refer to him, even in his presence, as anything but Mr. Bains.

The handshake is a bone crusher and, like a professor ushering a tardy student into a tutorial, Mr. Bains takes a seat and immediately begins to talk. After a while it's hard to think of this man as a farmer because not much about the land enters his conversation—no long reminiscences about the glory of nature or laments about the year some disease or other ran through his herd. But he would certainly talk all day about democracy, religion (his own and others), urban development, the spirit, machinery, history and the economy. Every topic worthy of discourse has been placed under an intellectual microscope to be studied, dissected, reassembled.

At the first meeting between David and Mr. Bains, he stage-manages a wide-ranging discussion designed to find out what David knows. Apparently satisfied with David's rudimentary knowledge of the Sikh religion, Mr. Bains turns to a test of politics, flinging names at him in quick succession, giving David few moment after each to offer his opinion. "Brian Mulroney. Glen Clark. Bill Vander Zalm," Mr. Bains fires out. "Richard M. Nixon."

"Asshole," David responds firmly. "Brilliant politically but an asshole."

Mr. Bains nods. David has passed a test. "Asshole," he agrees with emphasis. It is the final word.

Though Mr. Bains is ostensibly a dairy farmer, he spends much of his time pondering and considering. With Gurts now taking charge of the daily management of the farm, he finally has time to devote to matters of the mind. But even when his family was young and he and Darshan were establishing themselves as farmers, he spent every moment he could spare in the affairs of the Sikh community. It isn't a hobby for him, but an obligation. As a long-time director of the World Sikh Organization, he travelled the world consulting and mediating troubles.

When he arrived in Canada, the employment options for Giani Joginder Singh Bains were trucking and farming, not traditional pursuits of the mind. He drove briefly in the Fraser Valley, working for the trucking and gravel business of G.H. Singh and Sons Trucking, owned by Darshan's father. "It was hard for me. I didn't like it."

The choice of farming over trucking or employment elsewhere was an easy one. "Other jobs you have to lie. Here I'm my own boss. You milk the cows, sell the milk, feed the people." Instead of buying a truck and throwing in their lot with Darshan's relatives, they took some of the money Darshan's mother gave them as a wedding gift and purchased a small house with ten acres for $8,000. "Five per cent interest! That is what I paid and I bought my foundation. I saved some money, built a barn and bought more land. I was so lucky! The next year I got the quota." He remembers the day, probably the hour too; he recalls financial transactions dating back half a century with the same clarity. March 1, 1964, 201 pounds of milk produced that day. "So much is luck," he emphasizes, hands shooting up to heaven as if to try to yank some of that elusive stuff down to earth.

"No cheat, no lie—luck. The quota encouraged me to keep a dairy farm."

Darshan, perched on her special chair, piled high with cushions so she doesn't tax her fragile knees when she stands up, interrupts. "Yes, but who created the circumstances? Who created the luck?" She smiles at her husband triumphantly, as if she's nailed him on a particular point. "You could have gone in a different direction. Who created the circumstances?" Mr. Bains acknowledges Darshan with a shrug and veers off. "If you have no get-up-and-go, you work for somebody else."

Quotas across the country are like precious franchises, husbanded, guarded jealously and passed down from generation to generation. Farmers have been known to sit on quotas long after they've ceased to milk, giving them up only after being chased down by milk marketing boards demanding that they be sold and put back into circulation. Buying them today in B.C., if you can ever find one on the market, costs more than most farmers make in a year.

In Ontario, near where we live, a farmer milks a small herd of cows. It seems he's been a grandfather almost as long as we've been alive. He's not old so much as permanently shrivelled, growing down toward the earth with every passing year. He looks like he's been cured in a smoke house.

At 5:15 every morning the porch light flicks on, and two minutes later Harold pushes his feet into his black rubber Bulldogs and walks slowly to the barn. He whistles up the cows and props himself against the barn door waiting for them to push and shove their way frantically inside, bursting with milk, eager for food. They pass so close any one of them could trample him into the clay floor. He waits and eventually they sort themselves out, finding their own spots and burying their noses in the ancient wooden trough, swimming with silage. The process of milking, even with machines, takes him hours, as he moves slowly from one animal to the other. Half a day later he does it all over again. Harold has a quota. With children and grandchildren long grown and gone to Calgary, Vancouver and Toronto, he will die with that quota. It is as precious to him as the land.

Mr. Bains immediately saw the economic beauty of the quota system—if you had one. "B.C. has the best quota system in the world. It gives you a handle on production. It is supply management. Very successful to producer and public. Washington State surplus milk is sufficient for all Canada! That's why the quota system works, why it is so good here." He's not shy about having made an excellent living from his herd over the years. But if you ask him how much he paid for additional quotas after that first one, he draws back, his eyes open wide and he shakes his head.

"*I never bought one again!*" He laughs hugely. "Never again!"

Then he waits; he knows what's coming. "Frugal is at the top of his list," Darshan chuckles. "The very top." It's homage paid.

"She calls me frugal all the time," Mr. Bains agrees proudly.

David rises to the bait.

"So just how did you get more quota?"

He leans forward, happy to get to the real meat of the matter. "I make money by dealing. I buy land, sell land, buy cows, sell cows, buy machinery, sell machinery. I have a good excuse to stay in business because I milk cows. The quota comes, with the right deal, the quota comes."

Mr. Bains roars with laughter when David tells of an acquaintance who paid $75,000 for a prize dairy cow to upgrade his herd.

"Things are a little different in Ontario," he admits. "But not different enough to make it worthwhile to spend that kind of money on a cow."

"Maybe the cow is a good producer," David ventures.

"If I get a gallon more a day from a cow, so what?" Mr. Bains scoffs. "If I need more milk I'll just get another cow. Once my quota's filled, it's filled. I don't get more money for more milk once the quota's filled."

OUR FIRST CONTACT WITH Darshan Bains didn't follow any of the rules of preliminary research. Had we let her, Darshan would have taken our book in hand, dictated all the interviews, suggested an outline, and edited the final version just to make sure we got it right. Over the phone she's a big woman with a powerful, musical voice touched with just enough warmth to fool you into believing she will go along with your viewpoint for the sake of social nicety.

In person the physical picture is very different. Arthritis has contorted her hands, attacked her hips and knees and bowed her spine. She fully expects to be bedridden before long, but in the meantime she grabs at life, shakes it, alters it, slaps it around when need be. She talks quickly, throwing questions into her commentary, keeping you constantly off guard. There isn't a subject on earth she won't wade into, from bull semen to the lack of amenities at Canadian border crossings and along our highways. "We're stupid, the Americans aren't! They've got gas stations everywhere, rest stops, picnic tables. Look at us. You can drive for miles with no place to stop and go to the bathroom, eat your lunch, nothing! It's as if we're trying to hurry people along, get rid of them. It's stupid, don't you think?"

Though the Sikh religion has no strictures against women, few have exercised their rights to the limit. Nothing in the bible decrees that men and women must sit on opposite sides of the temple, but many do. Nothing says the women must cook the food and the men must serve it in the temple, but they do. Nothing prohibits women from becoming priests, but none have.

All the wretched stereotypes led us to expect a woman of Darshan's age, sixty-three, her cultural background and her gender to be retiring, indirect and deferential. But Darshan is so direct you feel impaled after five minutes with her. Out in the milking barn we would not have been surprised to hear her order the cows to stand and fill the buckets without the aid of a milking machine.

It is even more surprising to discover how devout she is, how the life of this forthright, completely modern Canadian woman is as close to the teachings of her faith as the words in the Sikh bible are to the pages they are written on. Children are one of her favourite topics. She marvels at her two sons, Gurts and Harbans, who works in Vancouver in the tourism industry. But she won't talk about their accomplishments or relate cute stories of their childhood. She is far more interested in the philosophy of guiding them through life, steering them through the obstacle course while maintaining a firm control at the helm.

"You have to be really strict. All the time. You need to give them constant reminders. All families should do it. My mom was always with us, always."

She says the last sentence with a laugh. Darshan was not a child easily contained, physically or intellectually. "My god, my mother didn't even let me go to the bathroom by myself!" She shrugs. "But that was the way. That's the way things were."

Darshan's mother discouraged friends. "I am your friends, she told me," she says. "Every weekend she took me someplace. Maybe dinner out. She was always there."

Darshan's father was one of the first Sikhs to come to Canada, and the family lived in Vancouver when Darshan was young. But her father yearned for the land. "My mother said to him, this is a fire that's not going out." Her father responded, "My children need a job. No job and they are idle, minds go all over the place."

Their first farm was in Agassiz, another Fraser Valley town. They had a few cows and her father also worked in his trucking business. The great flood of 1948 drove them out of their home. For weeks Darshan's father helped build the dikes that saved many towns. "We had to move the cattle to higher ground for three months; it was incredible!"

After the flood, the family moved to Chilliwack, where they were the only Sikhs. "You have to be strong," Darshan says, remembering the days when the five children walked to school, completely alone, a small island in the white valley farm community. They weren't thrilled: everyone else rode the bus. "My mother always said you've got to know who you are and be true to that. She told us it's okay to be different. She wouldn't let us go on the bus. She said, 'You will pick up garbage on the bus. You walk and other kids will walk with you. You will teach them first.'" She smiles at the memory of her mother, who could make reinforced concrete crumble with the power of her will. "She was something." And she was right. Eventually a few children joined Darshan and her brothers and sisters in the walk to school.

THE BAINSES FORCED US to come face to face with our own prejudices against monster homes and arranged marriages. They don't use either adjective when describing the new family estate or the nuptials of the two sons but, since we're white folk with roots in the west coast, the two words spring easily to our lips—monster and arranged. South Vancouver is full of overbuilt monstrosities, crammed against modest bungalows on prime land with colonnades, expensive clay tile roofs, porticos, three-car garages and bulging bow windows. Depending on which racial or national group bothers one the most, they are denounced as tasteless show homes of moneyed Greeks, Italians, Indians or Chinese.

The Bainses' new home/estate/castle exists in a different stratosphere than even the largest of those houses. When Darshan gives us directions, she cheerfully mentions it as a landmark. "If you see the house from the highway, you've gone too far." Others echo the comment but in a less friendly manner.

"There's no way you're going to miss that place—not if you've got your eyes open," directs one man, with a nasty edge to his voice.

David is the first to get a tour of The House. He arrives after spending five days with the Lallys. There he developed a taste for masala chai, Indian tea, but he craves coffee. He knocks at the Bainses' door at 6:00 a.m., in time for the morning milking, and Darshan quickly opens it. Mr. Bains takes one look at David and disappears. Returning, he thrusts forward a cup of rich, dark coffee, forever endearing himself to David.

When he learns that David once built his own small house, the milking plans are abandoned. "Gurts can look after the cows," Mr. Bains announces. "Let's get another cup of coffee. Then we're going to see the house."

Over the years, we've been in many houses that are under construction or being renovated. We've renovated several of our own, top to bottom, and we know how even a small project like a bathroom can occupy months of planning, shopping, examining estimates and supervising the work. Choosing paint colours, flooring, mouldings can suck up weeks. Erecting twenty thousand square feet is beyond imagining—it is a life work.

Despite its size, the house stands in reasonable proportion to the nine-thousand–foot mountains, streaked with snow, standing sentry in the background. When you have twenty thousand

332

square feet to play with and a 143-foot frontage, you may be forgiven for indulging in a few architectural flights of fancy. After looking at it for a while, David realizes that it is shaped like a temple without the ornamentation. And like a Sikh temple, it has welcoming doors opening at all four compass points.

"Yes," agrees Mr. Bains, "home is like a temple."

As tour guide, Mr. Bains, ambling happily around the unfinished, cavernous rooms in his ratty carpet slippers, is like a teenager with his first car. The list of features is imposing: the twenty thousand square feet include an attached four-car garage and unfinished basement running the full extent of the house, 450-amp electrical service—200 or less is normal—5 furnaces, 5 fireplaces, 14 bathrooms, 134 windows.

"I'm not supposed to ever develop this into living space," Mr. Bains says of the vast basement. "So they tell me." Then he pauses, deciding how much more he wants to say.

"One day this house will be full of children—if the boys do their jobs. Then we'll see.

"Did Darshan tell you they tried to make me tear down the other house?" he asks. David responds no and Mr. Bains launches into a common farmer's problem. When they want to build a new house on the farmstead, they're often forced to tear down the original. Usually the reason is to thwart illegal subdivisions on scarce B.C. farmland.

But Mr. Bains hates waste. "It's a perfectly good house. Too small for our family. Why should I tear it down?"

After years of fruitless bickering with the bureaucrats, the Bains, with the advice of a friendly official, concluded that "they weren't quite looking at things the right way" and hit upon an elegantly simple solution. If they called the old home a guest house, it didn't have to be torn down.

"It is now my guest house. Guests will stay there. I have a lot of guests. It is a guest house." Mr. Bains punctuates each repetition of "guest" with a firm nod.

The House is not just a giant home; it has a purpose far beyond luxurious shelter. Many generations of Sikhs will live here, families within families. "I want to create a tradition for my family. A place for them, an anchor. We could keep the house for a hundred years or more." Mr. Bains wants the house to be a sanctuary, where his family can be Sikhs in the fullest sense of the word, yet flourish in the greater world and in the family business, the dirty, mucky business of farming.

At the front of the house is the four-car garage, which connects to a large heated area for the repair of farm vehicles. The garage will shelter the cherished and cossetted vintage TransAm and Camaro given to Gurts and his brother Harbans on their graduations by Darshan's mother. Adjacent to it is a mud room, where workers can shed dirty coats and boots after a day in the fields or barn. It has its own washer and dryer—"You don't want to mix your farm clothes with your regular clothes." Tired people coming in from milking or shovelling manure tend to be a little careless, so the entry hall walls are lined with plywood instead of drywall. "You won't accidently put a boot through that," assures Mr. Bains, smacking the wall with his palm, "and it'll be easy to clean."

Five furnaces seems excessive, but Mr. Bains has a reason for every one of them. "I want to be able to keep our part of the house warmer. Old people get cold, you know." The master bedroom suite is actually a separate apartment, with a private kitchen—"in case we want a cup of tea,"—its own fireplace and sufficient wiring for a home theatre and an array of electronic gadgets. Everything has been carefully sized in order to accommodate Darshan should her arthritis confine her to a wheelchair.

That accounts for one furnace. Then there's one more for each son and his family, "in case the boys don't get along," or one wife prefers tropical while the other temperate. The boys are very close and Mr. Bains has little doubt that they will continue to be close—Darshan wouldn't tolerate otherwise. But families are another matter and most especially families of families. Accordingly, the boys' wings can be sectioned off, giving the families a buffer from each other.

Gurts's and Harbans's living areas have their own kitchens, dining rooms, master bedrooms, bathrooms, laundry rooms and on and on. "There's got to be room for cribs," Mr. Bains states emphatically. There's also a common area with a huge communal kitchen, eating area, laundry, children's play area and formal dining room capable of seating thirty, and three guest suites and a prayer room.

The central living and common areas are so enormous they require a separate furnace too, number four. The fifth exists as a back-up and may be called into play should they decide to develop the basement, which has the same square footage as the main floor. As it is, forty or fifty people could live comfortably in The House.

The House sits by itself on a slight rise. Every window has a view of hills, fields or breathtaking, intimate exposure to Mount Baker. You can walk completely around the second floor on a wide balcony, and below there's a covered outdoor area for children to enjoy during the west coast rainy season. Mr. Bains's office is on the main floor next to his personal worship area, and the family archive, museum and library are on the third. Another large balcony provides a place to stroll, and a bathroom and small kitchenette allow those worshipping or studying to spend the day up there without being disturbed.

Mr. Bains doesn't exactly say it, but he envisions a time when the family elders, and others in the community, will come here to spend time discussing faith and important issues. It may not happen during his life but that doesn't matter. Mr. Bains likes the idea that his descendants might think of him occasionally because he had the forethought to create the space.

The kitchen would make Emeril Lagasse weep with envy. Aside from great bowling-alley stretches of countertop and acres of specially designed cabinetry with nooks and crannies to tuck out of sight a platoon of appliances, there is a special room for cooking Indian food. "You know how it is. The smell is coming all over the house and your clothes, it is better in its own place," Mr. Bains explains. A unique venting system will whoosh away the pungent odours and disperse them across the fields.

As Mr. Bains talks about planning the house, security and safety pop up continuously in his conversation. It seems like a bit of overkill. During the first few days of David's visit, there is no hint that the Bains family has ever been the target of racism and it is hard to imagine anyone but the most dim-witted messing with either of the well-muscled boys. But logic argues otherwise. These are people who stride through life unapologetic about who they are, where they come from and what they believe. There's even a slight trace of defiance mixed with pride in the way the men of the family wear their turbans. It has never occurred to them that they might be anything other than what they are. And irritatingly, to some, they are extremely good at what they do. It isn't possible that these people haven't been rubbed over by the sandpaper of prejudice.

On the third evening David has dinner with the family. He sits at one end of the table. Darshan perches at the opposite end, eating little but concentrating on subtly directing Sarbjit, Gurts's wife, who has prepared and is serving the feast. "I don't know how long I've got left," Darshan told David earlier. "She needs to know what I know; someone has to take my place." It is a crash course in a new life. Within months of Sarbjit's arrival in Canada, Darshan had her enrolled in driving lessons and English courses, and she spends hours with her discussing issues—from politics to religion and raising children. And then there are the cows. Sarbjit is slender, graceful like a dancer, her hands and arms thin and delicate. She looks made for jewels and lushly coloured silks shot with silver and gold. In her wedding pictures she is hauntingly beautiful. In the barn, clad in cumbersome rubber boots and an oversized plaid shirt, she heaves milk buckets for the bawling, ravenous calves.

"I love it," she confides to Alison softly. "I never thought I would. I worried a bit about it. But I trusted my parents, I trusted Darshan." She lifts a bucket into the calves' pen and three recently weaned youngsters rush over as if it is the last drop of milk on earth. "Look at them, always so hungry."

"Kind of like Gurts," Alison jokes. Sarbjit claps her hands to her mouth trying to wrestle back an unladylike bellow of laughter.

"Yes," she gasps. "Yes, you're right." Her eyes flick to him at the far end of the barn. Gurts is moving purposefully from one cow to another, attaching the milking machines, making sure the suction is right, then quickly attending to the next. He straightens up for a moment and looks through the door of the milking area, down the long corridor where the cows gobble silage from concrete troughs and over to the corner where the weaned calves are penned. When their eyes meet—the tall, powerful dairy farmer and his ethereal Malaysian wife—the moment is so tender, so intimate Alison feels like an intruder.

At dinner Mr. Bains sits beside David so they can talk and he can press food on his guest. His tastes take some getting used to—not the exotic Indian ingredients, rather the combinations. At breakfast during Alison's visit he assures her that a mountain of pineapple chunks on top of scrambled eggs is an excellent repast. "Excellent!" he insists, ladling, to Alison's horror, a quantity on to her eggs, the juice running into the soft white and yolk of the eggs. Actually, it isn't half bad.

Gurts sits across from David saying nothing, focusing on his forking, which is prodigious. Sarbjit has made tandoori chicken, fragrant and rich. There are lots of delicious tid-bits brought out to sample, notably Mr. Bains's homemade buttermilk and yogurt, which calms the power of the tandoori spicing.

"Why all the security precautions?" David asks after a big gulp of buttermilk. For a moment the family takes on the aspect of grouse disturbed from cover before returning to placidity with a collective exertion of will.

"Mr. Bains hasn't slept between 11 p.m. and 4:00 a.m. for years," Darshan finally says in an uncharacteristically small voice. "He just sits in his chair and looks out the window."

"That's why I look so old," Mr. Bains adds gruffly, trying to lighten the moment.

With a little prompting the story unfolds. Late one December morning in 1991 they woke to find their main barn in flames, with all the cows inside.

"It was arson. We got the cattle out but the barn was destroyed," Darshan laments.

"Insurance?" David inquires.

"Ha!" barks Mr. Bains. "The bastards cancelled my insurance and refused to pay."

The insinuation was that the Bainses had torched their own

barn for insurance purposes. Never mind that it was an old policy, originally taken out in the sixties, which only covered the structure for $20,000, far less than its $80,000-plus replacement value.

"I showed them I had money in the bank. Didn't owe money. Had my milk quota. I even offered to take a polygraph!" says Mr. Bains, throwing up his hands. "They still didn't believe me."

The worst part of the near-tragic incident was not knowing who had done it or why. For six years the family hunkered down while Mr. Bains spent his nightly vigil at the window wondering and watching.

"We couldn't get over it," Darshan says simply.

Finally an acquaintance came forward to admit he knew the culprit and, more painful, to tell them that the information was an open secret in the community. A neighbour had burned the Bains' barn. It was economic opportunism, not racism.

"It was the land all along, he just wanted the land," sighs Mr. Bains. "He picked a very cold day to set the fire. He wanted to be sure the cattle were inside. He wanted to wipe us out."

There's little about human nature that surprises Darshan. She can understand the motivation behind the fire: greed is not difficult to grasp. "What really upset me was finding out that people knew. Some of them had known for eight years and didn't say anything. No matter how you look at it, that is very hard to think about.

"Would they have dared to do that if we weren't Sikhs?" Darshan asks. "I don't know."

White North Americans view arranged marriages with curiosity, horror and even a little fear. On the surface, they violate every tenet of freedom and carry the taint of slavery, of wretched, unwilling women being dragged into matrimony and shackled to a life of childbearing with a man they'd never met until the wedding day. One of Alison's favourite books as a child was *Around the World in Eighty Days*. The image of the poor Indian bride, married in childhood to a man she didn't know and forced to throw herself on the funeral pyre of her dead husband, has been indelibly printed on her soul. Darshan Bains is the first to be amused by the cultural anxiety that grips us when the subject is raised.

"Everyone has a problem finding a mate. Isn't that right?" she prods. "I'm right, aren't I? That's why you have to be so careful to select carefully. You have to think of many, many things. Young people don't know. They think they know, but they don't. That's why so many marriages break up. Because they weren't careful, they didn't *select* well."

It's hard to argue with Darshan, and not only because she's very good at pressing her point. Under her prying, we admitted that both of us had been previously married and divorced and that a little more care in the initial selection of our mates might have saved us considerable unhappiness. She was good enough not to look triumphant at the news.

In Darshan's view, there are many more issues than simply selecting a mate well so marital longevity is assured. "My dad was looking for someone committed for me. He had to be someone who could demonstrate he was committed." She laughs. "It wasn't easy, I tell you. My father was very, very fussy. He looked for a long time. Talked to people, got recommendations."

By the 1950s the Sikh community was already spread all over the world, with sizeable concentrations in England, Canada and the western United States, as well as Malaysia and several other Asian countries. Between her mother's and her father's families, Darshan's parents had ties to nearly every major Sikh community. Word spread.

"Then one day my uncle said to him, 'I think I know what you're looking for.'"

The young man her uncle proposed was an educated man from a family well respected in their community. Best of all he followed the teachings of the bible rigorously. Perfect. There was only one stumbling block. He had been in jail, twice.

Joginder Singh Bains was a political prisoner after the bitter partition of the Punjab in 1947. That interested Darshan's father right away. In his mind there was no separation between church and state; politics and religion could not exist in different spheres, but were joined philosophically, morally and historically. A Sikh who had been imprisoned for his political views was clearly a man of faith.

In the Punjab, Mr. Bains was considered a Sikh activist, a dangerous man to the ruling Hindus. He's amused now that a boy could have been thought dangerous enough to throw in jail. In 1949 he had been part of a demonstration protesting the partitioning of Pakistan from India, which ripped the heart out of the Punjab, placing the five hundred–year-old capital, Lahore, in the new country.

"We did not have a national government, it was a Hindu government. India was to be divided on language basis, that is what we were promised. Gandhi, Mountbatten, that is what they had told us. But it was lies, just lies. We trusted the Indian government and we took Gandhi at his word. Lord Mountbatten said in 1945 to the Sikhs, 'You will have your rights.' But Gandhi was against a separate province."

Darshan interrupts. "When it came to language it was very simple—my way or the highway. Gandhi gave the Sikh people no choice."

Mr. Bains was sentenced to a year, but after serving six months in prison, the charges were mysteriously dropped and he returned to university. His father, a devout man and a farmer, wanted all his children to go to school. "You see, he was not educated but he wanted us to be. All of us. But I was the only one." Sikh anger over the betrayal of the Indian government escalated, and in 1954 Mr. Bains was once again caught up in protests. During a huge demonstration in Amritsar near the sacred Golden Temple, thirty thousand people were arrested, many of them scholars, politicians, writers and students like him.

"One good thing, to be in jail, I was in charge of the library. That's why I came to Canada. I was reading, reading, always reading and Canada was a very wonderful place. Lots of land. Punjabi people love the land. Politician, doctor, lawyer, no matter. They are always looking for the land. They will work in the fields because they want to. In the summer here you can see them coming from the city.

"When you are educated, you want to get out. You want to know what's out there. So in jail I had time to read about Canada, about every place. I kept asking, 'What's out there?'" Jail gave him more than just time to learn about the world. Among his cellmates were people like Parkash Badal, now premier of the Punjab. Mr. Bains prepared for his M.A. in jail and was teaching in a Punjabi college when Darshan's uncle made the contact in 1955.

"This fellow in India is perfect for your family, perfect for Darshan," her uncle told her father. "He has five brothers and two sisters, and he is the only one who doesn't drink. All through his life he has kept his own philosophy."

Darshan's father quizzed his wife's brother up, down and sideways about the young man's character and his nature. "Will he cut his hair?" Darshan's father demanded.

"Off with my head if he does," responded Darshan's uncle.

"That's right!" assured her father. "What guarantee are you giving me that he is the person you say?" It was a very serious question, the most important one in the many hours of conversation about the young man from the Punjab. Her uncle did not respond quickly. The question was not asked lightly and the answer deserved thought. Darshan's father would never have asked it if he did not already hold his brother-in-law in high esteem, high enough to consider his recommendation of a husband for his daughter. In the end, her uncle could only offer faith in his own judgement that the young man would be suitable. It was enough for Darshan's father. The process began.

Emissaries were sent, more discussions undertaken and finally the marriage was arranged. But it would take nearly seven years before Darshan set eyes on her husband-to-be. "Thank God he is working," Darshan's father said to his nineteen-year-old daughter as the immigration process dragged on. He hoped that the young man's education and job would help offset his two arrests in the eyes of the Canadian officials.

After three years passed, some of Mr. Bains's friends tried to persuade him to give up and look for a bride at home. "I made a promise in front of God!" he shouts, pounding his hand on the living room coffee table, still outraged at the thought nearly forty years later. "They would have me break that!"

At Darshan's home, friends of the family also gently tried to suggest the same thing to her mother. "Oh God, she got so angry. 'Don't say that to me!' she'd tell them. It's funny they each had no idea they were saying the same thing. They didn't know each other and they were all those miles apart but they were saying the same thing. Amazing isn't it?"

Darshan's father died and still the process dragged on. Her mother wrote furiously to the minister of immigration, a woman, a *single* woman. "No wonder it's taking so long," her mother harrumphed. "How can a woman who's not married understand?"

Finally the letter came. Refused. It was a medical problem; supposedly Joginder Singh Bains had cataracts. This was news to Mr. Bains, who sought out an eye doctor in the Punjab for a second opinion. The man couldn't find any sign of cataracts or anything else wrong with his eyes.

"Perhaps they thought I was a communist. Maybe that affects your eyes, hmm?" Mr. Bains shrugs. "In my village it was divided, communism versus democracy." Which made the situation all the more ironic. "You see, I believe the Sikh religion is *based* on democracy. It *founded* democracy. The Sikh religion gave all kinds of rights to women, women have full freedom and rights. They worried that I'm a communist but I fought communism through religious philosophy."

With the new medical information in hand, Darshan's mother applied a second time. "At least immigration apologized," says Darshan. In late 1960 the flimsy blue airmail envelope arrived in Mr. Bains' village. Approved.

"I went straight to the church." Mr. Bains breathes deeply, savouring the memory of the excited, grateful man who had been waiting seven years to lay eyes upon his betrothed. He stares at the tiny woman sitting on a pile of cushions like a child on a throne. "I was so lucky. I wait almost seven years and it was worth it." For a moment, Darshan is once again the young girl who had endured an eternity for a husband she did not know.

Darshan's face twitches slightly. "I was so impatient but he knew. He knew because of his faith."

Mr. Bains prefers to see it as a temporal matter. What he knew and understood was politics and institutions. "I knew about *these* things," he explains earnestly. "The bureaucracy—bureaucrats are very dangerous. I knew the procedure more than her."

Darshan will have none of it. "It was written that you make your own luck and your luck goes with you." She turns to him and repeats what she has said before. "You created the circumstances. It was your faith. Your perseverence."

Throughout the years of waiting, Darshan's mother wouldn't allow her to see a photograph of her fiancé. "She told me that if I saw a picture I would see a different man than who he really was. But I wondered what he would be like, would he be handsome? I tell you, I was scared. I thought maybe he was really terrible, and that's why my mother wouldn't let me see his picture."

Nor was her mother about to permit Darshan to go to the airport and meet him on August 25, 1961. She begged, her brothers coaxed and finally her mother relented—slightly. "All right," she said firmly. "You may go but you may not speak. Not a word." It was better than nothing. It took more pleading to persuade Darshan's mother to let her get out of the car and hover near the airport entrance so she could catch a glimpse of her intended. Her brothers stayed with her and twenty-five-year-old Darshan's heart was thumping so hard inside her chest she was sure it resonated throughout the entire airport. Her brothers spotted him first.

"Hey, not bad. He's okay," Shorty, the youngest, opined. "Sssssh! Shut up!" hissed her older brother. "Mom's coming."

With appropriately downcast eyes, Darshan stood quietly, willing herself to look at him but only quickly and to say nothing. Mr. Bains left them for a few moments to attend to his baggage. Her mother turned to her with the first hint of doubt in her voice. It was Darshan's lone opportunity to back out.

"Are you okay, Dot? Did I make the right choice?" Darshan

smiled at her. "He's okay, Mom. But why didn't you just give me the picture and I wouldn't have worried all these years?"

"Because I didn't want you to form any impressions. I wanted your first impression to be when you came face to face."

Her brother interrupted, "C'mon, let her talk to him now." Darshan's mother quickly reverted to form. "Be quiet! We've come this far. I'm not making no boo-boo now." Her mother rented a motel room near the airport and put the word out about Mr. Bains's arrival. More than a hundred people, most from the areas near his village and now settled in Canada, came to greet him.

They married a few weeks later, and after the ceremony Shorty took him aside and said, "From now on she's yours. The job is done." There was both warning and encouragement in his words.

GURTS WAS MARRIED IN March 1998 and his younger brother Harbans in August 1998. "Harbs found his own girl," laughs Darshan. "Gurts, well, Gurts was a little slower."

Harbans, the more outgoing of the two, met his bride-to-be, Harpeet, five years earlier. Of course, she had to be acceptable to Darshan and Mr. Bains. The approval came quickly. As the younger son, Harbs decided to hold off his marriage as a gesture of respect for his brother. He didn't realize it would take so long. Darshan combed the entire world. Woman after woman was brought for consideration. Usually they came for tea with their mothers or a go-between. "Gurts won't talk if he doesn't like the girl," Darshan says with a mixture of pride and rue. As the years ticked by, there was more sipping than talking.

Then, in November 1997, a Sikh woman from the small Punjabi community in Malaysia visited Vancouver to search out a suitable match for her twenty-two-year-old daughter. The family was looking for a Sikh man who was established and followed the basic strictures. Word was passed and Gurts met Sarbjit for the requisite tea. "They pretended not to look at each other," recalls Darshan, "but then they sat talking for an hour. They talked and talked." Gurts, though obviously bowled over, was cautious. "She was okay," he said to Darshan. "Let's talk a couple of more times. Let's take it easy." Darshan gritted her teeth. In the end it had to be his decision; she would be patient.

They were engaged in December and married in Malaysia, with a reception later in British Columbia.

Gurts is his father in a slightly taller, more muscular package. Long-limbed, with big hands and broad shoulders, he looks like an athlete and walks with the bouncy grace of one, swinging from the hip, impatient to be where he's going before he has even left. Energy and vigour define him, seemingly ready to burst out from under his skin. Everything he does is in a hurry. He talks fast, laughs often and starts one job while putting the finishing touches on another.

Initially, Gurts treats David with the respect he'd accord a much older man, larding on the "sir" with the ardour of a fledgling military recruit. On the last day David spends with the Bainses, Darshan suggests he view the morning milking again. But when he arrives, Darshan has other plans. "Go with Gurts," she urges. "He's going to cut some hay for the cows. You should talk."

It is a glorious Fraser Valley morning, British Columbia at its best. Though the field is close to the highway, it's early and traffic is sparse, the noise unobtrusive. The air is so clear Mount Baker seems within strolling distance.

For a few minutes the two men stand on the edge of the field saying nothing, the forty-nine-year-old agnostic writer and the thirty-six-year-old turbaned Sikh who insists on calling David "sir." The warm sun caresses their shoulders and the sweet smell of dew on the long green grass surrounds them. "You should talk," Darshan instructed. But Gurts isn't the kind of man who flaps his gums just for the sake of exercise. David, wondering how to jump-start the conversation, idly comments on the hockey gear he's seen in the back of Gurts's truck.

Gurts brightens up considerably, telling David that he has played since he was five and now coaches a team of his own. He calls himself a "big-time Philadelphia fan," never missing a game if he can help it. "I was in Malaysia meeting my wife's family. My god, it was so hot. I was dying, just dying. But the worst part was no hockey. I was going crazy for a hockey fix. So I'm meeting all these people and getting to know the woman I'm going to marry and I can't stop thinking about the playoffs." Gurts laughs at himself. "Finally I went to a mall. Whew! I got my hockey fix. I was watching when Kasparaitis laid that hit on Lindros."

When David mentions that he's met Eric Lindros and knows his family, Gurts is off and running on what will be a more-than-two hour conversation.

"So what's the deal with him?" he questions. "Why can't that team win in the playoffs? I like the way he plays, but does he choke? Is he disruptive like people say? What's he like? And what about the Flyers' goaltending?"

Back and forth they go, David providing an inside tidbit or two, Gurts pressing for more. They stop for a contented breath. "Do you own this field?" David asks.

Gurts eagerly offers a history of the sixty-two acres they are standing on. "Dad's been watching this field since 1962. An older Sikh gentleman owned it. He wouldn't listen. They can be very stubborn. You may have noticed that. There's a lot of water in the field, we saw that. We told him he had to put drainage in if he wanted to grow anything but grass. He wouldn't listen."

The spot where they're standing is quite dry but Gurts shows David another patch, a hundred metres away, that seems identical but on close inspection is boggy even though there's been no rain for a couple of weeks.

"When you get a good rain, this is like a lake," explains Gurts. "We saw it. We told him. He planted strawberries anyway. Jeez!

"He'd jump down from his tractor and get stuck—mud over his boots. I'd have to drive over and rescue him. He kept at it for four years. Stuck again and again. He'd break axles and chains trying to get out. One time his tractor was stuck for five months." For a moment David and Gurts are laughing so hard he can't continue.

"And when it came time to pick strawberries, he couldn't get pickers to stand knee to thigh deep in mud and water. He was very stubborn, he kept at it for four years. He'd go by and I'd wave and smile. I'd say to myself, I shouldn't be thinking I told you so . . . but I told you so."

"Was it hard growing up here, being the only Sikhs?" David asks.

Gurts's smile thins and his eyes take on a Clint Eastwood glint. "It was hard at times. People would try to push us around. We'd get called names—you know the ones. But we were taught to be strong."

When David asks if the colour of turbans he and his brother wear, the blue symbolic of Khalsa warriors, is a coincidence, Gurts answers emphatically, "No!" and changes the subject back to hockey. It's time to get working, the hay needs cutting and Gurts isn't accustomed to standing around when there's something to be done. He mentions that he collects T-shirts and wonders if David can find anything unusual for him—maybe something from the CBC, where Alison occasionally works. David suddenly remembers he has a Newsworld baseball cap in his car and offers it. Gurts grins at him.

"I don't need one. Anyway, where would I put it?"